/ UNIVERSITY LIBRARY
W. S. U. - STEVENS POINT

W9-AOV-821

Leading Issues in International Economic Policy

Leading Issues in International Economic Policy

**Essays in Honor of
George N. Halm**

Edited by
C. Fred Bergsten
William G. Tyler

Lexington Books
D.C. Heath and Company
Lexington, Massachusetts
Toronto   London

Library of Congress Cataloging in Publication Data
Main entry under title:

Leading issues in international economic policy.

CONTENTS: Bergsten, C.F. Introduction.–Bibliography of the writings
of George N. Halm (p.   )–International money: Dale, W.B. The
International Monetary Fund and greater flexibility of exchange rates.
Tyler, W.G. Exchange rate flexibility under conditions of endemic inflation: a case study of the recent Brazilian experience. [etc.]
   1. International finance–Addresses, essays, lectures. 2. International
economic relations–Addresses, essays, lectures. 3. Halm, George Nikolaus,
1901–   –Bibliography. I. Halm, George

Nikolaus, 1901–   II. Bergsten, C. Fred, 1941–   ed. III. Tyler,
William G., ed.
HG3881.L39   332.4'5   73-2004
ISBN 0-669-86868-X

Copyright © 1973 by D.C. Heath and Company.

All rights reserved. No part of this publication may be reproduced or
transmitted in any form or by any means, electronic or mechanical,
including photocopy, recording, or any information storage or retrieval
system, without permission in writing from the publisher.

Published simultaneously in Canada.

Printed in the United States of America.

International Standard Book Number: 0-669-86868-X

Library of Congress Catalog Card Number: 73-2004

Contents

HG
3881
.L39

237550

List of Figures

List of Tables

Introduction

C. Fred Bergsten

In December 1971, in the wake of the Smithsonian Agreement to realign world currencies, the world took its first basic step toward reform of the international exchange rate mechanism since Bretton Woods by authorizing countries to widen the margins around the parities of their currencies from two to four-and-one-half percent. The membership of the International Monetary Fund had concluded that widening the "bands" would help dampen international flows of liquid capital, and provide a useful first move toward improving the balance of payments adjustment process by increasing the flexibility of exchange rates. The first modern proposal to widen the bands, and indeed to move toward limited flexibility to reconcile the fundamental debate between fixed and freely flexible exchange rates which had blocked adjustment reform, was made by George N. Halm in 1965.

In January 1971, the President of the United States created a Council on International Economic Policy, which he was personally to chair, in recognition of the importance of international economics to the United States in this period of history. He shortly thereafter appointed an Assistant to the President for International Economic Policy, who was also Executive Director of the new Council. The three closest advisors immediately chosen by the new presidential assistant were former students of George N. Halm.

These two events epitomize the remarkable influence of George Halm, Professor of International Economics at the Fletcher School of Law and Diplomacy for over a quarter of a century. His impact on international economic relations has been substantial, although he never held a governmental position. His writings, particularly on international monetary policy, but also on comparative economic systems, were influential throughout this period: in 1945, Lord Keynes wrote that he considered Halm's *International Monetary Cooperation* "decidedly the clearest and most objective analysis of the evolution and provisions of the Bretton Woods plans." A generation later, Halm's proposals provided the foundations when it became necessary to reform Bretton Woods.

Of even greater influence, however, was the spread of George Halm's thought through the thousands of American and foreign students who graduated from the Fletcher School into responsible positions in governments around the world, in banks and in industry, and in academia. George Halm taught many who were to become high officials in noneconomic positions the only economics they would ever learn, and inspired many who were to attain prominence in economic positions to pursue that field. The impact of such teaching is of course incalculable. But it can only be immense. As such, it is fitting tribute to a man who dedicated his entire life to teaching and his students.

As further tribute, some of George Halm's former students and closest academic colleagues present this Festschrift. To honor his contributions to all three major aspects of international economics—the monetary system, trade, and development—this book includes sections on each.

International Money

The international monetary system lies at the heart of the world economy. An effective monetary system is necessary to smooth the flow of world trade and payments. An ineffective monetary system will produce proliferating controls over trade and capital flows, which will gradually distort both national economies around the world and international political relations—as it has done in the late 1960s and early 1970s. The construction of a new monetary system is now the most urgent issue of international economic reform.

There are two central issues in the debate over monetary reform. One is whether the balance of payments adjustment process will seek to maintain fixed exchange rates, as in the Bretton Woods system, or move systematically to greater flexibility—and, if so, how. The first three chapters present an array of views on this issue.

The first paper is by William B. Dale (Fletcher '47), a key figure in all of the major international monetary developments of the past decade as U.S. Executive Director of the International Monetary Fund. It traces the development of the exchange rate issue through the history of the IMF, describes the weaknesses of the mechanism constructed at Bretton Woods and its breakdown in the late 1960s, and outlines the case for greater (though limited) flexibility as proposed by U.S. Secretary of the Treasury George Shultz at the Annual Meeting of the IMF in September 1972. The Shultz proposals are one key point of departure for the reform negotiations which are now underway to reshape the monetary system, and Dale explains both their rationale and how they would be implemented in practice to achieve better equilibrium among the world's trading nations, including greater flexibility for the exchange rate of the dollar.

A major question about small and frequent changes in exchange rate parities, the most common reform proposal, is how they would work in practice. None of the industrialized countries has any experience with such a regime. The second paper in this book, by Professor William G. Tyler (Fletcher '63) of the University of Florida and Kiel University in Germany, analyzes the most relevant case in existence: the "trotting peg" which has been maintained by Brazil since 1968. Tyler notes that this regime has been associated in Brazil with rapid economic growth, increased exports, reduced speculation against the cruzeiro, a reduction in the rate of inflation, and rapidly growing capital inflows. He is properly cautious in assigning causality, but concludes that the Brazilian experiment has succeeded and augurs well for similar systems elsewhere, adapted to meet the different needs and institutions of different countries.

The third paper on exchange rates is by Professor Charles P. Kindleberger of MIT (and formerly of the Fletcher School, as well), one of the strongest supporters of fixed exchange rates and the concomitant reliance on a single international money. In this essay, he focuses on the critical importance of "money illusion" in the analysis of international (as well as domestic) monetary phenomena, and concludes that money can function effectively in an international context only if it is sufficiently stable to justify such illusion—a strong argument against flexible exchange rates, at least for those currencies (particularly the dollar) widely used in international finance. The Kindleberger and Dale papers thus inter alia present opposite views on the appropriate exchange rate strategy for the United States in the future.

The other major issue of monetary reform concerns the financial basis for the new system—the liquidity, as opposed to the adjustment, issue. The intellectual consensus which has seemed to be developing in favor of Special Drawing Rights, the truly international money created since 1970 by the International Monetary Fund for the use of all of its participating members, has been frequently described elsewhere. The next two chapters of this book outline the major alternatives: the dollar and gold.

Professor Gottfried Haberler, formerly of Harvard and now Resident Scholar at the American Enterprise Institute, in a paper published previously in *Lloyd's Bank Review* in July 1972, believes that the dollar could again provide a stable basis for the monetary system if the United States checks inflation successfully and would offer some sort of purchasing-power guarantees to foreign dollar holders. He sees great difficulty in reforming the monetary system in ways which would make the dollar "just another currency," so is hopeful that a strengthened dollar standard will prevail. Under such a regime, other countries could of course choose whether to maintain a given exchange rate with the dollar or move to a new relationship with it.

Professor Don D. Humphrey, William L. Clayton Professor of International Economic Affairs at the Fletcher School, to the contrary, views the dollar standard as politically unacceptable to other important countries. However, he has strong doubts about Special Drawing Rights as well, and characterizes them as "fair weather" assets. Fearing an impasse if these are the only two alternatives, and agreeing with the view that official reserves must grow over time if international controls are to be avoided, he outlines a case for restoring gold to the central monetary role in the system—at a higher official price, of course—as a first-best political, if second-best economic, compromise.

Chapter 6 focuses the adjustment and liquidity issues from the policy vantage point of whether the United States should restore convertibility of the dollar into U.S. reserve assets. C. Fred Bergsten (Fletcher '61), Senior Fellow at the Brookings Institution, in a paper also published by the Committee for Economic Development, argues that the United States should agree to restore convertibility to get a reformed monetary system which would provide a new adjustment process, adequate growth of world reserves through creation of Special Drawing

Rights, a definitive elimination of the problem of the dollar overhang, and new means for dealing with liquid capital flows. In his view, the United States has major national interests which call for a sharp reduction in the international roles of the dollar—and much greater flexibility for the exchange rate of the dollar in the future. From a different perspective, Bergsten thus supports the position espoused by Dale in Chapter 1 and opposed by Kindleberger in Chapter 3.

The final monetary paper in the volume considers the problems of *private* international finance, the means by which traders and investors finance their daily transactions, rather than *public* international finance, the means by which national monetary authorities use official reserves to finance their countries' balance of payments surpluses and deficits. Written by Professor Fritz Machlup, of Princeton and New York University, it analyzes the new phenomenon of "stateless money"—how the Euro-currency markets unite lenders, borrowers, and currencies which may all come from different countries into a single market to carry out huge volumes of international business.

International Trade

If the monetary system must provide underlying stability to the world economy, trade policy is the flash point which could trigger massive and rapid disintegration of the international framework which has developed in the postwar period. Protectionist pressures have been growing since the end of the Kennedy Round in 1967, especially in the United States where organized labor is actively seeking drastic curbs on U.S. imports (and foreign investment by U.S. firms). Success for such efforts would trigger foreign retaliation on a like scale, and levy heavy costs on both the nonprotected sectors of all national economies and international political relations.

It is widely agreed that trade policy is unstable and that the initiation of a new round of international trade negotiations in pursuit of the general interest in freer trade is needed to prevent political success for those special interests which seek new trade restrictions. The first paper on trade policy, by Bernard Norwood (Fletcher '48), now Advisor at the Board of Governors of the Federal Reserve System and a senior member of the U.S. negotiating team during the Kennedy Round, proposes both substance and scenario for that new negotiation. The paper discusses inter alia the relationship between the U.S. trade balance and U.S. objectives in a trade negotiation, the central role which tariffs are likely to play in the negotiations despite all the talk about nontariff barriers and agriculture, the need to find alternative techniques to the linear tariff cuts of the Kennedy Round, and the imperative of prior congressional approval if the United States is to carry a credible position into the international negotiations.

Underlying all of these issues of trade policy are growing uncertainties, in both official and private circles, over the adequacy of existing trade theory. In the most theoretical piece in the volume, Professor Paul Samuelson of MIT (and also formerly of the Fletcher School) addresses one such question: whether differential profit rates among countries, under conditions of international capital immobility, undermine the conclusions which would be reached under the standard application of the theory of comparative advantage. He concludes that they do not, but raises a provocative point which may well stimulate further analysis and empirical investigation.

International Development

The third broad branch of international economic policy in the postwar period, in addition to money and trade, has been foreign aid. The relationship between the developed and the developing countries, however, has always encompassed far more than aid. Trade and private capital flows have been far more important than aid to the development of the lower income countries. All of these external factors have been subordinate to the internal policies of the countries themselves, although the external and internal features have often interacted closely. And economic development has been conditioned by the domestic and international political milieu within which it has functioned. The final section of this book addresses each of these three issues.

Professor Robert West, Director of the International Development Studies program at the Fletcher School, leads off with an analysis of one of the most pervasive and emotional issues of development: the perceptions in developing countries of their economic dependence on developed countries, and the effects of those perceptions on their internal economic policies and even their economic and political structures. Methodologically, this study breaks new ground through its skillful linkages between the international and domestic, and the economic and political, aspects of the problem. Empirically, it applies its hypotheses to twenty-eight developing countries in all parts of the world. Substantively, it reaches important new conclusions—presented with proper caution as to how widely they can yet be applied—on the significance of different manifestations of "foreign presence" in developing countries, on the central role of that presence in the domestic politics of such countries, and therefore on the close linkage between changes in their political regimes and changes in their national policies toward foreign involvement. Major implications may emerge for the theory of policy-making and the theory of revolution in developing countries. So may important considerations for the policies of both governments and multinational firms in the developing world.

One strategy for both developing and developed countries, to reduce some of the tensions highlighted by West, is to rely increasingly on the international private capital markets, relative to both foreign aid and direct investment, in channeling capital from rich to poor. In the second paper in this section, Ernest Stern (Fletcher '56) of the International Bank for Reconstruction and Development argues that portfolio flows have been too long neglected and that renewed emphasis on them could have highly desirable effects on the development process itself. For the increasing number of countries which can tap that source of funds, it would help them integrate more fully into the economic network of an increasingly interdependent world; even with modest success, it would help bridge the gap between the needs of the developing countries for external capital to meet their growth targets, during this Second Development Decade, and the amounts of concessional aid which are likely to be made available by the industrialized world. Stern suggests a number of steps, in both developing and developed countries, which could make the approach a reality.

The final chapter in the volume, by Jonathan Levin (Fletcher '51) of the International Monetary Fund, discusses one key aspect of the economic policies of many developing countries: the direct relationship between their government finance and balance of payments adjustment problems. He finds this a sharp contrast to the usually indirect relationship between the two policy issues in industrialized countries, where fiscal policies generally influence the external accounts primarily through aggregate demand management and only occasionally through temporary import surcharges and "border tax adjustments." In many developing countries, however, wide disparities in productivity exist between major exports and other activities; these countries' fiscal systems, as a result, tie government revenue needs to the exchange rate system itself, raising balance of payments complications beyond those presently facing the industrialized countries. The article highlights the need for fiscal reform in many countries, and illustrates one key area in which policy prescriptions for developed countries may not be applicable in the Third World.

Bibliography of the Writings of George N. Halm

Books

DIE KONKURRENZ. UNTERSUCHUNGEN ÜBER DIE ORDNUNGSPRINZI-
PIEN DER KAPITALISTISCHEN VERKEHRSWIRTSCHAFT. Munich and
Leipzig, 1929.

GELD-KREDIT-BANKEN. Munich and Leipzig, 1935.

MONETARY THEORY. A MODERN TREATMENT OF THE ESSENTIALS OF
MONEY AND BANKING. Philadelphia, 1942. 2nd ed., 1946 (India, 1951).

INTERNATIONAL MONETARY COOPERATION. Chapel Hill, 1945.

ECONOMIC SYSTEMS. A COMPARATIVE ANALYSIS. New York and Toronto, 1951, (Japan, 1955; Germany, 1960). Rev. ed., New York, 1960
(Spain, 1964; India, 1965; Brazil, 1965). 3rd ed., New York, 1968 (India,
1970).

GELD, AUSSENHANDLE UND BESCHÄFTIGUNG. Munich, 1951. 2nd ed.,
Munich, 1954. 3rd ed., Munich, 1957. 4th ed., Berlin, 1966.

ECONOMICS OF MONEY AND BANKING. Homewood, Ill., 1956 (Spain,
1959). Rev. ed., 1961 (Spain, 1963).

Co-arranger and editor, APPROACHES TO GREATER FLEXIBILITY OF
EXCHANGE RATES: THE BÜRGENSTOCK PAPERS, Princeton, 1970.

Pamphlets

IST DER SOZIALISMUS WIRTSCHAFTLICH MÖGLICH? Berlin, 1929 (Japan,
1931).

DER WIRTSCHAFTLICHE KREISLAUF UND SEINE GESETZE. Leipzig,
1934.

THE FOREIGN TRADE GAP (with Harry Hawkins). New York, 1949.

THE "BAND" PROPOSAL: THE LIMITS OF PERMISSIBLE EXCHANGE
RATE VARIATIONS. Special Papers in International Economics No. 6,
Princeton, 1965 (Germany, 1965).

INTERNATIONAL FINANCIAL INTERMEDIATION: DEFICITS BENIGN
AND MALIGNANT. Essays in International Finance No. 68, Princeton,
1968.

TOWARD LIMITED EXCHANGE-RATE FLEXIBILITY. Essays in International Finance No. 73, Princeton, 1969.

THE INTERNATIONAL MONETARY FUND AND FLEXIBILITY OF EX-
CHANGE RATES. Essays in International Finance, Princeton, 1971.

Articles in Periodicals or Collections
of Essays

"Das Zinsproblem am Geld und Kapitalmarkt." JAHRBÜCHER FÜR NATION-ALÖKONOMIE UND STATISTIK, 1926.

"Wirtschaftswissenschaft und Handwerkerpolitik." ZEITSCHRIFT FÜR DIE GESAMTE STAATSWISSENSCHAFT, 1927.

"Schumpeters Theorie der wirtschaftlichen Entwicklung." JAHRBÜCHER FUR NATIONALÖKONOMIE UND STATISTIK, 1927.

"Zur Frage der Überwälzung und Fernwirkung der Einkommensteuer." JAHRBÜCHER FÜR NATIONALÖKONOMIE UND STATISTIK, 1930.

"Über Konkurrenz, Monopol und sozialistische Wirtschaft." JAHRBÜCHER FÜR NATIONALÖKONOMIE UND STATISTIK, 1930.

"Wirkung der Besteuerung des Kartellgewinnes, in Das Kartellproblem." SCHRIFTEN DES VEREINS FÜR SOZIALPOLITIK, Vol. 180, 1930.

"Zum Problem der Lohnsenkung." SCHMOLLERS JAHRBUCH, 1931.

"Warten und Kapitaldisposition." JAHRBÜCHER FÜR NATIONALÖKONOMIE UND STATISTIK, 1931.

"Zwiedineck-Südenhorsts Kapitalbegriff." JAHRBÜCHER FÜR NATIONALÖKONOMIE UND STATISTIK, 1932.

"Kritische Bemerkungen zu Albert Hahns Volkswirtschaftlicher Theorie des Bankkredits." JAHRBÜCHER FÜR NATIONALÖKONOMIE UND STATISTIK, 1933.

"Further Considerations on the Possibility of Adequate Calculation in a Socialist Community." In COLLECTIVIST ECONOMIC PLANNING. Ed. by F.A. Hayek. London, 1935 (France, 1939; Italy, 1946).

"The International Monetary Fund." REVIEW OF ECONOMIC STATISTICS, 1944.

"International Measures for Full Employment." REVIEW OF ECONOMICS AND STATISTICS, 1950.

Zinspolitik und Wirtschaftstheorie," In WIRTSCHAFTSTHEORIE UND WIRTSCHAFTSPOLITIK. Festgabe für Adolf Weber. Berlin, 1951.

"John Maynard Keynes und die Marktwirtschaft." In WIRTSCHAFTSFRAGEN DER FREIEN WELT. Festgabe für Ludwig Erhard. Frankfurt, 1957.

Geldpolitik und Marktwirtschaft." In INTERNATIONALE WÄHRUNGS—UND FINANZPOLITIK. Berlin, 1961.

"Metamorphosen der Sozialismusdebatte." In NATURORDNUNG. Innsbruck-Vienna-Munich, 1961.

"Albert Hahn und John Maynard Keynes." ZEITSCHRIFT FÜR NATIONALÖKONOMIE, 1963.

"Gold-Value Guarantees." WELTWIRTSCHAFTLICHES ARCHIV, 1965.

"Säkulare Inflation." ZEITSCHRIFT FÜR DIE GESAMTE STAATSWISSENSCHAFT, 1965.

"The Case for Greater Exchange-Rate Flexibility in an Interdependent World." In ISSUES IN BANKING AND MONETARY ANALYSIS. Ed. by G. Pontecorvo and R. Shay. New York, 1967.

"Mises, Lange, Liberman: Allocation and Motivation in the Socialist Economy." WELTWIRTSCHAFTLICHES ARCHIV, 1968 (Venezuela, 1968).

"Widening the Band for Permissible Exchange Rate Fluctuations." In THE INTERNATIONAL ADJUSTMENT MECHANISM. Federal Reserve Bank of Boston, 1969.

"Will Market Economies and Planned Economies Converge?" In ROADS TO FREEDOM. Essays in Honor of Friedrich A.v. Hayek. Ed. by E. Streissler. London, 1970.

"Toward Limited Flexibility of Exchange Rates; Comments on Mr. Roosa's Paper; Comments on Mr. Johnson's Paper; Fixed Exchange Rates and the Market Mechanism." In APPROACHES TO GREATER FLEXIBILITY OF EXCHANGE RATES. Arranged by C. Fred Bergsten, George N. Halm, Fritz Machlup, Robert V. Roosa. Princeton, 1970.

"The Gliding Band for Variations of Exchange Rates." NEW ENGLAND ECONOMIC REVIEW, 1971.

Contributions to Encyclopedias

"Gross-und Kleinbetrieb; Monopolistische Bestrebungen in der Gegenwart." HANDWÖRTERBUCH DER STAATSWISSENSCHAFTEN, 4th ed., Jena 1928.

Zoll-und Subventionspolitik." INTERNATIONALES HANDWÖRTERBUCH DES GEWERKSCHAFTSWESENS. Berlin, 1932.

"Sozialisierung des Bankwesens." HANDWÖRTERBUCH DES BANKWESENS. Berlin, 1933.

"Exchange, Foreign." ENCYCLOPAEDIA BRITANNICA, 1946.

"Devaluation und Revalvation; Internationaler Währungsfonds; Währungsausgleichsfonds; Währungsblock." In HANDWÖRTERBUCH DER SOZIALWIS-SENSCHAFTEN. Stuttgart-Tübingen-Göttingen, 1954, 1959, 1961.

"Geld und Kredit." In SOWJETSYSTEM UND DEMOKRATISCHE GESELL-SCHAFT. Freiburg, 1969.

"Economic Systems," ENCYCLOPAEDIA BRITANNICA, 1969.

Contributions to Congressional Headings

Fixed or Flexible Exchange Rates?; Special Problems of a Key-Currency in Balance-of-Payments Deficit, in Factors Affecting the United States Balance of Payments, Joint Economic Committee, 1962.

Statement, in Outlook for United States Balance of Payments, Joint Economic Committee, 1963.

"The Band Proposal. The Limits of Permissible Exchange Rate Variations." Reprinted in GUIDELINES FOR INTERNATIONAL MONETARY REFORM. Joint Economic Committee, 1965.

Statement, in United States Quota Increase in the International Monetary Fund, Committee on Banking and Currency, 1965.

Statement and Reprint of "The International Monetary Fund and Flexibility of Exchange Rates" in The Balance-of-Payments Mess, Joint Economic Committee, 1971.

Leading Issues in International Economic Policy

Part I:
International Money

The International Monetary Fund and Greater Flexibility of Exchange Rates

William B. Dale

A quarter century ago last spring I had the good fortune to take George Halm's Fletcher School course in International Monetary Theory. That complemented the international trade course I had just taken from Paul Samuelson and became the basis of all my professional activity since. It is hard adequately to convey the impact of such an experience. It was in Halm's course that most of the students first had a glimpse of the IMF and IBRD, and of his conviction of their importance; for me, at least, that conviction left a hope of association with the Fund which has now been reality for a decade, and has been as rewarding as those first hopes promised. As an economist, George Halm was of course first rank—as a *teacher*, he was simply superb.

Of all the prices to which economists have since the beginning devoted their analytic talent, there is little doubt that two have the greatest quantitative importance: the interest rate (the domestic price of money) and the exchange rate (the foreign price of money).

Even for the United States, where the foreign sector as a proportion of GNP is unusually small, merchandise exports, almost at the annual rate of $50 billion or about 4 percent of GNP, are in rough terms not greatly different from the dollar volume of residential construction or gross farm receipts from marketings—far from inconsequential segments of the economy. For other countries, the relative size of the export sector is typically much larger. Only India among the 125 Fund members shows a marginally smaller percentage of GNP in exports of goods, with Mexico slightly higher than the United States. Among other industrial countries, Japan—even now, somewhat surprisingly—with around 12 percent of GNP as goods exports, or three times the U.S. figure, shows the lowest rate, while other industrial countries range up to figures approaching 40 percent for the Netherlands and several points more in the case of Belgium. A few developing countries heavily dependent on primary product exports (e.g., Malaysia) show still higher proportions and some of the smaller economies

The views expressed in this article are those of the author. As this is written in January 1973, the views of the International Monetary Fund on exchange rates and a number of other matters are of course under active review with a view to reform of the international monetary and economic system. The views expressed here are consistent with the contemporary views of the U.S. government on these matters, and any appearance otherwise is unintended.

3

whose activity centers to an extraordinary extent on oil have exports from two-thirds of GNP to higher than GNP itself! Indeed the weighted *average* of Fund members, excluding the United States, shows merchandise exports in the vicinity of 15 percent of GNP or almost four times the U.S. proportion, and this figure—which has been growing—may be a low estimate. These few crude comparative figures do not of course take any account of often large international service transactions, nor of what can be large, growing, and at times volatile capital movements. The export percentages, moreover, do not directly deal with the frequently-observed phenomenon—which may be thought of as a modern basis of mercantilism—that exports can be a leading edge not only of growth, but perhaps more importantly, of structural modernization.

Where a single price—the exchange rate—has profound effects on output, employment, profitability, growth, and the economic structure in such large segments of so many economies, it could hardly be surprising: (1) that officials are not too inclined to take bold leaps into new and operationally uncertain territory—however attractive elements of analysis or even philosophy may appear; (2) that controversy should from time to time arise among countries about these questions, either as to decisions on particular exchange rates or, even more, as to the whole mechanism by which exchange rates are determined and the philosophy that underlies it; or (3) that domestic interests, not infrequently taking a distinctly political tone, become important factors in the exchange rate equation.

The domestic and foreign prices of money also have a common peculiarity which distinguish them from other prices: for reasons of history or substance, or both, the position is that governments cannot avoid taking responsibility for these prices in the sense of either trying directly to determine them (at any rate to limit their size or movement) or more indirectly recognizing that the combined influence of public policies as reflected in the evolution of national economic conditions have a marked impact on these prices even when their proximate determination is left to essentially free markets. In the case of the exchange rate, history evolving from the gradual movement away from full-bodied money quite naturally left the tradition that direct governmental determination of the basic price, which was anticipated would be pretty enduring, was the natural and expected state of affairs. Only after national financial systems had been modernized and progressively disentangled from commodity money were anything like floating rates even technically feasible, but for the most part tradition and the views of business people and officials continued to be against it.

It has been said often that military planners are always fighting the last war. That old aphorism may not be fully fair to modern military planning, but it is largely applicable to the financial planners at Bretton Woods. They were planning for the last peace.

The exchange rate regime they provided called for stable reference rates fixed officially, from which market rates would not be allowed to depart by more than one percent, with "competitive exchange depreciation" protected against and each change in the reference rate the subject of international discussion and decision-making. The structure of the exchange rate provisions, like the arrangements as a whole, were naturally a compromise. Thus, traditional notions of sovereignty were respected in that only a member country itself could make a proposal to change its par value although the Fund has the power (in Article XII, Section 8, which has not been used explicitly) to "communicate its views informally to any member on any matter arising under this Agreement," not excluding its views on the member's par value or exchange rate policy. Moreover, the Fund by a two-thirds majority of the weighted voting power may publish a report made to a member on policies or conditions of that member which "directly tend to produce a serious disequilibrium" for members; again, the power has not been used.

Traditional views of sovereignty were again provided for by structuring the legal arrangements so that a new par value introduced by a member against the objection of the Fund does not constitute, as a technical legal matter, a breach of international legal obligation. In such a case, the member is automatically ineligible to make drawings from the Fund unless the Fund takes the initiative to decide otherwise.[1] Eventually, such a difference can, if the Fund so decides, result in compulsory withdrawal of the member, though no serious consideration has ever been given to compelling withdrawal of a member on grounds of exchange rate behavior. But the point here is that an unauthorized par value produces unhappy consequences, not a breach of law.

The only criteria provided in the Articles to guide par value changes were that changes were to be made to correct a "fundamental disequilibrium," that "competitive exchange depreciations" were to be avoided, and that "exchange stability" (meaning exchange *rate* stability) was an objective to be promoted. No full-scale effort was ever made to define with any precision the concept of fundamental disequilibrium. This was consistent with two important premises of the system: that the use of exchange rate change as a means of adjustment should not be encouraged, at least until other measures of adjustment had been utilized as far as possible, and that formal initiatives for par value changes were reserved for each country itself. It was however, always understood that indicators of fundamental disequilibrium need not be limited to imbalances shown by balance of payments data. Equally admissible were indications that external balance was being maintained at the cost of domestic economic performance (e.g., in terms of unemployment or price increases) that the country itself regarded as unacceptable, with the Fund expected to be willing to concur with the country's judgments as to the practical range of domestic performance to be regarded as acceptable.

Yet the system did not provide affirmative signals as to when either adjustment action should be initiated, and by whom, or when such action should take the form of exchange rate change. The Fund's annual consultation procedure, as did discussion elsewhere such as in Working Party 3 of OECD and in BIS meetings at Basle, provided opportunity for substantive consideration of the policies of members, and these no doubt had a certain influence at times. Fund financing beyond the gold tranche could be denied, as could financing for deficits from other sources, and this could lead to devaluations perhaps. There was the scarce currency clause for possible optional use to put pressure on surplus countries, but it was structured on what proved to be a relatively narrow base of use of Fund facilities for payments financing and was thought to involve both punitive aspects, which are extremely difficult to invoke in relations among nation states, and the danger of provoking a measure of unhelpful economic warfare.

For most of the first quarter century of the Fund's history, the exchange rate mechanism—and more generally the adjustment process—was thus somewhat permissive, less than fully consistent, and perhaps used less (or at any rate later) than would have been optimal. Yet the international monetary system as a whole worked extraordinarily well. Without doubt this was because the United States was in a position where persistent external deficits, if not too large, played a useful role in providing reserves for the system as a whole, in redistributing reserves among the main countries and in promoting the achievement and continuation of convertibility in Europe and the progressive liberalization of trade and payments. Consistent with these trends, and no doubt extremely helpful to them, were the central role acquired by the dollar in terms of its use as vehicle and intervention currency, and a preoccupation with building confidence as a basis for continuing convertibility—a preoccupation which contributed to the idea that among industrial countries, at any rate, par value changes should be viewed as a last resort when all else had failed. By the mid-sixties, it was common for officials to refer to the system as one of "fixed" (not "stable") exchange rates.

Meanwhile, it is worth mentioning that while devotion to "the par value system" as it was understood at the time was marked on the part of the Fund, a pragmatic and openminded attitude was being displayed toward problems of individual member countries in adhering fully to the prescribed system, and toward departures from it. Thus, when the policies toward drawings from the Fund in the first credit tranche and beyond were formulated in 1955 and 1957, respectively, drawings by countries not observing their exchange rate obligations under the Articles were not excluded. Indeed, since 1957, the policy has been that drawings would be approved for programs likely to achieve "the enduring stability of the exchange rate at a *realistic* level" (emphasis added). And, over the years, realism—including realism attained where necessary because of domestic economic circumstances by floating or frequently adjusted rates which are not par values—has in practice been a much more important operative standard than stability in the cases of drawings and stand-by arrangements on the part of a number of developing countries. Moreover, in the second half of the sixties, the Fund evolved the practice in a few cases of formally urging countries, where it thought the circumstances warranted this, to adopt free exchange rates; and in a number of stand-by arrangements with developing countries suffering from high rates of inflation, the Fund has had understandings as to certain quantitative factors (e.g., price changes or net official reserves, or both) which would be utilized in determining the timing and amount of exchange rate changes on the part of countries whose rates were not based on operational par values and which could not therefore legally be approved by the Fund.[2] In such cases the practical considerations were mainly two: to avoid deepening price distortions and to avoid proliferating controls, while seeking control over inflation through improvement in the traditional aggregative instruments of domestic policy.

These pragmatic views, however, were evolved with respect to individual cases of countries which were regarded as involving aberrations, and therefore as being outside the framework of the normal features of the system. It was not until almost the end of the sixties that the first real stirrings of official interest in somewhat greater exchange rate flexibility occurred, both inside and outside the Fund.

A rather dramatic shift in official attitudes had occurred by 1969-70. As late as 1966 it was possible for a major OECD report[3] on the international adjustment process to be written by officials with only a brief mention—consistent with the view of the time—of exchange rates as an adjustment measure of last resort. The documents of the Fund reflected essentially the same view. Moreover, I well remember reading George Halm's 1965 Princeton paper on wider margins and thinking it was an interesting piece of analysis, but obviously hardly practical.[4] In those years, open-minded official consideration of greater exchange rate flexibility was not only not on, but the subject was essentially taboo.

Events in the last few years of the decade changed all that quite quickly. Academic writing on the subject came with greater frequency, urgency, and appeal. The sterling exchange rate in the end could no longer be defended by policies that were practical at home, and the devaluation of November 1967 occurred, with a certain number of other currencies moving at the same time due to the impact of the sterling change itself or taking advantage of the occasion to make needed changes while minimizing the national political trauma. The SDR negotiation of 1966-69 occurred, and succeeded in among other things making the world safe for a U.S. external equilibrium, but although there were U.S. surpluses stemming from heavy short-term capital inflows in 1968-69, it became progressively more evident that this necessary condition was doing little or nothing to bring about the kind of correction in the world's payments situation that was needed. The Bonn Ministerial Conference in the fall of 1968 for the first time placed two important exchange rates on the table for open and explicit official consideration at a high political level, and in the ensuing year both the Deutsche mark and the French franc par values were moved appreciably, one up after a temporary float, the other down in a straight par value change. At the same time, it was becoming more and more clear that the growth in both the volume and volatility of private funds which had shown their willingness to move internationally, through the intermediary of the Euro-dollar market and otherwise, was likely to continue and to pose augmented problems for the management of reserve positions and domestic financial situations, at least in some countries. New and often inventive policy responses were devised, some of which relied to a certain extent on restrictions of various types.

Early in 1969, work began in the Fund to investigate the desirability of somewhat greater exchange rate flexibility in the system as a whole. The subject was regarded as sufficiently sensitive and controversial, however, that the subject was handled in an unusually informal and off-the-record manner. Essentially personal discussions on the basis of highly informal and tightly-held discussion papers were held for several months in the spring and summer of that year, with the executive directors not consulting with or reporting to their national authorities in the usual manner. While these discussions were not intended to do more than open up some preliminary consideration of a subject which had been taboo for so long, they did succeed in illuminating some elements of the exchange rate landscape. At the same time, government officials in capitals were for the first time proceeding to canvass systematically the implications of greater rate flexibility.

These efforts to open up the subject enabled it in 1970 to be brought into the open, in the form of the Fund report on "The Role of Exchange Rates in the Adjustment of International Payments." That report, and the process of consideration leading up to it, was perhaps notable more for the fact that it was a first effort to deal on an official cooperative level with the subject than for any dramatic new directions that were pointed. Indeed, the Report was criticized by Professor Halm himself[5]—with justice in my view—for its failure to formulate practical affirmative guidelines for changes in par values, "except those that could not be avoided anyway." Those who participated in the completion of the report got a taste of how varied and how strongly-held are governmental views on this subject. At a time when other elements of the international monetary and economic system were not similarly up for review, it is not easy to push ahead with major changes in a field like exchange rates. Moreover, in 1970 the United States was one of the principal protagonists of examining the merits of greater flexibility, but it was necessarily far from clear that the United States itself would in any circumstances be willing to alter its own par value (in terms of gold) at all, and this factor led to an appearance to others that flexibility might impinge mainly on them.

By 1972, full-scale reform of the international economy was under consideration in all its aspects—and of course the Smithsonian realignment had occurred, the dollar's convertibility into gold was a thing of the past, and wider margins up to 2 1/4 percent above and below par values or the new central rates were being used by a number of countries—including a surprising number of developing countries, given the tendency for their broad views to be in opposition to margins for the system as a whole which are any wider than necessary. Moreover, with the present Canadian float now two and a half years old and with sterling having now floated, further experience with currencies of substantial developed countries on a floating regime was being accumulated.

In these conditions, the 1972 Fund Report on Reform took a somewhat more affirmative tone and view toward greater exchange rate flexibility than did the 1970 report.[6] Moreover, while the 1972 report was carefully and diplomatically phrased, it demonstrated a much greater willingness openly to reveal major differences of approach, philosophy and view than has any previous Fund report. The 1972 report was the opening act of a fundamental reform debate, and sharp differences were to be expected.

As this is written, about New Year's 1973, consideration of reform of the international economic system has been launched within the forum of the so-called Committee of Twenty within the Fund, while negotiations on trade barriers are to be undertaken in the GATT. Rules and practices in all the features of the international economy are likely to form part of the broad negotiation which has been put in hand, so that the Committee of Twenty will have to address itself at an appropriate stage to the question of the consistency between rules and practices with respect to trade and investment that have been under development in GATT and elsewhere, and the substantive features of the international adjustment mechanism, in particular, to which it will itself have been devoting a major part of its effort. Indeed, major organizational change in the context of reform of the system is in no way excluded, which could adjust significantly the area of responsibilities of the several international organizations concerned, perhaps notably the Fund and GATT. With a very wide purview in mind, the terms of reference of the Committee of Twenty includes taking full account of the interrelationships between its work and rules and practices concerning trade, investment, and development that may be developed elsewhere.

In considering the design of the exchange rate mechanism to be installed in the future system, one must have constantly in mind the links between this feature and each of the other main elements of the system—the extent, conditions, and form of convertibility of officially-obtained holdings of foreign exchange into other assets such as SDRs; the nature and form of the intervention mechanism by which margins around central values of currencies are maintained;[7] and the role to be played by the several reserve assets in the system, to mention only three. Only a system in which each element is consistent with and supportive of each of the others is likely to prove successful and durable.

In his address to the IMF Annual Meeting in the fall of 1972, Secretary Shultz set out an outline of main points which presented a broad framework for negotiation covering exchange rates, reserves, the adjustment mechanism, controls over capital and other balance of payments transactions, related (i.e., trade) negotiations, and institutional implications. The American view on exchange rates is premised on a recognition that most countries prefer, for the system as a whole, to base themselves on a fixed point of reference for their currencies which has at any given time been established with international concurrence through the Fund. Such rates, with limited margins for market fluctuation of rates from them, carry the corollary of a commitment to defend them through action in the market and through a balanced system of convertibility.

Thus, floating rates as the organizing principle of the system as a whole are not under active consideration. Countries generally have declared themselves to be unwilling to see exchange rates for trade and other current account transactions altered more than by modest amounts by the market pressures that they envisage might, at least at times, be brought to bear by capital movements. Another dimension of the same point is that countries are not prepared to commit themselves to foreswear under all circumstances intervention in the exchange markets for their currencies. Still a third dimension is that countries in general take the view that current account transactions, and trade in particular, are more important than others and that exchange rates—by implication both spot and forward rates—should be kept as stable as possible for these transactions. Indeed, many countries (with which the United States is in dissent on this matter) would prefer capital controls or dual exchange markets to the current account rate fluctuations that variable capital flows may bring, and in this context they would seek a suitable degree of monetary policy autonomy— which in fact may in many cases be relatively modest—behind a wall of capital controls. Besides, one view somewhat prevalent among officials in a number of countries is that enhanced exchange rate flexibility may itself bring about still a greater augmentation of the volatility of capital flows.

But irrespective of the actual degree of market exchange rate fluctuation which will in fact be associated with international provisions envisaging greater flexibility, the critical point is to develop a system that produces exchange rates (in terms of both central values and market rates) which both *are* within reasonable limits from equilibrium rates and are perceived by the markets to be that way. Put another way, an ideal exchange rate mechanism would be one in which, except for unusual events such as a natural catastrophe or a sudden and unexpected wage explosion, exchange rate changes would not typically be large enough and predictable enough to engender large-scale speculative activity. This has led some proponents of variants of the crawling peg systems to assert that very small and very frequent movements in central values, even when they proved to be in the wrong direction, would be a good thing, so that markets would be accustomed to movement and any correction in direction or size of a given movement could be corrected in a subsequent movement in a long series. Whatever merit there might be in such an approach, which in certain respects has been applied with good results in several high-inflation developing countries such as Brazil,[8] there is little likelihood of it being used generally as a system where the need for it is not so compellingly clear. There remains, however, the need for a system which will promote payments equilibrium as a positive operational goal with commitments and incentives which countries will respond to, so that the contentious problems of relations, and the waste and distortion of resources, brought on by a system of continuing and deepening disequilibrium can be avoided.

Though it is one of the purposes of the Fund Agreement "to shorten the duration and lessen the degree of disequilibrium in the international balances of payments of members," there is no doubt that the inadequacies of the adjustment process, more particularly in recent years, have underlain the failure of the international monetary system. It has often been said that the heart of the problem lay not with the system, but with the unwillingness or inability of countries to adapt the network of their policies so as to make the system work. Perhaps so—the spirit may have been willing, but the flesh was weak. It was admittedly not an impossible system, just one which was progressively more ill-at-ease with the realities of modern life in a world of nation states greatly aware of their mutual interests in economic life, but also increasingly pre-occupied with profound problems of national identity and with domestic issues of novel and transcendent difficulty. In a word, while isolationism was much too pessimistic a word to describe the mood of nations in regard to international economic relations, they seemed not prepared to come up to the standard of conduct which the existing rules of the game implied. At just this time, the tremendous and deepening disequilibrium involving a huge U.S. deficit matched by surpluses elsewhere came into the forefront. The United States, as always during the postwar period (and in particular having in mind the SDR reform), resisted powerfully the idea of adjustment by formally devaluing against gold. Other countries found it excruciatingly difficult to accept either revaluation of their currencies against gold or to stay fixed against gold while the United States devalued. Having focused for so many years on the relationship with the dollar as the de facto pivot of the system, they found it extremely hard to accept the necessity of adjustment against it. Yet nothing else would do to right the central difficulty that had arisen and was rapidly growing worse.

Given the agreed need for reform, there is a question to what extent the system as such, or to what extent the performance of its members, are the main candidates for reform. Idealism aside, there can be only one answer—the system must in some sense represent the weighted average views and commitments of its members and a system which presumes greater willing or autonomous national devotion to its objectives than is likely to exist in practice cannot endure. Viewed in this way, the superior international economic and monetary system can be seen as a decision-making mechanism which optimizes the tradeoff between the international and national considerations.

Ideas of this kind lay behind the main thrust of the U.S. proposals for reform of the system. These proposals are premised on several conclusions about the nature of the international economy at present:

1. The great majority of countries wish to have an exchange rate mechanism basically designed on the assumption of central values for currencies, which in turn implies that in most situations margins of a certain size from these values will be maintained.
2. Many countries, perhaps chiefly on noneconomic grounds, want a system in which convertibility of officially-held dollars (and other currencies) is provided for or more generally in which surpluses and deficits of the official settlements balance of payments of the United States, as for other countries, results in more or less corresponding gains and losses of U.S. reserves. This attitude reflects in considerable part a recent emphasis on both greater symmetry in the system and on a desire for greater influence of the international community acting jointly over the level and growth of aggregate world reserves.
3. The adjustment process is both the most difficult and the most important of the problems of the international economic system. For any system to work with reasonable smoothness and harmony, it will have to avoid excessive reliance on ad hoc judgmental decisions regarding the need for adjustment measures in the manner of the system as it has operated in the past generation.
4. The system will also have to provide adequate room for disequilibria that will clearly develop from time to time without requiring or being premised on "fine tuning" with respect to the external balance which is beyond both the capabilities and the desires of national authorities.
5. The system must, as a practical matter, allow adequate scope for national policy-making, in particular in the choice of adjustment measures, without sacrificing the fundamental requirement that adjustment be accomplished.
6. The system, in terms of its central design, should be based on liberal and progressively freer (including more equitable) arrangements for both trade and capital transactions.

Perhaps the most novel single feature of the U.S. proposals lies in the suggestion that reserve data should be used as an objective indicator to determine the need and location of requirements for adjustment in the system. A detailed paper, submitted to the Deputies of the Committee of Twenty in

November 1972 has been published and need not be reviewed here.[9] But four aspects of use of reserve indicators deserve mention. First, they can provide signals of the need for adjustment. Second, they can point without emotion to the country or countries that need to initiate adjustment action, and in the process can avoid what in the past have at times been fruitless and heated debates over whose "fault" imbalances have been. Third, reserve criteria can form the basis, as existing arrangements have been unable to, for international measures to provide enforcement action in cases where adjustment steps are not adequately taken. Fourth, reserve criteria can provide critically important linkages between the adjustment process (and the exchange rate mechanism in this context) and other features of the system, so that consistency and durability of the whole structure can be reasonably assured. In this connection, the linkage between the adjustment process and the reserve system, convertibility or other features of official financial settlement, and the supply and demand for various forms of reserves represent the major problem, a problem which the Bretton Woods system to date has not adequately met.

Two other points about the U.S. proposals for the use of reserve indicators are important. They are not a proposal for a fully automatic statistical system. Room would remain for discussion and analysis, using all available data and methods of analysis and appreciation, and such discussion could overturn the strong presumption that adjustment action is required on the part of a given country on the basis of the behavior of its reserve situation. But from a decision-making point of view, strong presumption of a requirement to adjust would have to attach to the signals provided by reserves. While the presumption would be rebuttable, it is definitely the intention to put a strong burden of proof on the country which wishes to represent that the adjustment action suggested by the indicator is unnecessary. If the indicator were used only to precipitate international discussion of *whether* adjustment action were necessary, without a strong presumption that it was, experience of past years indicates that the performance of the adjustment process would be little improved.

Second, the use of reserve indicators would enable the system to adopt a broader and more helpful definition of the equilibrium which is to be pursued—not merely the absence of official settlement imbalances, but in principle a level and direction of official settlements imbalances consistent with moving the world at a reasonable pace toward an optimal distribution of reserves.

It has been suggested, among others by Fred Bergsten,[10] that a basic balance indicator would be preferable to a reserve indicator. I don't think so. While a series of statistical and technical problems admittedly exists for a reserve indicator, there would be no fewer such problems for a basic balance standard, and in addition the figures are subject to significantly greater delays. The opportunities for fatal inconsistencies to emerge would be much greater. Second, a basic balance indicator suggests either controls over short-term capital movements or a completely separate official financing arrangement for them, or perhaps both. Neither of these implications seems to me desirable. It may be noted in passing that a recent Fund staff effort to assess, against historical experience, the performance of a number of possible indicators of the need for adjustment did not show the basic balance indicator to be significantly better than several forms of reserve indicators.[11]

The U.S. proposals do not envisage greater exchange rate flexibility as an objective in itself or as necessarily being the result of the reform, except that margins in the range of those determined at the Smithsonian would continue to be available to countries. So far as central values are concerned, they would be more readily available than past traditions have indicated as an adjustment measure, but it is envisaged that countries would have a considerable measure of discretion in choosing the techniques and policies of adjustment—though as stressed above, it would be of importance not to permit this scope for choosing measures to be translated into failure or delay in meeting the basic adjustment obligation.[12]

Another feature of the U.S. proposals as to the exchange rate mechanism is its express desire to gain for the dollar the same range of possibility for intramarginal fluctuation, and thus the same range of capability for market management, as has in principle been available to other countries since December 1971. The gains to be expected from wider margins have been fully examined in many other writings, and will not be pursued at any length here. They concern mainly the room to influence short-term flows by market incentives, scope for a reasonable degree of national monetary policy autonomy, and a potentiality of easing the movement from one central value to another. But as is well known, in practice the scope for market fluctuation of the dollar vis-à-vis other currencies has been only half that which any other pair of currencies could have. This is due to the use of the dollar as the world's principal intervention currency. The desire of the United States for the same freedom of action as others have gained as to margins, combined with the expectation that others would not want to double their own margins to achieve this result, yields the probability that in order for the U.S. desideratum to be realized, some form of multicurrency intervention mechanism—at least in part—might well be necessary. Such practices have become familiar to a certain extent in the arrangements of the Common Market countries to operate their "snake in the tunnel." To the extent, which could be regarded as considerable, to which arrangements of this type resulted in a reduced use of the dollar as the exclusive medium for official intervention, the result would be considerably greater symmetry in the system—with respect to both exchange margins and more broadly to the role and treatment of currencies in the operations of the system.

The final point to be made about U.S. views on the exchange rate mechanism is that they envisage a role for fluctuating exchange rates to which the Fund could give its legal approval. While such floats are not seen as likely to become so widespread and durable as to constitute "the system," there is no strong reason either to regard them as so much an aberration, and so reprehensible, as to leave them deliberately outside the legal pale. Moreover, while floats may well more often than not be properly described as "temporary," in the sense of constituting interludes between the determination of central values with reasonable confidence, there seems no strong reason to insist that each incident of floating must be short-lived in some rigorously defined way. On the contrary, there are a number of examples—mostly of developing countries—in which floating of one kind or another has been utilized over a number of years and has doubtless represented the most sensible approach to reconciling domestic with international interests. For one thing, forms of floating may, in some cases of countries tending toward deficit, enable countries to avoid what could be competitive depreciation in order to establish a central value that errs on the side of establishing fully adequate credibility in the market—a phenomenon which, notwithstanding that there has been an absence of rate changes characterized as "competitive depreciation," has not been unknown in the past twenty-five years. The stress in the U.S. proposals, however, is on international surveillance of the policies and practices of floaters, in particular in cases where floats endure more than a fairly brief period.

A central preoccupation of the Bretton Woods exchange rate mechanism was to preclude competitive depreciation. But that mechanism lacked guiding operative standards to determine when and where adjustment initiatives were required, and during much of its history it tended to form traditions which resulted in over-rigid exchange rates. With the increasing rapidity of change which is characteristic of modern life in all its dimensions, shifts in the structure of industry and demand—as well, no doubt, as the greater scope for differential rates of price increase which recently higher rates of inflation all over the world have offered—have increasingly resulted in undervaluation without devaluation. Even in cases where undervaluation by this process have not been egregious, they have tended to become cumulatively large as countries feel more comfortable from every angle running a balance of payments situation which tends rather more toward surplus than toward deficit. Such surpluses, without trying to assign fault or causes and without regard to whether they are large or small, have tended to result in cumulatively large U.S. deficits and in overreliance on dollars in reserves.

In the design of the reformed system for the future, a system in which official balances of dollars will be freely convertible into other reserve assets from U.S. holdings, the central issue is to design criteria to result in adjustment initiatives which are equitable, effective, and consistent with the sustained health of the international monetary system. It is this role that the U.S. proposals for reserve criteria aim to fulfill.

Exchange rate changes in the reformed system would be available as a normal and expected adjustment measure, if the country concerned wished to use this technique. Some countries—in particular those with smaller than average foreign sectors—would no doubt more often want to adjust by bringing prices in the foreign sector into proper alignment with those at home. Countries with large foreign sectors may often prefer to conduct their domestic policy so as to insure that domestic prices are kept or brought into line with prices in the foreign sector. Under the U.S. proposals, each would be permitted to do so, provided the overriding objective of taking effective adjustment action is met.

Exchange rate flexibility as such is not an overt objective of these proposals, but the expectation would be that in fact somewhat greater flexibility will result from their application. We believe the system will function more effectively as a result.

Notes

1. This provision has become operative only once, in the case of a par value change by France in 1948, which was opposed by the Fund on the ground that it was not devalued sufficiently to permit the elimination of discriminatory restrictions. The Fund acted to restore normal French drawing facilities in 1954. As a result of this incident, the Fund in 1948 took a decision recognizing "that the extent of the change in par value, necessary to correct a fundamental disequilibrium, cannot be determined with precision and that in reaching a decision on a member's proposal to change its par value . . . the member should be given the benefit of any reasonable doubt. . . . due consideration should be given the views of the member regarding the political and social consequences of a change in par value greater than the one proposed."

2. An interesting anomaly in the Fund's legal structure is that it has the power to approve multiple rates (Article VIII, Section 3), but lacks legal authority to approve unitary floating exchange rates or other exchange systems which do not have at least one exchange rate based on an operative par value. The result is that the distinctions between exchange systems which the Fund is empowered to approve, and those it cannot, are to a certain extent arbitrary, accidental or even capricious. Thus the present practices of the United Kingdom, Canada, and Brazil are outside the law, while the dual market systems of France and Belgium have been approved by the Fund. At the extreme, the Fund can approve any exchange system involving floating rates, so long as there are at least two rates, but a unitary float is beyond its power to approve.

3. THE BALANCE OF PAYMENTS ADJUSTMENT PROCESS, A Report by Working Party No. 3, Organization for Economic Cooperation and Development, Paris, 1966.

4. George N. Halm, THE BAND PROPOSAL: THE LIMITS OF PERMISSIBLE EXCHANGE RATE VARIATIONS, Princeton Special Papers in International Economics No. 6, January 1965.

5. George N. Halm, THE INTERNATIONAL MONETARY FUND AND FLEXIBILITY OF EXCHANGE RATES, Princeton Essays in International Finance, No. 83, March 1971.

6. REFORM OF THE INTERNATIONAL MONETARY SYSTEM, a Report by the Executive Directors to the Board of Governors, International Monetary Fund, Washington, D.C., August 1972.

7. The term "central value" has recently been coined to refer to defined reference exchange rates, such as par values under the Articles of Agreement of the Fund or central rates as provided for in the post-Smithsonian arrangements, but the term is deliberately expressed in other words with the intention of avoiding the evocation of the historical and emotional associations of those earlier phrases.

8. See Chapter 2 in this volume on the recent Brazilian exchange rate experience, by Professor William G. Tyler.

9. As an Appendix to Chapter 5 of the ANNUAL ECONOMIC REPORT OF THE COUNCIL OF ECONOMIC ADVISERS.

10. C. Fred Bergsten, REFORMING THE DOLLAR: AN INTERNATIONAL MONETARY POLICY FOR THE UNITED STATES, Council on Foreign Relations Paper on International Affairs No. 2, September 1972, esp. pp. 50-51.

11. Other interesting conclusions of this study were that efforts to adjust basic balances for cyclical factors worsened their performance as indicators and that the performance of general indicators of domestic price movements (wholesale and consumer price indexes) was little better than random. Reserve and basic balance indicators (without cyclical adjustment) were among the best performers and while all indicators fell well short of "perfection" in the test, the best performers were judged to show a record substantially better than the actual performance of countries in the past decade.

12. In this connection, note needs to be taken of recent work by two of the most able students of the question (Price Competitiveness in Export Trade Among Industrial Countries, by Helen B. Junz, Federal Reserve Board, and Rudolf R. Rhomberg, International Monetary Fund, Discussion Paper No. 22, January 9, 1973, Division of International Finance, Board of Governors of the Federal Reserve System) to the effect that the lags in effectiveness of exchange rate changes may be longer than have been commonly supposed—perhaps up to five years for full results. This places further stress on prompt corrective action and also on the capacity of the system to accommodate imbalances during the lag period.

2

Exchange Rate Flexibility Under Conditions of Endemic Inflation: A Case Study of the Recent Brazilian Experience

William G. Tyler

I. Introduction

Recent discussions of the crawling peg and greater exchange rate flexibility have generally presumed relatively stable economies and, subsequently, rather small exchange rate adjustments.[1] The "band proposal," for instance, presupposes that exchange rate fluctuations will occur within a rather narrow range, say 4 percent, of an established par value for a country's currency.[2] Yet given the seemingly endemic inflation existing in many of the world's less developed countries, it appears doubtful that minute exchange adjustments around a certain par value could resolve the problem of balance of payments for such inflating countries. If there is a clear long-term tendency in a country's nominal exchange rate, certain questions are raised as to the applicability of the band proposal or the crawling peg.

Recent Brazilian exchange policy provides a good case study by which to examine some of the issues raised by the use of a crawling peg in a rapidly inflating country. In August 1968 the Brazilian monetary authorities initiated a policy of devaluing the cruzeiro every four weeks or so instead of on a more infrequent and irregular basis. After some three years of the mini-devaluation policy,[3] some preliminary conclusions are possible, and the purpose of this chapter is to examine the Brazilian experience with greater exchange flexibility. On the whole, the mini-devaluation policy appears enormously successful.

For a country characterized by seemingly chronic inflation, whatever its causes, the choice is not one between a fixed exchange rate and exchange adjustment. The very fact that inflation continues intractably rules out changes in domestic prices and incomes as a means of adjustment. Barring uncommon circumstances, the exchange reserves for a country under a fixed exchange rate with inflation greater than that of its trading partners dwindle, and international credit dries up. Direct controls also serve only temporarily as expedients. Eventually a change in the exchange rate is necessitated. Thus, the choice

The research was completed in September 1971 while the author was Visiting Fulbright Scholar at the Getulio Vargas Foundation in Rio de Janeiro. In addition, he is also grateful to Kenneth King, Denio Nogueira, Alberto Rodrigues, and Carlos von Doellinger who were helpful in discussing several problems with the author. He also thanks the many helpful officials and economists of the Central Bank and Finance Ministry who provided indispensible information and counsel.

ultimately for a country experiencing high rates of inflation on a continuing basis is not between a fixed exchange rate and exchange rate adjustment; rather, the choice is between different methods of exchange adjustment.

There are basically four alternative methods of exchange adjustment available to the rapidly inflating country. A deficit country can employ infrequent devaluations; more or less continual devaluations as exemplified by a mini-devaluation policy; a flexible exchange rate with government intervention to stabilize the market, discourage speculation, and iron out irregularities in an otherwise smooth transition for a secularly depreciating rate; or, finally, a freely fluctuating exchange rate. Although some would argue that the freely fluctuating, market-determined rates constitute the most preferable method of exchange adjustment, the differing degrees of managed flexibility implied in the mini-devaluation and interventionary flexible exchange rate regimes appear better than the awkward rigidity of the system of large infrequent devaluations.[4] As such, managed flexibility provides something of a second best. For a number of a priori and theoretical reasons the method of continual adjustment is conceptually superior to the system encompassing large, infrequent, last resort type devaluations.[5]

The policy of the International Monetary Fund in recent years has evolved to reflect the superiority of continual exchange adjustment so far as less developed countries are concerned. The Fund for some time has maintained an informal, "case by case" dichotomy in its interpretation of acceptable balance of payments adjustment measures. One set of adjustment rules is considered appropriate for the developed, industrial countries, while another, more liberal, set of rules of good balance of payments behavior is applied to the less developed countries.[6] The Fund has been lax in insisting that newly admitted, less developed member countries establish a par value for their currencies.[7] Still more important has been the gradual modification of the Fund position and policy with respect to flexible exchange rates for less developed countries. Initially the Fund's position was one of begrudging tolerance, but more recently it has changed to one of downright advocacy and promotion of greater exchange flexibility for less developed countries under certain conditions.[8] That exchange rate adjustment has been commonplace during the postwar period has been demonstrated by a recent study done under the auspices of the Fund. It was calculated that 96 of the IMF's 109 member nations underwent at least one devaluation between the end of 1948 and 1967.[9] The IMF seems to have recognized that, if exchange adjustments are to be made, attention must be given to what constitutes the best way to make such adjustments.

II. Brazilian Growth and Exchange Rate Policy

In the period since World War II the Brazilian economy has experienced remarkable growth and rapid industrialization. Spurred by high rates of industrial growth, Brazil's GDP grew at an annual average rate of about 6 percent from 1947 until 1962. Accompanying this growth was persistent inflation. As is seen in Table 2-1, during the mid-1950s growth slackened, inflation accelerated until 1964, and the economy stumbled through a period of stagnation and crisis. It was only toward the end of the 1960s, owing in great part to efficacious financial and economic policy, that high rates of growth were restored.[10] Inflation was gradually brought under control and, importantly, exports began to grow after nearly a twenty year period of virtual stagnation. Since the military take-over in 1964, one important area of financial policy reform, contributing to the economy's resurgence, has been exchange policy.

The Brazilian experience with exchange policy has been varied, witnessing several types of exchange regimes and differing degrees of controls since the end of World War II. The import exchange rate has frequently differed rather drastically from the export rates because of the use of bonuses, changes, and auctions which have resulted in the frequent de facto existence of multiple

Table 2-1
Macro Performance of the Brazilian Economy, 1947-1970

	GDP (%)	GDP per Capita (%)	Industry (%)	Agriculture (%)	Exports (US $1000)	Rate of Inflation[1] (%)
	Growth Rates					
1947-1950[2]	6.8	4.4	5.5	4.3	1,196	10.6
1951-1955[2]	6.8	3.8	7.7	5.1	1,488	15.6
1956-1960[2]	6.9	3.8	10.1	3.8	1,334	20.6
1961	10.3	6.7	10.6	7.6	1,403	33.3
1962	5.3	2.1	7.8	5.5	1,214	54.8
1963	1.5	−1.5	0.2	1.0	1,406	78.0
1964	2.9	−0.2	5.2	1.3	1,429	87.9
1965	2.7	−0.4	−4.7	13.8	1,595	55.4
1966	5.1	1.8	11.7	−3.2	1,741	38.8
1967	4.8	1.5	3.0	5.7	1,654	27.0
1968[3]	8.0	5.0	13.2	1.5	1,881	28.1
1969[3]	9.0	5.6	10.8	6.0	2,311	21.7
1970[3]	9.5	6.5	11.1	5.6	2,739	19.8

Sources: Centro de Contas Nacionals of the Fundaçao Getúlio Vargas, CONJUNTURA ECONÔMICA, and COMÉRCIO EXTERIOR DO BRASIL. Data were adapted from the introductory article in H. Jon Rosenbaum and William G. Tyler, eds. CONTEMPORARY BRAZIL: ISSUES IN ECONOMIC AND POLITICAL DEVELOPMENT (New York: Frederick A. Praeger, 1972).

Notes:
1. Implicit deflator used in the national income accounts.
2. Annual averages.
3. Preliminary estimates.

exchange rates. The import exchange policy in the postwar period has been used in two principal fashions—as a revenue tool and as a policy to promote development via import substituting industrialization. Indeed, exchange policy bore the burden of being the primary protectionist instrument until the system of specific tariffs, which was rendered ineffective by inflation, was reformed into a more meaningful system of ad valorem tariffs with the General Tariff Reform of 1957.[11] The export exchange policy has been erratic, but until recently seems to have hindered export diversification and expansion.

Some five phases of Brazilian postwar exchange policy can be identified. The first phase (1946-1953) was characterized by abuse-prone import licensing and a fixed exchange rate which become increasingly overvalued owing to domestic inflation. The period 1953-1959 witnessed an elaborate set of multiple exchange rates.[12] On the import side, several categories were established according to "essentiality," and auctions were used to allocate the foreign exchange alloted to the different categories. A third phase from 1959 to 1964 entailed attempts at exchange unification with respect to both imports and exports. Various import and export items were transferred to the free market exchange rates. Gradually, however, the attempts of exchange unification and reform disintegrated. The free rate became in effect the official exchange rate and devaluation was again allowed to lag behind price increases. To partially ameliorate the effects of the resultant exchange overvaluation, the monetary authorities resorted to a system of making partial, de facto devaluation through the use of exchange premiums (*bonecos*) that varied according to product.

A fourth phase in postwar exchange policy lasting until August 1968 was initiated in 1964 with new attempts to unify the exchange system. At that time there were three distinct exchange markets: (1) the bank rate, used for official transactions abroad; (2) the so-called manual rate, used in the exchange houses for tourism ends; and (3) the black or "parallel" market, used for unauthorized transactions. The exchange reform of 1964 united these different exchange rates into one market for foreign exchange. In August 1967 the monetary authorities took action tantamount to reestablishing the black market when it stopped selling dollars to all comers. A black market appeared literally overnight. In this fashion, as was the case in the third phase, exchange unification took place in the initial stages only to later retrogress into a less unified system.

In August 1968 the monetary authorities devalued and announced that they would henceforth follow a new devaluation policy. Instead of devaluing infrequently (every twelve months or so) devaluations began to occur more frequently and in smaller amounts. This can be seen in Table 2-2, which shows changes in nominal exchange rate between the devaluation of December 26, 1964 and September 1, 1971. From the initiation of the mini-devaluation policy to September 1, 1971 there were twenty-four exchange rate devaluations averaging 1.6 percent in nominal terms and occurring on an average of every forty-four days. The time between adjustments has been in no case less than two weeks nor more than two months.[13]

Table 2-2
Nominal Exchange Rate Adjustments, December 12, 1964-September 1, 1971

Date of Devaluation	New Exchange Rate[1] (Cr$/US$)[2]	Increase in Nominal Exchange Rate (%)	Numbers of Days Since Previous Devaluation
December 12, 1964	1.850	–	–
November 16, 1965	2.200	19.35	286
February 13, 1966	2.700	24.09	421
April 1, 1968	3.200	16.87	313
August 27, 1968	3.630	13.35	170
September 24, 1968	3.675	1.36	27
November 19, 1968	3.745	1.89	55
December 9, 1968	3.806	1.63	31
February 4, 1969	3.905	2.61	57
March 17, 1969	3.975	1.78	43
May 13, 1969	4.025	1.25	55
July 7, 1969	4.075	1.23	55
August 27, 1969	4.125	1.23	51
October 10, 1969	4.185	1.23	37
November 13, 1969	4.265	1.91	41
December 17, 1969	4.325	1.30	34
February 4, 1970	4.380	1.37	40
March 30, 1970	4.460	1.81	56
May 18, 1970	4.530	1.55	49
July 10, 1970	4.590	1.32	52
July 24, 1970	4.620	0.65	14
August 18, 1970	4.690	1.50	56
November 4, 1970	4.780	1.90	48
December 22, 1970	4.920	1.86	33
February 9, 1971	5.000	1.63	49
March 19, 1971	5.080	1.60	38
May 3, 1971	5.160	1.60	45
June 6, 1971	5.250	1.74	37
August 5, 1971	5.370	2.28	59

Source: Banco Central do Brasil, BOLETIM, various issues. The data were published in the BRAZIL HERALD, August 7, 1971.

Notes:

1. The exchange rate used is the "buy" rate, i.e., the rate at which cruzeiors are bought with dollars.

2. The figures given are in new cruzeiros. With the devaluation of February 1967, the decimal point in the cruzeiro was moved three places to the left—transforming the monetary unit into the New Cruzeiro. In 1970 the term New Cruzeiro was officially dropped, changing the name back to the cruzeiro—minus of course the three zeros.

Reasons given for the initiation were the desires to stop adverse movements of speculative capital and improve export performance.[14] After three years, it would appear that the objectives of the mini-devaluation policy have been met. We will now turn to an evaluation of the mini-devaluation policy, examining in turn its effect on trade performance, capital flows, inflation, and exchange policy administration.

III. An Evaluation of the Mini-Devaluation Policy

Trade Performance

With the possible exception of freely fluctuating exchange rates, the avoidance of the exchange rate overvaluation per se cannot properly be considered an effect of a certain type of exchange policy regime. In both the periodic and mini-devaluation regimes the selection of an exchange rate is discretionary.

The desire to avoid further overvaluation of the cruzeiro was clearly expressed by the Brazilian government shortly after the 1964 military take-over. Numerous official statements appeared stressing the importance of maintaining a "realistic" exchange policy in order to eliminate distortions and promote exports.[15] In view of the evidence such statements appear illusory and misleading.

To examine the drift of exchange policy we estimate real exchange rates through deflating nominal export exchange rates by the Brazilian wholesale price index.[16] The resultant exchange rate is then adjusted for dollar inflation.[17] As can be seen in Figure 2-1 and Table 2-3, even allowing for dollar inflation, the real exchange rate was allowed to fall approximately 40 percent between the military coup in March 1964 and June 1971. Discounting the exceptional and chaotic first few months of the rule of the post-1964 government, it is evident that a considerable decline occurred during the governance of the Castelo Branco administration—exactly that period during which commitments to a policy of "realistic" exchange rates were most vocal. From January 1965 to January 1967 the real exchange rate was permitted to fall by about 30 percent. The large devaluation of February 1967, which succeeded in increasing the real exchange rate by nearly 20 percent, was insufficient to raise the real exchange rate to its previous level. Between the initiation of the mini-devaluation policy in August 1968 (which began with a real devaluation of about 12 percent) and June 1971 the dollar inflation adjusted real exchange rate was permitted to fall by some 10 percent. This decline was most pronounced between mid 1969 and mid 1971.

Offsetting the decline in the real export exchange rate has been the implementation of a host of fiscal incentives for export—mainly for manufactured products. These tax incentives have been estimated in August 1971 to have an average value equal to some 50 percent of the domestic retail price for

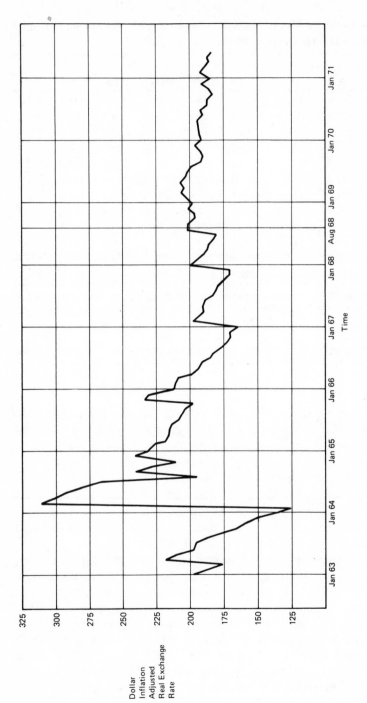

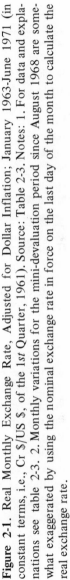

Figure 2-1. Real Monthly Exchange Rate, Adjusted for Dollar Inflation; January 1963-June 1971 (in constant terms, i.e., Cr $/US $, of the 1st Quarter, 1961). Source: Table 2-3. Notes: 1. For data and explanations see table 2-3. 2. Monthly variations for the mini-devaluation period since August 1968 are somewhat exaggerated by using the nominal exchange rate in force on the last day of the month to calculate the real exchange rate.

Table 2-3

Real Monthly Exchange Rates:[1] **January 1963-June 1971 (In Constant Terms, i.e., CRS/USS, of the 1st Quarter, 1961)**

| | 1963 | | 1964 | | 1965 | | 1966 | |
	N.D.I.A.[2]	D.I.A.[3]	N.D.I.A.	D.I.A.	N.D.I.A.	D.I.A.	N.D.I.A.	D.I.A.
January	197.9	198.9	134.2	135.5	228.7	231.0	204.3	213.7
February	185.5	185.9	125.8	126.4	224.8	227.5	200.4	211.2
March	175.3	175.1	312.5	313.8	216.1	218.9	197.5	208.2
April	220.6	219.9	300.2	301.1	213.1	216.7	188.5	198.9
May	211.3	211.3	294.1	294.4	210.9	215.3	183.3	193.6
June	199.3	199.9	282.2	282.2	208.6	214.4	180.3	190.6
July	194.2	195.4	264.5	265.6	203.3	209.2	174.7	185.9
August	186.9	187.6	194.4	195.0	200.4	206.2	171.6	183.3
September	176.0	176.5	238.5	240.2	198.3	204.2	167.4	178.8
October	165.3	166.1	226.9	228.7	193.3	199.3	163.3	173.4
November	160.0	161.1	210.6	212.1	226.6	234.5	162.2	171.8
December	150.0	150.5	239.6	241.3	222.0	231.1	161.6	171.1

Sources: Data from Banco Central do Brasil, BOLETIM, various issues; CONJUNTURA ECONÔMICA, various issues; and the U.S. FEDERAL RESERVE BULLETIN, various issues.

Notes:

1. Differing only slightly from the rate for non-manufactures (except coffee) and for imports, the export exchange rate for manufactures is presented. The nominal exchange rate

industrial exports.[18] Combining the dollar inflation adjusted real exchange rate and the tax incentives for export, as is done in Table 2-4 on a quarterly basis, the real domestic currency remuneration for Brazilian exporters of manufactures rose 67 percent from the first quarter 1964 (when the real export exchange rate was uncommonly low) to the fourth quarter 1970. Comparing the first quarter 1961 with the final quarter 1970, we find a still considerable increase in real exporter remuneration of 33 percent. The implementation of the fiscal incentives for export has had the effect of initiating, or rather broadening, a system of multiple exchange rates. In addition to what amounts to a separate, and lower, coffee export exchange rate, the fiscal incentives provide a premium to exporters of manufactures.[19] Disregarding tariffs and the fiscal incentives for export,[20] imports are made at essentially the same rate as non-coffee exports.

It is difficult to fathom the effects of the mini-devaluation policy on imports, but they appear to be rather insignificant. Estimates of import functions are fraught with all the well-known problems of time series analysis, but such estimates for Brazil suggest a low import elasticity with respect to the exchange rate.[21] Furthermore, in examining monthly import totals there was no readily evident or identifiable variation of imports over the devaluation cycle despite the

1967		1968		1969		1970		1971	
N.D.I.A.	D.I.A.	N.D.I.A.	D.I.A.	N.D.I.A.	D.I.A.	N.D.I.A.	D.I.A.	N.D.I.A.	D.I.A.
155.3	164.9	184.9	198.2	179.4	198.6	166.3	192.9	159.8	185.2
186.0	197.2	180.0	194.4	181.9	202.1	166.1	193.3	159.8	192.6
183.7	194.2	176.0	190.4	185.1	206.8	166.8	194.5	158.7	189.9
180.4	190.0	173.8	188.2	183.1	204.9	166.8	194.5	156.3	187.1
180.0	190.4	172.0	186.6	184.3	207.9	167.1	195.2	155.8	187.8
178.5	189.7	168.4	183.1	179.3	203.0	163.4	191.2	154.0	183.0
172.4	183.6	165.8	180.9	178.6	202.4	163.8	192.8		
171.3	181.7	186.3	202.5	176.1	199.7	160.2	187.8		
168.8	179.3	184.3	201.1	169.8	192.9	156.3	187.7		
165.7	175.8	179.9	196.3	167.3	190.7	156.7	189.6		
162.7	172.8	180.0	197.3	168.0	192.7	159.1	187.6		
161.7	172.7	182.3	200.1	170.3	196.0	162.4	191.3		

used is that in force on the last day of the month. All values are given in old (i.e., pre-1967) cruzeiros.

2. Nondollar inflation adjusted exchange rate. It is calculated by deflating the nominal exchange rate by the Brazilian wholesale price index.

3. Dollar inflation adjusted real exchange rate. It is calculated as:

$$\frac{\text{N.D.I.A. exchange rate x U.S. wholesale price index}}{100}$$

widespread belief that exchange speculation was manifested in part through trade flows. The frequency of devaluation does not seem to have appreciably affected imports.

It is hypothesized that exchange rate policy has played a major role in contributing to Brazil's success in export expansion and diversification in recent years. In addition to the level of the real exchange rate, oscillations in that level also have important determining effects on export behavior. With the method of large periodic devaluations to adjust the exchange rate, a degree of uncertainty and risk is interjected into the expectations of exporters that is not evident under a system of continual exchange rate adjustment. The exporter is exposed to an additional risk that he does not face in the domestic market—the exchange risk. In the domestic market sales prices can presumably rise with production costs, but in the export market unit local currency receipts are fixed because of constancy of the nominal exchange rate. When a devaluation occurs, export prices in local currency are once again fixed at a new, higher level. To predict his profit margin the exporter must be able to accurately forecast the size and time of the devaluations.

The unevenness in exporter profitability under a regime of large, periodic

Table 2-4
Real Remuneration to Brazilian Industrial Exporters, 1961-1971 (In Constant Terms, i.e., CR\$/US\$, of the 1st Quarter 1961)

	Dollar Inflation Adjusted Real Effective Exchange Rate[1] (R)	Index of Remuneration to Industrial Exporters via the Fiscal Incentives for Export[2] (T)	Rate of Real Effective Remuneration[3]
1961			
I	.201	100.00	.201
II	.223	100.00	.223
III	.196	100.00	.196
IV	.214	100.00	.214
1962			
I	.209	100.00	.209
II	.200	100.00	.200
III	.216	100.00	.216
IV	.218	100.00	.218
1963			
I	.161	100.00	.161
II	.170	100.00	.170
III	.179	100.00	.179
IV	.164	100.00	.164
1964			
I	.160	100.00	.160
II	.211	100.00	.211
III	.191	101.00	.193
IV	.211	103.00	.217
1965			
I	.205	103.00	.211
II	.198	104.00	.206
III	.199	109.02	.217
IV	.202	119.07	.241
1966			
I	.202	119.07	.241
II	.192	119.07	.229
III	.188	119.07	.224
IV	.177	119.07	.211
1967			
I	.177	121.97	.216
II	.184	129.57	.238
III	.182	129.57	.236
IV	.178	129.57	.231

Table 2-4 (cont.)

	Dollar Inflation Adjusted Real Effective Exchange Rate[1] (R)	Index of Remuneration to Industrial Exporters via the Fiscal Incentives for Export[2] (T)	Rate of Real Effective Remuneration[3]
1968			
I	.184	129.57	.238
II	.177	129.57	.229
III	.173	135.74	.235
IV	.183	135.74	.248
1969			
I	.186	135.74	.252
II	.190	135.74	.258
III	.189	141.90	.268
IV	.192	141.90	.272
1970			
I	.195	141.90	.277
II	.192	141.90	.272
III	.189	141.90	.268
IV	.189	141.90	.268
1971[4]			
I	N.A.	149.61	—
II	N.A.	149.61	—

Sources: Ministério da Fazenda, BOLETIM DO COMÉRCIO EXTERIOR, various issues; CONJUNTURA ECONÔMICA; FEDERAL RESERVE BULLETIN; and Tyler, "Export Diversification and the Promotion of Manufactured Exports in Brazil," pp. 139-41.

Notes:

1. Instead of using the nominal exchange rate to calculate the real exchange rate, an effective exchange rate for manufactured exports was estimated and employed. The effective exchange rate incorporates exporter earnings from varying export bonuses which were widespread before 1963. It was calculated by dividing the cruzeiro value of manufactured exports by their dollar value. All values are in (new) cruzeiros.

2. The estimation of the magnitude of the tax incentives for export is explained in Tyler, "Export Diversification and the Promotion of Manufactured Exports in Brazil," pp. 122-41. As quantified, the index of tax incentives represent the remuneration for manufactured export in comparison to domestic prices. The tax incentives include those credits or rebates allowed for the tax on value of industrial product (IPI), the circulation tax (ICM), the business income tax, and the tax on financial operations. An estimation of the drawback has been excluded from the index.

3. The real effective remuneration to manufactured exporters is calculated as:

$$\frac{R \times I.}{100}$$

4. At the time of this writing (September 1971) export data for the beginning months of 1971 were not yet available owing to a major revision in the classifications of the Brazilian trade statistics.

devaluations accompanying continuing inflation is demonstrated graphically for a firm in Figure 2-2. Beginning in time t_1, should the producer export, increasing unit losses will be incurred until the devaluation occurs at time t_2. From t_2 to t_4 exports for the firm will be profitable with varying profit margins depending upon the rise of production costs and magnitude of the devaluation at t_3. From t_4 to t_5 export is once again unprofitable.

Frequent devaluations or continual depreciation accompanying the intended inflation do much to remove the uncertainty and exchange risk confronting the potential exporter. Export profitability is no longer subject to a seemingly arbitrary decision and is more easily predictable. Assuming that inflation, depreciation, and the exporter's increase in production costs all proceed at the same rate, a line representing local currency unit receipts for exports will parallel that depicting production costs in Figure 2-2. The greater evenness in unit local currency export receipts and the greater predictability of profit margins are believed to be important in promoting exports. The elimination of the on-again-off-again nature of export profitability brought by the large, period devaluation permits the exporter to make plans and marketing arrangements for selling his

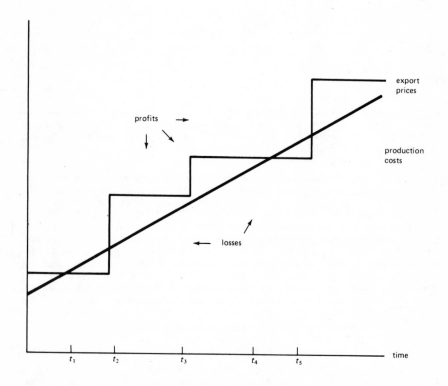

Figure 2-2. Export Prices and Production Costs in Local Currency

products in international markets. It also assures the buyer of a greater dependability of supply.

The argument that a more steady real exchange rate is more conducive to export expansion than one characterized by greater oscillations finds support in the Brazilian case. Between January 1963 and the initiation of the mini-devaluation policy in August 1968 the average monthly variation in the dollar inflation adjusted amounted to a noteworthy 7 percent, while from then until June 1971 the average monthly variation registered a more modest 1.5 percent.[22] At the same time, as suggested in Table 2-1, Brazilian exports were experiencing a considerable expansion. The effect of exchange policy in contributing to the recent export success constitutes an interesting and important question.[23]

To analyze the impact and test the importance of exchange rate policy for exports two different approaches were employed. First, a series of in-depth interviews was made with some thirty-five manufacturers to examine the determinants of export behavior and the effectiveness of policy.[24] Respondents were chosen according to differing export performance, firm size, product, and nationality of firm ownership. Almost without exception firms brought up and stressed the importance of the mini-devaluation policy in diminishing entrepreneurial risk by enabling them to more accurately predict export profitability. Furthermore, many firms emphasized that the implementation of the mini-devaluation policy was an indication of the government's sincerity in promoting exports and providing support for exporting firms. Since the overall direction of change in the dollar inflation adjusted real exchange rate since mid-1967 has been less pronounced than the monthly, or short-term, changes, questions regarding the level of the exchange rate did not yield consistent and significant results.

A second approach in examining the effect of the mini-devaluation policy on export performance employed the use of regression analysis in an attempt to explicate variance in manufactured exports. While the results of such an analysis indicated the importance of the exchange rate variable, nothing could be concluded from the regression analysis as to the importance of the frequency of devaluation. Using quarterly data from 1961 to 1970, the following regression equation was estimated:[a]

$$\log X_1 = -13.577 + 1.415 \log X_2 + .005 X_3 + 2.634 \log X_4$$
$$(-3.386) \quad (2.628) \qquad (.546) \qquad (1.430)$$

$$+ \quad 1.238 X_5 - .037 X_6$$
$$(1.405) \quad (-2.184)$$

$$R^2 = .90 \qquad\qquad\qquad D.W. = .91$$

[a]The t values appear in parentheses beneath the regression coefficients. The estimated Durbin-Watson statistic indicates a problem of significant autocorrelation of residuals.

where:

X_1 = constant dollar value of Brazil's manufactured exports

X_2 = dollar inflation adjusted real effective exchange rate manufactured exports

X_3 = absolute (i.e., without signs) percentage variation in X_2

X_4 = fiscal incentives for export

X_5 = total world imports

X_6 = proxy variable for Brazilian industrial capacity utilization (residuals from time trend regression line for industrial production)

The independent variables X_2 and X_6 are statistically significant at the 5 percent level, while X_4 and X_5 are significant at about the 15 percent level. Although the exchange rate variable X_2 was seen to be significant and possessing a high elasticity of 1.4, the test for the importance of the mini-devaluation policy proved inconclusive. Variable X_3, reflecting quarterly fluctuations in the real effective exchange rate regardless of sign, was not statistically significant. Nor did it even demonstrate the theoretically "correct" negative sign (albeit it did have a very low regression coefficient of .005). As expected, both the recession-boom effect and the fiscal incentives, along with the real exchange rate, proved to be important determinants of Brazil's manufactured exports.[26]

Speculation and Short-term Capital Flows

A paramount question for flexible exchange rates is whether speculation is stabilizing or destabilizing. While there is much theoretical literature supporting both possibilities, the empirical work is somewhat limited and ambivalent.[27] The speculative flow issue is possibly the most damaging charge against continual exchange adjustment for an inflating country. With a freely fluctuating rate the argument can be made that speculation will be destabilizing. Since there is no doubt about the general direction of the exchange rate, there will be no incentive to hold liquid assets in the depreciating currency. Therefore, the argument runs the exchange rate will be bid down below its equilibrium level. As such, the flight of capital will actually precipitate the action it anticipates, i.e., the exchange depreciation.

Under a policy of discretionary devaluation by the monetary authorities the destabilizing speculative flow problem also exists. In fact the longer the period between devaluations and the greater their magnitude the greater will be the problem around the time of the expected devaluation. The periodic devaluation method has a speculation cycle all of its own. Prior to an anticipated devaluation speculators switch into foreign currency at an overvalued exchange rate, wait out the devaluation, and afterwards switch back into local currency at the new rate, thus realizing a windfall gain of the amount of the devaluation. If interest rate policy provides for positive real interest rates, the gain is twofold. High nominal interest rates are earned, allowing the speculator to convert a nominal gain in interest receipts into a real gain through propicious exchange speculation.

With the crawling peg approach of frequent devaluations coupled with a policy of maintaining positive real interest rates, the devaluation-speculation cycle is eliminated with, say, monthly devaluation. Exchange speculation becomes unprofitable if the nominal interest rate is greater than the nominal exchange depreciation, provided interest is not earned on deposits of only a few days duration. For example, assuming both inflation and exchange depreciation of some 2 percent monthly, a nominal interest rate greater than 2 percent monthly will render exchange speculation unprofitable. With a relatively open exchange system a real short-term interest rate greater than that existing in other capital markets, a net inflow of short-term capital can be expected. The resultant inflow of short-term capital, however, may tempt the monetary authorities to diminish the rate of exchange depreciation. Such a decline in the real exchange rate ceteris paribus would tend to make local currency short-term debt instruments still more attractive to foreigners, increasing the short-term capital inflow and providing further problems of monetization for the authorities.

With a freely fluctuating rate and persistent inflation the fear of destabilizing speculative capital flows also appears to be overstated. In addition to the applicability interest rate condition, as stated above, speculation, as Friedman and others have convincingly argued,[28] will tend to be stabilizing when the actual exchange rate differs from the equilibrium rate. Furthermore, inflationary expectations in many lesser developed, inflating countries provide a certain stability in preventing a panic which would result in massive capital flight and subsequent excessive exchange depreciation.

In examining the Brazilian case, it is apparent that the institution of the crawling peg has not resulted in adverse speculative flows. In fact the heavy movement of capital that was witnessed around the time of devaluation under the previous, periodic jolt method of devaluation is no longer present.[29] At the same time, however, it is impossible to precisely isolate, either quantitatively or qualitatively, the effects of the mini-devaluation policy on exchange speculation and capital flows in the Brazilian balance of payments. A number of policies and financial sector reforms have also had a balance of payments impact. As such it is impossible to disentangle the effects. Nevertheless, by examining some of these other policies and occurrences along with developments in the external accounts, we can form some judgments as to both the total effects of financial policies and the specific influence of the mini-devaluation policy.

Major changes have been made with respect to interest rate policy and capital markets. As shown in Table 2-5, real interest rates in Brazil's highly compartmentalized financial markets have undergone appreciable changes in the last ten years. Faced with legal restrictions on interest rates, the early 1960s witnessed

Table 2-5
Real Interest Rates in Brazil, 1960-1970[1] (In Percentage per Annum)

Year	Commercial Bank Loan Rates	Banco do Brazil[2] Loan Rates	Letras de Cambio[3] Rates to Borrower	Commercial Bank Deposit Rates	ORTN[4] Rates to Holder	Letras de Cambio Rates to Holder
1960	-7.4	-15.2	9.9	-19.3		-6.4
1961	-11.8	-18.0	10.9	-23.9		-7.9
1962	-17.5	-25.0	5.5	-31.6		-14.6
1963	-25.6	-35.0	-2.8	-41.0		-23.1
1964	-30.1	-37.5	-4.9	-45.9		-24.5
1965	-14.1	-21.7	14.1	-34.4	-1.9	-13.3
1966	-2.3	-9.1	24.2	-26.2	6.1	-5.5
1967	4.5	-5.1	16.1	-20.7	1.4	2.3
1968	7.6	8.4	17.7	-16.6	5.3	4.3
1969	8.4		19.3	-13.7	1.7	6.2
1970			19.9 (May)		2.0	6.8

Source: Computed from various unpublished reports and information provided by the Brazilian Central Bank. Calculations and data were taken from Don Syvrud, "Interest Rate Structure and Policies in Brazil—1960 to 1970," unpublished paper prepared for AID, 1970.

Notes:

1. To estimate real rates of interest nominal interest rates have been deflated by the general price index (Index No. 1 in CONJUNTURA ECONÔMICA).

2. The Banco do Brasil is an unusual combination of a private and public bank. Having both some characteristics of a commercial bank and a government financial institution, it is not to be confused with Brazil's Central Bank.

3. Letras de Cambio are private sector financial instruments.

4. The ORTN (readjustable treasury bonds) are adjusted by the monetary correction index of the National Monetary Council. ORTN came into existence only in 1965.

increasingly negative real interest rates as the inflation accelerated.[30] As part of the stabilization measures undertaken by the government, monetary correction was extended to the major financial instruments in 1965-1966. Monetary correction to adjust for inflation, coupled with greater than anticipated success in reducing inflation, resulted in turning real interest rates from negative to positive in 1966 for the recently created, readjustable treasury bonds and in 1967 for commercial bank loans. Since 1968 the monetary authorities have employed incentives in an attempt to induce commercial banks to reduce their loan rates.[31]

Further institutional changes have occurred in the nascent Brazilian stock market. The government has undertaken numerous measures, such as an income tax deduction for stock purchases and the exemption of capital gains from taxation, to stimulate the development and later to bolster the level of the stock market. In 1969 the subsidy provided in the form of income tax deductions alone amounted to some Cr.$ 212.1 million; this amount exceeded the year's news issues.[32] Brazil's resurgence of economic growth plus the institutional measures propping up the market have given rise to an unparalleled stock market boom. From December 1968 to August 1971 the BV index of prices for stocks listed on the Rio de Janeiro exchange increased by over 18 times its December 1968 value.[33]

As can be seen from Table 2-6, the capital account in Brazil's balance of payments has witnessed important changes in recent years. Since the initiation of the mini-devaluation policy and other financial reforms, a net autonomous inflow of foreign capital has increased continually, accounting for overall balances of payments surpluses since 1968. Importantly, net private foreign loans and financing have risen dramatically.[34] Short-term (i.e., less than 365 days) private borrowing and lending activities are included under both the items for "Loans and Financing" and "Other."

Table 2-7 presents a disaggregation of short- and medium- and long-term capital flows. For the latter, both inflows and outflows can be seen. Care must be used, however, in interpreting the short-term vs. medium- and long-term inflows. The categories have been subjected to some changes and are not entirely comparable on a yearly basis. For example, the apparent fall in net short-term capital inflow from 1968 to 1969 is overstated owing to the reorganization of the categories to transfer some flows previously included under item II to item IA2.

The important errors and omissions item in the balance of payments presumably is reflective to some degree of unregistered and unmeasured short-term capital movements. Despite the variability of errors and omissions, in recent years they have displayed lesser negative magnitudes. Not surprisingly, the preliminary estimates of the balance of payments for 1968-1970 contained errors and omissions of higher positive magnitudes. As revisions of the payments estimates were made, increases in net inflows were made in the private capital account (along with lesser changes in the service account).

Table 2-6
The Brazilian Balance of Payments, 1961-1970 (In Millions of U.S. Dollars)

	1961	1962	1963	1964	1965	1966	1967	1968	1969	1970
Exports (FOB)	1,403	1,214	1,406	1,430	1,596	1,741	1,654	1,881	2,311	2,739
Imports (FOB)	-1,292	-1,304	-1,294	-1,086	-941	-1,303	-1,441	-1,855	-1,993	-2,526
Current Account Balance	-261	-423	-147	102	283	-33	-277	-503	-269	-622
Net Autonomous Capital Movements	327	245	13	92	79	205	66	541	850	1,068
Private Capital	224	187	42	67	75	133	84	569	757	891
Direct investment	108	69	30	28	70	74	76	61	124	108
Direct reinvestment	39	63	57	58	84	85	39	–	–	–
Loans and financing	346	178	93	54	113	180	304	337	604	944
Amortization	-210	-188	-141	-100	-132	-145	-211	-218	-197	-298
Other, including some short-term net capital flows	-59	65	3	27	-60	-61	-124	389	226	137
Non-Accommodating Government Capital	53	33	-54	-9	4	72	-18	-28	93	177
Loans and financing	183	165	169	172	250	328	226	246	449	519
Amortization	-117	-122	-229	-178	-172	-205	-233	-266	-336	-351
Errors and Omissions	49	-140	-120	-126	-31	-19	-34	-1	-20	39
Surplus (+) or Deficit (−)	115	-318	-254	68	331	153	-245	32	549	545
Commercial Arrears	-68	163	14	57	-182	-44	-8	–	–	–
Accommodating Government Financing	-47	155	240	-125	-149	-109	253	-32	-549	-545

Source: Banco Central do Brasil, BOLETIM, various issues. Recent data and some revisions were kindly supplied by the Balance of Payments Division of the Central Bank.

The capital inflow and resultant balance of surpluses have greatly increased Brazil's foreign exchange reserves and presented the monetary authorities with the problem of monetizing the inflow of foreign credits. By the end of 1970 Brazil's holdings of liquid foreign assets had risen to an unprecedented high of US$ 1.9 billion, or approximately two-thirds of her 1970 CIF imports.[35]

The increases in foreign reserves have had a considerable expansionary impact on domestic credit. In 1970, for example, such increases amounted to Cr.$ 2,917 million as compared to a total increase in the money supply of Cr.$ 7,509 million (an increase of 26.5 percent when compared to the money supply in 1969). From the ratio of changes in reserve money to changes in the total money supply a money multiplier of 1.9 was estimated. As such, the foreign reserve accumulation accounted for an increase in the money supply of some Cr.$ 5,522 million—an amount equal to nearly three-fourths (i.e., 73.6 percent) of the increase in the total money supply.[36] Given a monetary budget the authorities have sought to sterilize the increase in foreign reserves through contractionary domestic operations. Sterilizated measures have tended to push interest rates up, while, on the other hand, the lower foreign interest rates (and resultant capital inflow) have tended to have an offsetting depressant effect on interest rates in Brazil.

The mini-devaluation policy and other institutional changes have brought about an opening up of the economy which in turn has constituted a necessary condition to the sizable recent influx of foreign capital. The Central Bank's Resolution 63 has provided a mechanism to channel relatively short-term foreign credits to Brazilian firms through the commercial banking system.[37] Other foreign credits are registered under Law 4,131 and Instruction 289. The inflow of such capital has contributed greatly to the recent growth in Brazil's foreign debt. During 1970 external indebtedness increased to US$ 5.295 million of which about 75 percent was accounted for by private sector increases of foreign exchange borrowing, in great part of a short- or medium-term nature.[38] This can be observed in Table 2-8.

The sizable net inflow of short- and medium-term capital since 1968 reflects a number of factors. Interest rate policy has brought about positive real interest rates and a credit squeeze. Such conditions have resulted in a classic inflow of short- and medium-term capital. Such borrowing, however, has not taken the form of highly mobile international capital seeking higher interest rates. It has resulted from local (foreign and domestic) firms, feeling the pinch of the credit squeeze, seeking and acquiring short- and medium-term loans abroad. Foreign firms especially have increasingly resorted to this practice; flows of capital between parent company and subsidiary alledgedly have accounted for much of the borrowing.[39] Changes in administrative ground rules, coupled with the favorable foreign investment climate, have made it attractive for foreign subsidiaries to bring money into Brazil as loans rather than having it registered as foreign investment. Much of such borrowing operations have been through U.S.

Table 2-7

Capital Flows in the Brazilian Balance of Payments, 1964-1970 (In Millions of U.S. Dollars)

	1964		1965		1966	
	Inflow	Outflow	Inflow	Outflow	Inflow	Outflow
I. Medium and Long Term Capital	398	345	476	482	688	575
A. Private Capital	104	115	202	211	290	253
1. Direct Investment	28	–	70	–	74	–
2. Loans and Financing	61	98	113	132	180	145
3. Other	15	17	19	79	36	108
B. Government Capital	294	230	274	271	398	322
1. Loans and Financing	160	179	250	172	328	205
2. Other	134	51	24	99	70	117
II. Short-Term Capital (net)	29	–	0	–	11	–
III. Total (I ÷ II) (net)	82	–	–	6	124	–

Source: Unpublished data kindly provided by the Balance of Payments Division of the Brazilian Central Bank.

banks operating in Brazil. Because of a quirk in U.S. tax laws, American banks have a competitive edge over European banks.

Another apparent factor accounting for the recent short- and medium-term net capital inflow has been the stock market boom. As suggested in Items IA1 and II of Table 2-7 and the errors and omissions item of Table 2-6, the frenzy of activity in the stock market since 1968 appears to have dampered capital outflows.[40] In addition, it has been alleged that much foreign capital has found its way into the Brazilian stock market.[41]

A third factor is the advent of the mini-devaluation policy. While it is natural that short- and medium-term capital flows to where there exists a liquidity shortage, prior to 1968 such short- and medium-term capital flows were impeded for Brazil by the exchange rate regime. The unpredictability of exchange rate devaluation injected an element of uncertainty into the decisions of bankers, corporate treasurers, and speculators. The mini-devaluation policy, coupled with reforms in interest rate policy, resulted in a greater openness of the economy's balance of payments.

To further analyze the determinants of capital inflows in the Brazilian balance of payments the following linear regression equation was estimated:

$$F = 334.19 + 9.50\,i + 553.11\,D$$
$$\qquad\qquad (1.83)\quad (4.23)$$

$$R^2 = .90 \qquad\qquad \text{D.W.} = 2.06$$

1967		1968		1969		1970	
Inflow	Outflow	Inflow	Outflow	Inflow	Outflow	Inflow	Outflow
637	532	801	621	1,291	610	1,766	795
404	284	479	271	815	227	1,109	332
76	–	81	20	139	15	129	21
304	211	337	218	604	197	944	298
24	73	61	33	72	15	36	13
230	248	322	350	476	383	657	443
226	233	246	266	449	336	519	351
4	15	76	84	27	47	138	92
–	75	361	–	169	–	77	–
27	–	541	–	850	–	1,068	–

where F represents private medium- and long-term capital inflows, i equals the real rate of interest paid to holders of *letras de cambio* (commercial paper), and D represents a dummy variable for the mini-devaluation policy. Annual data from 1964 to 1970 was utilized, with t values indicated in parentheses below the regression coefficients. Both independent variables are statistically significant—D at the 1 percent level and i at a little over the 10 percent level. Care, however, must be used in interpreting D. It must be remembered that during the period of the mini-devaluation policy other factors have also been important.

On the whole, it would be incorrect to attribute the marked improvement (i.e., inflow of foreign credits) of Brazil's capital account in its balance of payments solely to the initiation and administration of the mini-devaluation policy. Clearly many factors are involved. Political repression has brought a more attractive investment climate for foreign capital. Interest rate policy and other financial reforms have rationalized Brazil's money markets. Nevertheless, we can say more for the mini-devaluation policy other than merely that it did not result in adverse speculative activity. In addition to drastically reducing, if not eliminating, exchange speculation, the mini-devaluation policy, as one of many financial reforms, has contributed to opening the economy more to an influx of capital beneficial to Brazil's growth. Brazil's capital account in its balance of payments has become increasingly important in the past few years. (In 1970 the net autonomous capital inflow was equal to over 40 percent of FOB imports.) While the mini-devaluation policy itself has been significant in increasing the capital inflow the rate of discretionary exchange depreciation also plays an

Table 2-8

Selected Items in Brazil's Foreign Indebtedness (Millions of U.S. $)

	Year End 1969	Year End 1970
Foreign Currency Loans	1,604.7	2,284.6
Resolution 63	432.5	653.2
Instruction 289	373.5	381.2
Law 4,131	798.7	1,250.2
Total Foreign Indebtedness[1]	4,403.3	5,295.2

Source: Banco Central do Brasil, BOLETIM, Junho 1971, pp. 4-12. Unfortunately, data for prior to year end 1969 are unavailable.

Note:

1. In addition to foreign current loans, Brazil's total foreign indebtedness includes debt resulting from the financing of imports by international agencies and foreign governments, AID program loans and official compensatory borrowing.

important role, and may present problems for the monetary authorities. Given a level and structure of interest rates, if the real exchange rate is allowed to fall, capital will tend to flow to Brazil, since repayment is made in cheaper foreign exchange. Effectively, this spreads the interest rate differential between Brazilian and international money markets still more.

Inflation

Another charge frequently made against the use of flexibility in exchange rate is that such flexibility will inevitably lead to inflationary tendencies. Without the ironclad discipline of a fixed exchange rate government authorities will supposedly be unable to resist the inflationary temptations of irresponsible monetary and fiscal policy. One respected writer has argued that "a wide range of countries . . . are not to be safely trusted with a floating exchange and that the fixed exchange . . . is in many countries the sole surviving barrier to almost unrestrained inflation."[42]

The neglected element of the exchange-flexibility-leads-to-inflation argument is that it ignores the fact that under the present adjustable peg system, as exemplified by the rules of the IMF, exchange rates are also subject to alteration in the event of "fundamental disequilibrium." Without unquestionable fixity in exchange rates, thus forcing balance of payments adjustment via the noxious medicine of adjustment in domestic prices and incomes (and/or direct controls), the "ironclad discipline" of the fixed exchange rate is nonexistent. The question becomes one of degree. Does infrequent periodic exchange adjustment result in fewer inflationary tendencies than a system of continual exchange adjustment? Even if the answer to this question is affirmative, the costs of such a method of infrequent exchange adjustments may outweigh any benefits accruing in reducing inflation, especially if the exchange rate adjustments are necessarily large.

One might argue in addition that large infrequent exchange rate adjustments tend to be more inflationary than more gradual adjustments owing to the inflationary jolt given to the economy by a large devaluation. Following such a devaluation price and wage adjustments are usually made. The elimination of large devaluations spreads out the inflationary impulse resulting from exchange depreciation. Furthermore, with mini-devaluations the devaluation excuse to raise prices and increase wages is removed. Other pretexts have to be found by businessmen and labor leaders.

There is some suggestive evidence that this inflationary jolt argument connected with devaluation applies in Brazil. In examining the military government's four large devaluations of December 26, 1964, November 16, 1965, February 13, 1967, and April 1, 1968, it was found that in all cases the rate of inflation (as measured by the cost of living index) for the three months following the exchange rate adjustment exceeded that for the three months prior to the devaluation. In only one case was the difference less than 10 percent.

Whether infrequent or continual devaluations are slightly more or less inflationary is not a question of great concern in the Brazilian case. Whichever type of exchange regime the monetary authorities adopt, Brazil—given its present institutional and economic circumstances—will continue to experience inflation greater than its trading partners. If chronic inflation is a fact, the question is one of selecting the best overall system of exchange adjustment.

The Brazilian experience suggests the incorrectness of the argument that frequent changes in a country's exchange rate will result in unbridled inflation. What is important is not so much the exchange regime per se but the nature of the monetary and fiscal policies accompanying the exchange regime.[43] As was seen in Table 2-1, the Brazilian rate of inflation has not accelerated sharply since the initiation of the mini-devaluation policy in August 1968. If anything, inflation has decreased slightly—not as a result of the mini-devaluation policy, but of other policies. In the Brazilian case the use of more or less continual exchange adjustment has not resulted in a series of irresponsible monetary and fiscal measures. In my opinion financial and economic policy in Brazil has probably never been better. The implementation of the mini-devaluation regime is merely one indication of the soundness of such policy.

Administrative and Political Dimensions

While the rate of inflation in large part depends upon the suitability of financial policy, there are reasons to believe that in Brazil the administrative and political constraints to this implementation of such financial policies are eased to some measure by the mini-devaluation policy. When compared to the periodic jolt method of annual devaluation, the Brazilian mini-devaluation policy offers advantages of increased independence in monetary policy, apparent greater ease in devaluing and maintaining a certain real exchange rate, and increased protection from accusations of administrative abuse and corruption.

With the previous system of large periodic devaluation serious constraints in the administration of policy were encountered by the Brazilian monetary authorities. The devaluation cycle was accompanied by events resulting in considerable pressures and a subsequent loss in monetary policy independence.[44] Following a devaluation large inflows of foreign capital occurred which were accounted for in large part by subsidiaries of foreign firms receiving loans from their head offices abroad. Such a capital inflow resulted not only in the problem of monetizing foreign credits in cruzeiros but also a clamor among Brazilian firms for increased access to credit. Therefore, while the accepted noninflationary monetary doctrine would be to sterilize the increase in foreign reserves through offsetting domestic credit contraction, political realities, stressing the unequal distribution of benefits and the discrimination against less well-connected national enterprises were translated into strong pressures militating not only against such contraction but in favor of expansion. These pressures in general proved irresistible, thus serving to scuttle anti-inflationary monetary policy in the months following a devaluation despite the initial good intentions and resolutions of the monetary authorities. As the devaluation cycle wore on, other pressures arose. With approaching devaluation foreign subsidiaries began to repay loans from their head offices. Since these firms did not contract new loans from abroad, they exerted pressure on the Brazilian monetary authorities to supply the credit required to maintain their production. Once again the pressures were expansionary. Since the initiation of the mini-devaluation policy, monetary policy has exhibited greater independence from these pressures associated with the devaluation cycle.

The mini-devaluation policy is also important in overcoming nominal exchange inertia and reducing the political pressures associated with devaluation. Despite the fact that exchange rate selection under both the periodic and mini-devaluation policies is a discretionary matter, political constraints appear to differ under the two systems. There is a definite political resistance to a once-in-a-while, large devaluation. A large infrequent change in the exchange rate is seen as cataclysmic event—an explicit admission of failure by the government. In addition to the discomfiture caused by the political embarrassment of a large devaluation, the government may have other reasons for delaying or reducing devaluation. It may find that it has its own budgeting and financial interests at stake as an importer. In the Brazilian case considerable imports are made by government enterprises.[45]

On the other hand, such pressures for delaying or reducing devaluation are not so readily apparent with the mini-devaluation policy.[46] Small changes are far less dramatic than large changes. By introducing high degree of automaticity into exchange rate policy, Brazilian policymakers have shielded themselves from political pressures attendant with devaluation and have succeeded in diffusing devaluation as a political issue.

The initiation of the mini-devaluation policy in Brazil has also diminished the scope for administrative abuse and corruption. With no obvious large windfall gains possible for insiders with access to privileged information concerning devaluation, the suspicions and accusations of administrative malféasance at the time of devaluation are diminished. Under the previous exchange devaluation regime, rumors and accusations were rife, questioning government integrity and threatening political consequences.[47] With the mini-devaluation policy the automaticity of the system succeeded in diffusing a potentially political issue.

Concluding Remarks

While there are certainly some problems encountered, the Brazilian mini-devaluation policy has been a success. Far from generating massive capital outflows and unbridled inflation, as some might suspect, the application of the mini-devaluation policy in Brazil has been instrumental in stimulating exports, eliminating the speculation-devaluation cycle, providing greater autonomy and effectiveness for monetary policy, and easing the administrative and political burden of devaluation. The Brazilian experience with exchange policy provides not only an example to be emulated by the monetary authorities in similarly situated developing countries; it serves as another indication that greater flexibility in exchange rates can have beneficial consequences.

Notes

1. See, for example, George N. Halm, "Toward Limited Exchange-Rate Flexibility," Essays in International Finance, International Finance Section, Princeton University, No. 73 (March 1969); John H. Williamson, "The Crawling Peg," Essays in International Finance, International Finance Section, Princeton University, No. 50 (December 1965); Stephan Marris, "The Burgenstock Communique: A Critical Examination of the Case for Limited Flexibility of Exchange Rates," Essays in International Finance, International Finance Section, Princeton University, No. 80 (May 1970); E. Ray Canterbery and John T. Boorman, "The Crawling Peg and Exchange Stability," CANADIAN JOURNAL OF ECONOMICS 3, 2 (May 1970).

2. The most complete discussion of the band proposal is contained in George N. Halm, "The 'Band' Proposal: The Limits of Permissible Exchange Rate Variations," Special Papers in International Economics, International Finance Section, Princeton University, No. 6 (January 1965).

3. Another analyst has termed the recent Brazilian exchange adjustment policy the "trotting peg" as distinct from the crawling peg. See Juergen B. Donges, "Brazil's Trotting Peg: A New Approach to Greater Exchange Flexibility in Less Developed Countries," American Enterprise Institute Special Analysis No. 7, August 1971. After my research was completed, the Donges study was brought to my attention by Clement H. Donovan, to whom I am grateful. Donges also concludes that the mini-devaluation policy has had beneficial effects.

4. Although the differences between each of the four alternative methods of exchange adjustment enumerated are those of degrees along a continuum, both the mini-devaluation policy and regime of the flexible exchange rate subject to official intervention can be quite similar. It depends in the first case on the frequency of devaluation and the extent to which devaluations correspond to changes which would occur in a market determined rate. In the second case, it depends on the nature and magnitude of official intervention in the exchange market.

5. See William G. Tyler, "A Taxa de Câmbio 'Cadente' e a Inflação Endêmica (The Sliding Exchange Rate and Endemic Inflation)," REVISTA BRASILEIRA DE ECONOMIA 22, 4 (December 1968): 80-93.

6. An attempt to defend this hypothesis is contained in William G. Tyler, "Balance of Payments Adjustment in Less Developed Countries and the International Monetary Fund," Ph.D. dissertation, Fletcher School of Law and Diplomacy, 1969.

7. As of September 1967 there were 23 member countries within the Fund—constituting nearly one-fourth of the total membership—that had not established par values. All 23 were less developed countries. Ibid., p. 22.

8. Ibid., pp. 222-28.

9. Margaret G. de Vries, "Exchange Depreciation in Developing Countries," INTERNATIONAL MONETARY FUND STAFF PAPERS 15, 3 (November 1968), p. 562. In 84 of these cases nominal exchange depreciation amounted to more than 30 percent.

10. The performance of the economy from 1968 to mid-1971 has been so favorable that some Brazilian government economists have begun to speak of the "Brazilian economic miracle." Given certain lingering problems and a more modest appraisal of the economy's long-term outlook, such judgments appear somewhat premature. At least it would seem that the 9 percent rate of GDP growth, which has been estimated in the last few years and is now frequently discussed as a target rate, is unsustainable. See the introductory article of H. Jon Rosenbaum and William G. Tyler, eds., CONTEMPORARY BRAZIL: ISSUES IN ECONOMIC AND POLITICAL DEVELOPMENT (New York: Frederick A. Praeger, 1972).

11. For an analysis of Brazilian commercial policy, see Joel Bergsman, BRAZIL: INDUSTRIALIZATION AND TRADE POLICIES (New York: Oxford University Press, 1970).

12. For an analysis and discussion of Brazilian exchange policy and its effects, see Donald L. Huddle, "Balanço de Pagamentos e Contrôle de Câmbio no Brasil," REVISTA BRASILEIRA DE ECONOMIA (March 1964), and Donald L. Huddle, "Balanço de Pagamentos e Contrôle de Câmbio no Brasil: Eficácia, Bem-Estar e Desenvolvimento Econômico," REVISTA BRASILEIRA DE ECONOMIA (June 1964). See also Alexandre Kafka, "The Brazilian Exchange Auction System," REVIEW OF ECONOMICS AND STATISTICS (August 1956).

13. The Brazilian exchange rate is currently defined in terms of the U.S. dollar. Shortly after the United States took measures to float the dollar on August 15, 1971, the Brazilian monetary authorities decided for the time being to stick with the dollar, i.e., not to revalue the cruzeiro in terms of the dollar. As such, Brazil will receive a de facto partial devaluation as European (and Japanese) currencies are up-valued in dollar terms.

14. Interviews with various officials at the Finance Ministry, Central Bank, and Banco do Brasil have led me to conclude that the primary reason for initiating the mini-devaluation was the speculative flow issue.

15. See for example Ministério de Planjamento e Coordenação Geral, PROGRAMA DE ACÃO ECONÔMICA DO GOVÊRNO (Rio de Janeiro, 1965). Such statements were also made prior to the 1964 coup—as exemplified in Celso Furtado's PLANO TRIENAL of 1962.

16. The real exchange rate estimated here is that for exports of industrial products. It differs only slightly from that for nonmanufacturing exports (except coffee) and that for imports.

17. This approach does not exactly correspond to the precept of purchasing power parity. Dollar inflation was used rather than developing an adjustment factor employing rates of inflation of Brazil's trading partners weighted by the percentage of Brazil's trade going to them. Since the United States accounts for about 30 percent of Brazil's exports, dollar inflation was used as the adjustment factor. Based upon the notion that the wholesale price index is more representative of price movements for internationally tradeable commodities than the consumer price index, the U.S. wholesale price index was selected to represent dollar inflation. Two monthly, real exchange rates are presented in Table 2-3—one without adjustment for dollar inflation and one with.

18. For a description of the fiscal incentives for export the reader is referred to William G. Tyler, "Export Diversification and the Promotion of Manufactured Exports in Brazil," mimeographed study prepared for AID, 1969, pp. 122-41. It should be noted that Brazil's indirect taxes on manufactured products are very high in relation to other countries.

19. For manufactured exports themselves there exists a multitude of different effective rates, because the tax incentives which are based on the industrial product tax (IPT) differ according to product.

20. For an attempt to analyze the combined effects of fiscal incentives, tariffs, and exchange rates in Brazil see Joel Bergsman, "Foreign Trade Policy

and Development," in CONTEMPORARY BRAZIL: ISSUES IN ECONOMIC AND POLITICAL DEVELOPMENT, H. Jon Rosenbaum and William G. Tyler, eds. (New York: Frederick A. Praeger, 1972). Accounting for effective rates of protection and tax subsidies for export in the price deflators, Bergsman estimates "real" exchange rates for exports and imports. With estimates of exports and import elasticities he then calculates a "free trade exchange rate" from which he estimates both net protection and explicit export taxes. He concludes that in recent years the Brazilian economy has been opened up substantially. Net protection expressed as a percentage of his "free trade exchange rate" reached its lowest point in the postwar period, falling from 87 percent in 1963 to 22 percent in July 1970. Similarly, implicit export taxes have also fallen—from some 35 percent of the "free trade exchange rate" in 1963 to a more modest 12 percent in July 1970.

21. See Samuel Morley, "Import Demand and Import Substitution in Brazil," in THE ECONOMY OF BRAZIL, Howard S. Ellis, ed. (Berkeley, California: University of California Press, 1969). See also Paul G. Clark and Richard Weisskoff, "Import Demands and Import Policies in Brazil," mimeographed paper written for AID, 1966.

22. As is explained in the notes to Figure 2-1, this latter figure contains an upward bias.

23. It is quite clear that exchange rate policy had little or nothing to do with the increase in export receipts for some of Brazil's primary product exports. Coffee export receipts, for example, grew from US $708 million in 1967 to $939 million in 1970.

24. The great part of these interviews were made in connection with a larger study. See Tyler, "Export Diversification and the Promotion of Manufactured Exports in Brazil." Later efforts up-dated and broadened the sample of firms to include some nonmanufacturers. The interviews were structured in such a way so as to allow firm officials to bring up and discuss what they considered to be the most crucial export incentives for their firm. Only afterwards were specific questions directed to the various incentives (fiscal, exchange, credit, and procedural).

25. For a more detailed methodological explanation and interpretation of an earlier econometric attempt to explicate Brazilian manufactured export behavior, see William G. Tyler, "Manufactured Export Promotion in a Semi-Industrialized Economy: The Brazilian Case," JOURNAL OF DEVELOPMENT STUDIES, forthcoming.

26. It is interesting to note that an earlier attempt at analysis using 1961-1968 data failed to reveal the importance of the more recent fiscal incentives. See ibid. The high elasticity of the tax incentives (2.6) indicates that in the short run the fiscal incentives have been nearly twice as effective in stimulating exports as an exchange rate devaluation of the same amount. In the longer run, as the indirect affects of the fiscal incentives wear off, it is expected that the elasticity of X_4 will approach that for the real exchange rate.

Combining the real exchange rate and fiscal incentives into the real rate of effective remuneration to Brazilian industrial exporters, as presented in Table 2-4 and represented here by X_7, the following regression equation was estimated employing quarterly data from 1961 to 1970:

$$\log \quad X_1 = 3.857 + 1.616 \log X_7 + .001 X_3 + .008 X_5 - .035 X_6$$
$$(3.551) \ (2.775) \qquad (.139) \quad (6.364) \quad (-3.380)$$

$$R^2 = .88 \qquad\qquad\qquad\qquad \text{D.W.} = .90$$

Variables X_7, X_5, and X_6 are statistically significant at the 5 percent level. As before, X_3 is insignificant.

27. Conflicting conclusions, for example, have been drawn in different studies of the free exchange rates during the inter-war period. See Ragnar Nurkse, INTERNATIONAL CURRENCY EXPERIENCE: LESSONS OF THE INTER-WAR PERIOD (Geneva: The League of Nations, 1944) and S.C. Tsiang, "Fluctuating Exchange Rates in Countries with Relatively Stable Economies: Some European Experiences After World War I," INTERNATIONAL MONETARY FUND STAFF PAPERS 7, 2 (October 1959). Nurkse argues that speculation during the 1920s was predominately destabilizing and therefore concludes that the experience with free exchange rates was adverse. On the other hand, Tsiang, in an analysis of several countries, concluded that speculation was not generally destabilizing. Other case studies of flexible exchange rates have also found that speculation has performed a stabilizing role. See S.C. Tsiang, "An Experiment with a Flexible Exchange Rate System: The Case of Peru, 1950-54," INTERNATIONAL MONETARY FUND STAFF PAPERS 5, 3 (February 1957), and Rudolf Rhomberg, "Canada's Foreign Exchange Market: A Quarterly Model," INTERNATIONAL MONETARY FUND STAFF PAPERS 7, 3 (April 1960).

28. Milton Friedman, "The Case for Flexible Exchange Rates," in his ESSAYS IN POSITIVE ECONOMICS (Chicago: University of Chicago Press, 1953), p. 175, and James E. Meade, "The Case for Variable Exchange Rates," THREE BANKS REVIEW, September 1955.

29. Although monthly balance of payments data are not available, officials at the Central Bank in conversations have stressed the heavy capital account flows around the 1965, 1967, and 1968 devaluations. Such fluctuations have apparently disappeared with the mini-devaluation policy.

30. For the best available discussion of Brazilian interest rate policy in the early and mid-1960s, the reader is referred to Leif Christoffersen, "Taxas de Juro a Estrutura de um Sistema de Bancos Comerciais em Condições Inflacionárias," REVISTA BRASILEIRA DE ECONOMIA 23, 2 (June 1969). Christoffersen, a former student of George N. Halm, computed the average rates of return on loans for a sample of Brazilian commercial banks and compared such rates with the average annual loans outstanding. He found that despite

lending at negative real interest rates commercial banks profited considerably from the high rates of inflation. Credit was made available to the commercial banks at still lower nominal interest rates, i.e., higher negative real rates, by the quasi-public Banco do Brasil. This is suggested in Table 2-5.

31. Measures designed to provide such incentives have included Central Bank Resolutions 79, 114, and 134 of January 1968, June 1969, and February 1970, respectively. The relative ineffectiveness of these incentives is due to the use of various and ingenious evasive devices, e.g., compensating balances, on the part of the commercial banks.

32. At the average export exchange rate for 1969, the Cr.\$ 212.1 million equals more than US\$ 50 million. The amount of this fiscal subsidy to the stock market was calculated by adding the tax exemptions registered by firms to those applicable to individuals under the provisions of Decree-Law 157, which provides the legal basis for individual income tax exemptions for stock market purchases. New stock issues registered at the Central Bank in 1969 totaled Cr.\$ 141.8 million. Although complete data were not available at the time of this writing, it appears that also in 1970 the value of the direct fiscal subsidy exceeded the amount of new issues. Data for these calculations were taken from the Banco Central do Brasil, RELATÓRIO, 1970, May 1971.

33. Calculated from information in Banco Central Do Brasil, RELATÓRIO, 1970 and the JORNAL DO BRASIL, August 22, 1971.

34. Public medium- and long-term borrowing also rose considerably in 1969 and 1970. Such increases have been due primarily to the expanded Brazilian lending operations of the World Bank and the Inter-American Development Bank.

35. Banco Central do Brasil, RELATÓRIO, 1970, p. 133. The \$1.9 billion figure sharply contrasts to the \$245 million and \$199 million worth of reserves held by Brazil in 1964 and 1967. Data are available in the International Monetary Fund, INTERNATIONAL FINANCIAL STATISTICS, various issues. Calculations made from data in Banco Central do Brasil, RELATÓ RIO, 1970, p. 45.

36. A method to estimate the impact of foreign reserve accumulation on prices is discussed in James W. Foley and J. Peter Wogart, "Inflationary Factors Inherent in Stabilization Programs: The Argentine and Brazilian Cases," mimeograph. Foley and Wogart utilize coefficients estimated in regression equations linking price and money variables.

37. Resolution 63 of the Central Bank was promulgated by the National Monetary Council on August 17, 1967. Its text is available in the Banco Central do Brasil, RELATÓRIO, 1967.

38. Banco Central de Brasil, BOLETIM, Junho 1971. Of the US\$ 2,284 million worth of credits owed at year end 1970 some 66 percent was due for repayment within the next twelve months, while 85 percent scheduled for payment within two years.

39. This is the judgment of various officials in the Central Bank. Nearly all of the borrowing under the provisions of Instruction 289 is accounted for by credits to foreign firms. Resolution 63 was an attempt to offset the facility of foreign firms to take advantage of Instruction 289 by providing more equal access to short- and medium-term foreign credits. However, it appears that foreign firms have been more successful also in utilizing Resolution 63.

40. Regrettably, only data on the *net* short-term capital movements were available.

41. Although I have no concrete evidence as to foreign credits being applied in the Brazilian stock market, this operation along with a few examples has been revealed to me by several investment bankers and stockholders.

42. Jacob Viner, "Problems of Monetary Control," Essays in International Finance, International Financial Section, Department of Economics, Princeton University, 1964, p. 33. Since the United States falls within Viner's wide range of countries not to be safely trusted with flexible exchange adjustment, Viner presumably would also include Brazil in that category.

43. This argument has been made not only with respect to inflation, but to speculative capital flows as well. See Charles P. Kindleberger, "Flexible Exchange Rates," in MONETARY MANAGEMENT, prepared for the Commission on Money and Credit, 1963.

44. This position was described to me by various Brazilian central bankers and officials connected with the Ministry of Finance.

45. Prior to 1965 the operating deficits of public enterprises were sizable and contributed greatly to the budget deficits of the federal government. As such, several officials in the Central Bank have alleged that budgetary matters played an important role in delaying devaluation. Public utility rate increases associated with the "corrective inflation" of the 1964-1968 period plus measures designed to increase the operating efficiency of public enterprises have served to reduce their deficits and lessen the budgetary burden of the government. Consequently, such pressures for avoiding devaluation have been alleviated. For an analysis of corrective inflation see Howard S. Ellis, "Corrective Inflation in Brazil, 1964-1966," in THE ECONOMY OF BRAZIL, Howard S. Ellis, ed. (Berkeley: University of California Press, 1969).

46. One central banker remarked that a major contribution for facilitating devaluation was made by getting the news of devaluation off the front page of the newspapers.

47. For an example of the controversy and accusations of corruption raised by a sizable devaluation, the reader is referred to a perusal of the Brazilian newspapers during the two weeks following the 1967 devaluation (February 13, 1967) of 24 percent. Editorial comment in the Rio daily O GLOBO was especially vehement.

Money Illusion and Foreign Exchange

Charles P. Kindleberger

Widely introduced into the literature on domestic monetary theory, money illusion has only recently entered into the theoretical analysis of international monetary questions. As is well known, money illusion is the view generally regarded as irrational or mistaken, when prices are changing, that behavior should be guided by money quantities, such as money income or money wealth, rather than real variables, i.e., money variables deflated for changes in price levels. What counts are price changes, not expectations of price changes. In *The Course and Control of Inflation After World War I,*[1] Ragnar Nurkse mentioned that the initial reaction to the rise in prices in the Central and East European inflation after the war was to spend less while waiting for prices to decline again. Savings increased with rising prices because of inelastic expectations. With money illusion and inflationary incomes, people would save a higher proportion of incomes, and also spend more, under the illusion that their incomes had risen.

The purposes of this paper are (1) to review the major steps in the expanding discussion of money illusion in international questions; and (2) to suggest that money functions effectively, in international context as in domestic, only under conditions of stability such as to justify the "illusion" that wealth and income measured in money are equivalent to real wealth and real income respectively. In a word, money illusion is less a sign of irrationality than its absence is a symptom of monetary pathology.

Money illusion was first raised to a prominent position in the discussion of foreign exchange by Sidney Alexander in his debate with Machlup over the impact of devaluation on the balance of payments under conditions of full employment.[2] It will be recalled that Alexander stated that the current account in the balance of payments represented the difference between income and expenditure—which he called "absorption." If income exceeded absorption, the current account showed a surplus; if absorption was in excess of income, the current account necessarily was in deficit. With less than full employment and sufficiently high elasticities of demand, devaluation of the currency would raise the local-currency value of exports and reduce that of imports, at least relative to one another. The increase in production for export and of import-competing goods would raise income through the foreign-trade multiplier. If the marginal propensity to save was positive, income would rise more than absorption, and

I acknowledge with gratitude the comments of Donald G. Heckerman and Richard Marston.

51

the balance of payments would improve on balance, although the final improvement would be less than the "impact effect" produced initially, because of the spillover of increased income into imports. Under full employment, however, the increase in output from the "idle resources" effect could not be counted on. Increased exports and increased production of import-competing goods could not take place unless there was an original decrease in absorption brought about by depreciation, which released resources to the foreign trade sector. Alexander cited three possible sources of reduced absorption brought about by devaluation: income could be redistributed by the rise in export and import prices, especially to the extent that the wage good was imported or exported, and real wages fell to the benefits of profits, with higher rates of savings. Or with higher foreign-trade prices, firms and households might undertake to save more at every level of national income in order to restore the real value of their money balances. Or firms and households might suffer from money illusion, as prices and money incomes arose as a consequence of the impact effect of expanded exports and reduced imports, and save more because of higher money incomes, despite unchanged real incomes.[3]

Alexander dismissed money illusion, the real-balances effect and income distribution as unlikely to be significant factors in decreasing absorption as a result of devaluation, and was inclined to think that the prospect of improving the balance of payments under full employment by devaluation was small. His reasoning with respect to income redistribution was not that wages would be pushed up by labor, but rather that the increased profits of exporters and import-competitors would probably result in new investment, adding to investment absorption what had been subtracted from consumption. None of his critics argued with the dismissals of the real-balances effect or money illusion. Carlos Diaz-Alejandro, on the other hand, noted that income redistribution had made an important contribution to balance-of-payments improvement under conditions comparable to full employment in an Argentine case.[4] There was no discussion of the possible extent of money illusion, or of the possibility that it might exist in considerable degree immediately following a devaluation and wear off through time.

The next major discussion of money illusion in a theoretical context was given by Ronald McKinnon and in connection with optimum currency areas. Robert Mundell had introduced the concept of an optimum currency area as an area of appropriate size, larger than a single person and presumably smaller than the world, which had a single money (or what comes close to the same thing, a set of fixed exchange rates) within the area, but fluctuating exchange rates with the outside world.[5] Mundell's criterion for an optimum currency area was factor, and especially labor, mobility. With labor mobility, a region could maintain full employment and balance-of-payments equilibrium through the use of monetary and fiscal policy and exchange rate adjustment. Local unemployment in any part of the area would be cured by migration. Where migration was excluded for any reason—political or cultural differences, or distance—a separate currency area was needed; there was no other way to eliminate local unemployment while preserving the balance of payments. It was assumed that depreciation would improve the balance of payments and appreciation worsen it, either adopting Machlup's approach, or assuming idle resources and in either case sufficiently high elasticities.

McKinnon's approach to the optimum currency area questioned whether in fact exchange rate changes would alter the balance of payments in the absence of money illusion.[6] Implicitly his model operates with income redistribution, dismissed by Alexander, although the absorption issue is not raised. If an economy has little trade with the outside world, the impact of exchange rate changes on the price level and real income will be ignored. This is money illusion, which in the international context, could be called exchange illusion. For open economies which trade a great deal with the outside world, on the other hand, a devaluation will produce an increase in the prices of foreign trade goods and a reduction in real income which would be noticed. Full employment is implicitly assumed and also that the factors affected have sufficient market power to resist decreases in real rates of return. In these circumstances, the absence of money illusion means that money wages and prices will rise in proportion to the depreciation, and the balance of payments will not improve. Alexander called this type of economy "homogeneous" and emphasized that some nonhomogeneity was needed to produce a change in the balance of payments when the exchange rate was altered. When the economy was homogeneous, in the absence of money illusion, McKinnon held that it was not sufficiently large to constitute an optimum currency area, and should combine with other units until an economy sufficiently closed to experience money illusion was formed.

It is not clear in McKinnon's analysis whether the presence or absence of money illusion is a "go/no-go" matter, with a critical threshold as a country passes a given degree of increasing openness, or whether there are degrees of money illusion. If a threshold exists, it may be presumed to differ for different countries, and to change with recent experience. Openness is presumably measured by some ratio such as $\frac{(X+M)}{2}$ Y (the average of exports and imports to national income). If it be granted that openness is continuous, it is not clear whether the capacity of factors to alter market prices when commodity prices change is all or nothing, or again divisible. In some situations, as in de Gaulle's France of 1958, the working class experienced no money illusion whatsoever, but the depreciation of the franc was effective in improving the balance of payments because market forces and government successfully resisted attempts by workers to raise wages.

Absence of money illusion and existence of capacity to affect wage rates through collective action are responsible for the "structural inflation" of Latin

America, in which depreciation of the currency fails for long to improve the balance of payments because it stimulates more inflation.[7] They are also implied by Harry Johnson when he asserts that a system of flexible exchange rates will not work effectively in a "banana republic" because it is well understood in such countries that the level of living is determined by the foreign-exchange price of bananas, not the price in local currency.[8]

But while international-trade economists have brought money illusion into discussions of foreign exchange only recently, historians and economists have been faced with the issue for some time. In some models, money illusion applies not to a country as a whole, or a factor, but to a sector, such as households. The illustration dealt with the world economic depression. Money illusion was needed to correct an error in reasoning which was introduced by Keynesian economic analysis, an error which had not been presented in earlier analysis.

In his essay "Conditions of International Monetary Equilibrium,"[9] Ragnar Nurkse criticized the United States for devaluing the dollar in 1933 at a time when the balance of payments of the country was in current-account surplus. Using a Keynesian model, he argued that the existence of a balance-of-payments surplus on current account meant that the international transactions of the country were expansionary. In these circumstances it was a beggar-thy-neighbor action to allow (or force) the dollar to depreciate. Nurkse's view was criticized by Alvin Hansen, who noted that the appreciation of the dollar prior to 1933, as the Argentine peso, Australian pound, pound sterling, yen, etc., depreciated, applied strong downward pressure to United States prices and income.[10] The balance of payments remained in surplus because the deflationary price pressure reduced United States income (which improved the balance of payments) faster than appreciation hurt it. Price deflation from the foreign trade sector was transmitted to the American economy without the necessity for a balance-of-payments deficit.

Implicit in this view is a model in which money illusion is needed to modify the results of Keynesian analysis. In the latter, it is assumed that any foreign impact on domestic prices in the United States can be ignored, since the loss for the producer will be matched by a gain for his customers. If the producer suffers a monetary loss and cuts his spending, the consumer experiences an increase in real income and increases his spending—ignoring income redistribution effects which might alter the average propensity to save. On this showing, price changes transmitted from abroad would have no impact on spending or on national income except through the balance of payments.

But this view, which flew in the face of pre-Keynesian analysis, reckons without money illusion and perhaps without dynamic effects. Assume that the United States produced 1.2 billion bushels of wheat and exported 200 million bushels. Appreciation of the dollar reduces the price of wheat from say $1 to 50 cents, and cuts the value of wheat exports from $200 million to $100 million. With a multiplier of about 2, United States national income is reduced by $200 million. This ignores the impact of the price decline on the 1 billion bushels sold on the domestic market, on the ground that the loss of $500 million in incomes of wheat farmers, is offset by an increase in the real income of households, which consume bread, or of millers and bakers who stand between the farmer and the consumer. The reduction in farm spending on this showing is offset by the increase in urban spending. Money illusion, however, is likely to delay the recognition of the increase in real income of millers, bakers and households for a considerable period, while the loss of real and money income of the farmers is instantaneous, occurring even before the wheat is harvested. Deflation in the agricultural sector can also generate dynamic forces such as bank failures, leading to further deflation. The decline in the prices of cotton and wheat as a result of the appreciation of the dollar loosed strong deflationary forces far beyond those implied by the foreign trade multiplier.

The point is seen at its sharpest in the contradiction in W.A. Lewis' treatment of price declines in the world depression. At one point he notes the role of falling prices of agricultural products in spreading deflation from agricultural countries to the agricultural sectors of developed countries and beyond.[11] At another he records the Keynesian view that price changes cannot lead to changes in spending or income or output since decreases in spending on the part of producers suffering from price declines will be matched by increases in spending by those whose real income has increased as a result of lower prices.[12] The contradiction can be resolved by recognizing that money illusion is present in the former case, but not in the latter.

The issues of the existence and importance of money illusion in the adjustment process under exchange rate changes and in the spread of depression through price declines have not been resolved in the economic literature, but the question of money illusion has recently arisen in a new connection—in the impact of exchange rate flexibility on foreign investment. Replying to a statement that flexible exchange rates present exchange risks and therefore reduce international trade and investment in a world of risk aversion, Donald Heckerman states in an interesting paper that this, so far as investment is concerned, is predicated on the existence of money illusion.[13] It is not clear whether this is intended as a definitive refutation of the proposition, on the a priori ground that money illusion is irrational, and irrationality has a limited Darwinian survival value. The argument runs as follows: a rational investor maximizes the value of his investment portfolio not in terms of money, but in terms of real goods and services, i.e., money values deflated by relevant price indexes. To maximize only money values, even after taking into account the risk of exchange rate changes on foreign investments, is to suffer from money illusion. An investor therefore will make estimates of the prices of securities in various currencies, the likely course of foreign-exchange rates and the expected course of general prices. It is especially important for him to estimate the outlook for his own currency, and for the course of prices in his own country, since myopia and money illusion are most probable here. A utility-maximizing consumer-investor is not content to invest in his own currency to eliminate exchange risk, since he cannot at the same time eliminate the risk that the domestic price level will rise more than price levels in other countries. Only if he has domestic money illusion, therefore, will fixed exchange rates increase international capital mobility by eliminating exchange risks. With money illusion absent, exchange risk must be compared with relative prospective price changes, and there is no presumption that an investor has invested efficiently by keeping his portfolio in domestic securities.

In part, Heckerman's argument was developed as a counter to a theory of direct investment put forward by Robert Aliber, who made exchange risk the central ingredient in a theory of investment. In Aliber's model, investors regard one currency at a time as the strongest world currency, and are willing to pay premia for securities—equities as well as debt—denominated in that currency.[14] Corporations which issue securities in the dominant currency have an advantage over corporations with securities denominated in other currencies, in that their securities command higher prices, and they can issue them more cheaply than can corporations issuing securities in nondominant currencies. The former can therefore buy up real assets abroad at higher prices than local companies which issue securities and debt in local currency.

Midway between these positions is a possible compromise, which would hold that the outcome is different for debt and for equities. Investment in real assets abroad is relatively free of exchange risk, since it is anticipated that any change in the foreign-exchange rate will be offset without significant lag—or with a lag short enough to be unimportant to the ordinary corporate investor—by an opposite change in the price of the real assets. This is self-evident for internationally-traded goods where the law of one price applies; when the pound sterling is devalued, the prices of wheat, copper, and oil rise immediately by the full extent of the depreciation. It is not so clear for items such as wool, tin, and rubber, in which sterling countries serve to a considerable degree as price-makers, instead of price-takers, to use Metzler's expression. Nor is it so clear in producing assets, unless the economy adjusts to the exchange rate change homogeneously. Plant and equipment would presumably adjust in value to exchange depreciation by increases which would be fullest in import-competing industry (where the country was a price-taker), next in export industry, and last in purely domestic lines. But industry as a whole ignores these subtleties and the accounting rule generally is to assume that real assets abroad are not "exposed" to exchange risk, on the ground that the price of the assets will change oppositely to the exchange rate, and in proportion—the assumption of homogeneity in effect. Assets and liabilities fixed in money are exposed to risk, and can be netted, usually for current assets only. Between plant and equipment and inventories of imported materials on the one hand, and net current assets on the other stand such items as inventories of finished goods designed for the local market which may or may not be subject to price changes consequent on exchange rate changes, depending upon a variety of considerations such as price control, market power, labor intensity and the like. Accounting practice differs as to whether inventories are included with assets fixed in money, or those subject to price adjustment. But there is no exchange illusion in plant and equipment.

On this showing flexible exchange rates would not inhibit foreign direct investment, except to the extent that plant and equipment must be accompanied by net current assets which bear an exchange risk—as may be the case, for example, in such goods as sewing machines or tractors which are sold on installments in an economy which cannot provide the credit locally. It would inhibit capital movement through debt.

There is a counter argument on debt, however, which asserts that in the absence of money illusion, interest rates will adjust to the rate of inflation. This is as likely under a flexible exchange rate system as under fixed rates. If the relative rate of inflation in Country B is 3 percent higher than in Country A, the interest rate will presumably be 3 percent higher. This will not stimulate excessive capital movements in long-term debt, to be sure, because in the long run, the exchange rate may be expected to depreciate at the rate of three percent a year.

All these considerations postulate equilibrium rates of exchange at the times transactions are made and reversed. Mundell once suggested that inflation abroad led to excessive capital movements in debt because lack of money illusion led to higher than appropriate interest rates.[15] But this is only true if there is exchange illusion, i.e., the belief that inflation can proceed at a higher rate in one country than another without the exchange rate being adjusted.[16] It can happen, to be sure, that exchange rates may adjust more slowly than interest rates to differences in relative inflation. This would mean that inefficient capital movements would be stimulated, if investors had either money illusion, or the supersophistication which recognized that exchange rates adapted to inflation at a different rate and slower than interest rates.

If exchange rates stay at overvalued or undervalued rates persistently, inefficient capital movements may also take place in equity investments in real assets. At one point, I thought that the tendency of the prices of real assets to adjust to foreign-exchange-rate changes meant that they adjusted to overvaluation and undervaluation. The undervaluation of, say, the mark and overvaluation of, say, the dollar raised the price of real assets in Germany so that they did not appear cheap to American investors comparing the prices of real assets in the United States and Germany. This view is mistaken, however, as Thomas Horst pointed out to me in a seminar. The price of real assets in Germany may or may not rise by the full degree of undervaluation of the mark relative to the dollar. If they do not, German assets appear cheap relative to American assets in the eyes of United States corporations. If they do, the American investor is indifferent as between United States and German assets, but German investors find German assets capable of being bought by Americans very high priced, and are unwilling to buy them. This leads the owners of fixed assets who want to sell them to offer them instead to foreign investors. The likelihood is an outcome somewhere between rising the full amount of the relative undervaluation of the market, and no increase at all, with some incentive by asset owners to sell them abroad, and some incentive by U.S. investors to buy undervalued fixed assets in Germany. In this circumstance, if a movement from fixed to flexible exchange rates means that exchange rates will be less overvalued and undervalued and more nearly at equilibrium levels, the change will produce a reduction in capital flows, but one which is efficient for world welfare.

If, on the other hand, one believes that departures from equilibrium rates will occur under systems of fixed exchange rates, as a result of inflation, or under flexible exchange rates as a result of misinformed speculation, Heckerman is undoubtedly right that, in the absence of money illusion, a system of flexible exchange rates does not interfere with international capital flows. The question then becomes an empirical one, whether or not there is money illusion in international (trade and) investment.

I see little way of resolving the question. In the first Bologna conference on international monetary arrangements, largely on the price of gold, Lord Robbins and James Meade differed on a fundamental point, whether they would be willing to receive their salaries in sterling if the pound were freely floating. Meade said he would be happy to be paid in pounds; Lord Robbins stated that he would want dollars.[17] The point at issue could have been whether Meade agreed with Robbins that the pound was likely to depreciate in the long run; the context made it clear that the debate was about money illusion in the Alexander and McKinnon senses. If Meade has money illusion and Lord Robbins does not, it is hard to make general statements to the effect that everybody or nobody is subject to money illusion.

In international investment, a number of classifications of foreign investors have been made based on their size, experience, and sophistication. A handy one yields the taxonomy of (1) domestic firms with foreign operations; (2) multi-national corporations; and (3) international corporations. The first regards its foreign investments as merely incidental to its main preoccupations in the home country; the second tries to act everywhere as a good citizen of the country where it is; the third tries to maximize income and wealth worldwide without regard to nationality, whether that of the home country or those of host countries.[18] The three classes of firm are likely to behave differently along a series of dimensions—with respect to acceptable rates of return, personnel selection for foreign subsidiaries, research and development location, reinvestment of profits earned locally, and a number of operating policies, including attitudes toward exchange risk. On exchange risk, it was hypothesized that domestic firms with foreign operations regard all currencies outside the home country as subject to risk, but not the home currency.

The national corporation is usually hedged in foreign exchange, is seldom long of foreign currencies, and is ready to go short when a foreign currency is under attack. It will not take a short position in the currency of the parent company and does not, in fact, recognize that it has an exchange position when it holds net assets denominated in money in that currency.[19]

The multinational corporation regards it as a breach of good citizenship to go short of the currency of a country where it has an investment. It is long of most currencies, hedged in weak ones, but like the national firm, likely to ignore the fact that it can have an exchange risk in the home currency. The international corporation, on the other hand, is aware that effective maximization of its wealth may require it to go long or short of any currency, including that of the head office. It calculates its net worth in a single currency as *numéraire*, but that process does not mean that it ignores changes in value of that *numéraire*.

In this typlogy, the national corporation with foreign operations and the multinational corporation both have money or exchange illusion. Only the international corporation does not. The classification is based on casual empiricism. Such evidence as there is confirms the observation that at the level of corporate sophistication of recent years, most companies investing abroad exhibit attitudes and adopt rules of thumb which have elements of irrationality about them and which imply the existence of money and exchange illusion.

Virtually every investigator of international business has noted that firms tend to make strong distinctions between foreign currencies and the home currency. After an initial start, subsidiaries abroad must rely on reinvested profits and local financing.[20] Only large companies are prepared to furnish dollar financing to their foreign subsidiaries after the start, and a Canadian company investing abroad reiterates that the parent firm would furnish no Canadian dollars to its subsidiaries.[21] Accounting practice, as already noticed, takes account of exposure only in foreign exchange, and does not question the net exposed position in the currency of the parent company. It has in fact been argued by Stephen Hymer that all corporations are national ones with foreign operations, rather than multinational companies or international in the sense of the taxonomy above. Balance sheets and profit and loss statements are denominated in a national currency, equity shares are priced in it, and the corporate management is committed to maximize income and wealth in that currency only, without regard to the question whether some other currency is stronger and that by holding it in the management would one day have a higher value for its assets expressed in its normal *numéraire*. American management cannot be criticized for holding dollars, nor British management for holding sterling.[22] This is not patriotism but exchange illusion, which seems to be implicit in the current practice of international investment.

Increasing sophistication in the handling of international corporate finance, resulting in a wide-ranging periodical and monographic literature on exchange risk,[23,24] does not yet reach to the advocacy of regarding net current assets in the domestic currency as exposed, and at risk. That degree of sophistication may ultimately be achieved. When it does, the world economy will have dispensed with the use of money.

For money illusion is the essence of money. When it is gone, money fails to play its part as a store of value and standard of deferred payment, though it may still function as a medium of exchange and unit of account.[25] In countries with persistent inflation, savings take the form of real investment, and are thereby distorted from optimal allocation; contracts are made in foreign exchange, or tied to price indexes. Money is dethroned, and when this occurs, the transactions costs of doing business include those of calculating, along with the prices of goods and of securities, plus those for foreign goods and assets, the present and expected value of foreign exchange, and future price levels at home and abroad. The absence of money illusion is pathological, not normal. Put another way, conditions of unstable prices which are economically pathological, dispel the illusion which is necessary to make money function effectively, both domestically and when the need arises, in balance-of-payments adjustments brought about by the infrequent divergences of national price levels. With money illusion absent, international trade and investment require searching and scanning techniques, plus estimating in the future, which are comparable to trying to conduct efficient trade under barter. Linear-programing, decision-theory, and similar sophisticated devices backed by computers may make it possible, but the necessity increases the economies of firms of large size, and the risk of gross error and hence gross waste. Moreover, adjustment through exchange rate changes will not work. Far better to stabilize price levels, and exchange rates (or move the latter discontinuously) and reduce the necessity for forecasting anything more than the prices of goods and securities. Money illusion is needed. It requires stable monies.

This essay is to honor George Halm, and a postscript may be added on the relation of money illusion to his interest in a wider band for exchange rates. On a previous occasion, I suggested that the possibility of destabilizing speculation in the short run, and the need for rate adjustment in the long run, meant that the band was pessimal therapy, providing as it does, short-run instability and long-run lack of exchange rate change. The crawling peg of Williamson met the requirements of the system better than Halm's band.[26]

But it may be worth contemplating what the two reforms do for money illusion. Here the wider band may do less harm than the crawling peg, since it may be possible to preserve money illusion with the band, though not with the crawling peg. This insight may confuse cause and effect, since in a world of differing Phillips curves and differential inflation, exchange rates must change to preserve balance-of-payments equilibrium. Whether less harm is done to the preservation of the money illusion necessary for the efficient use of money in the world economy with the crawling peg than the discontinuous moving peg is an empirical question, the answer to which probably changes with time, place, experience, and sophistication. It is nonetheless important for being virtually unknowable.

Notes

1. Ragnar Nurkse, THE COURSE AND CONTROL OF INFLATION AFTER WORLD WAR I, (Princeton, N.J.: League of Nations, 1946).

2. S.S. Alexander, "Effect of a Devaluation on a Trade Balance," STAFF PAPERS, Vol. II (April 1952), pp. 263-78, reprinted in American Economics Association, READINGS IN INTERNATIONAL ECONOMICS (Homewood, Ill.: Richard D. Irwin, Inc., 1967), pp. 359-88.

3. Tsiang and Machlup added two more: Tsiang suggested that with a fixed money supply and higher prices and money incomes, firms and households would need more transactions balances and bidding for them would raise the rate of interest, leading to a higher rate of saving; Machlup observed that changing the exchange rate would lead to a new and more efficient allocation of resources, which implies higher incomes from which more could be saved, but this involves an index-number problem. See S.C. Tsiang, "The Role of Money in Trade-Balance Stability: Synthesis of the Elasticity and Absorption Approaches," AMERICAN ECONOMIC REVIEW 2, 5 (December 1961): 912-36, reprinted in American Economic Association, READINGS IN INTERNATIONAL ECONOMICS, op. cit., pp. 389-412; and F. Machlup, "Relative Prices and Aggregate Spending in the Analysis of Devaluation," AMERICAN ECONOMIC REVIEW 45, 3 (June 1955): pp. 255-78.

4. See Carlos F. Diaz-Alejandro, EXCHANGE-RATE DEVALUATION IN A SEMI-INDUSTRIAL COUNTRY: THE EXPERIENCE OF ARGENTINA, 1955-1961 (Cambridge, Mass.: The MIT Press, 1966).

5. See Robert A. Mundell, "A Theory of Optimum Currency Areas," AMERICAN ECONOMIC REVIEW 51, 4 (September 1961): 657-65. Mundell is not aware of the money-illusion point, saying on page 663:

The thesis of those who favor flexible exchange rates is that the community in question is not willing to accept variations in its real income through adjustments in its money wage rate or price level, but that it is willing to accept virtually the same changes in its real income through variations in the rate of exchange.

6. R.I. McKinnon, "Optimum Currency Areas," AMERICAN ECONOMIC REVIEW 53, 4 (September 1963): 717-25. For a more developed statement, see Gordon C. Winston, "Money Illusion: Devaluation and Supply Rigidities," Research Memorandum No. 23, Center for Development Economics, Williams College, Williamstown, Mass., July 1968.

7. See the essays by D. Felix and J. Grunwald in A.O. Hirschman (ed.),

LATIN AMERICAN ISSUES (New York, Twentieth Century Fund, 1961), pp. 81-124.

8. See H.J. Johnson, "The Case for Flexible Exchange Rates–1969," in Federal Reserve Bank of St. Louis, REVIEW 51, 6 (June 1969): 12-24.

9. See Ragnar Nurkse, "Conditions of International Monetary Equilibrium," ESSAYS IN INTERNATIONAL FINANCE, No. 4, Princeton, N.J., Spring, 1945, reprinted in American Economic Association, READINGS IN THE THEORY OF INTERNATIONAL TRADE (Philadelphia: Blakiston and Co., 1949), pp. 3-34.

10. Alvin H. Hansen, "Fundamental Disequilibrium," in S.E. Harris, ed., FOREIGN ECONOMIC POLICY FOR THE UNITED STATES (Cambridge, Mass.: Harvard University Press, 1948), pp. 379-83.

11. W. Arthur Lewis, ECONOMIC SURVEY 1939-1949 (Philadelphia: Blakiston and Co., 1949), pp. 55-56.

12. Ibid., p. 46.

13. See D.G. Heckerman, "Exchange Rate Systems and the Efficient Allocation of Risk," to be published in the proceedings of a symposium on trade, growth and balance of payments, held at the University of Chicago in December 1970.

14. Robert Z. Aliber, "A Theory of Direct Foreign Investment," in C.P. Kindleberger (ed), THE INTERNATIONAL CORPORATION: A SYMPOSIUM (Cambridge, Mass.: The MIT Press, 1970), pp. 17-34.

15. Robert A. Mundell, Testimony before the Republican Balance of Payments Seminar, CONGRESSIONAL RECORD, February 6, 1968, p. 6 of reprint.

16. Economic historians are becoming aware that the low interest rates in Europe during the great depression (1873 to 1896) were a reflection of lack of money illusion on the part of lenders and domestic borrowers. See Hans Rosenberg, GROSSE DEPRESSION UND BISMARCKZEIT (Berlin: Walter de Gruyter & Co., 1967), p. 42. Whether foreign borrowers, such as Czarist Russia and Latin America, had exchange illusion and were unaware that they were able to borrow at such cheap rates because they would have to repay in deflated monies, has not been explored.

17. Randall Hinshaw (ed.), MONETARY REFORM AND THE PRICE OF GOLD: ALTERNATIVE APPROACHES (Baltimore: Johns Hopkins Press, 1967), pp. 123-24.

18. See C.P. Kindleberger, AMERICAN BUSINESS ABROAD (New Haven: Yale University Press, 1969), pp. 179ff.

19. Ibid., p. 182.

20. See for example, Judd Polk, Irene W. Meister, and Lawrence A. Veit, U.S. PRODUCTION ABROAD AND THE BALANCE OF PAYMENTS, A SURVEY OF CORPORATE INVESTMENT EXPERIENCE (New York: The Conference Board, 1966), pp. 38ff.

21. See E.P. Neufeld, A GLOBAL CORPORATION: A HISTORY OF THE INTERNATIONAL DEVELOPMENT OF MASSEY-FERGUSON LIMITED (Toronto: University of Toronto Press, 1969), pp. 86, 90, 349, etc.

22. See Stephen H. Hymer, "The International Operations of National Firms: A Study of Direct Investment," Ph.D. dissertation, MIT, Cambridge, Mass., 1960.

23. See for example, books of readings such as Lee C. Nehrt (ed.), INTERNATIONAL FINANCE FOR MULTINATIONAL BUSINESS (Scranton: International Textbook Co., 1967); and David B. Zenoff and Jack Zwick (eds.), INTERNATIONAL FINANCE FOR MULTINATIONAL BUSINESS (Scranton: International Textbook Co., 1967), and David B. Zenoff and Jack Zwick (eds.), INTERNATIONAL FINANCIAL MANAGEMENT (Englewood Cliffs, N.J.: Prentice-Hall, Inc., 1969).

24. See, e.g., Bernard A. Lietaer, FINANCIAL MANAGEMENT OF FOREIGN EXCHANGE: AN OPERATIONAL TECHNIQUE TO REDUCE RISK (Cambridge, Mass.: The MIT Press, 1971).

25. It should be noted that in periods of inflation, more rather than less money will be held by asset-holders, as all seek for liquidity as a path to acquiring real assets and reduce security holdings. See Charles-Albert Michalet, LES PLACEMENTS DE ÉPARGNANTE FRANÇAIS DE 1815 Á NOS JOURS (Paris: Presses universitaire de France, 1968).

26. C.P. Kindleberger, "The Case for Fixed Exchange Rates, 1969," in Federal Reserve Bank of Boston, THE INTERNATIONAL ADJUSTMENT MECHANISM, Boston, 1970, p. 107.

Prospects for the Dollar Standard

Gottfried Haberler

After more than half a year of turmoil in the exchange markets and extensive floating, the international monetary system again came to rest on 18 December 1971—at least for the time being. It took President Nixon's bombshell of 15 August 1971, the imposition of an import surcharge, official declaration of the inconvertibility of the dollar into gold, innumerable high-level conferences and several summit meetings, to bring about a large realignment of currency values and an optional wider 'band' (around par values or 'central rates of exchange') which has been accepted by most countries.

The questions I shall discuss are: In what respect is the present system different from what we had before 15 August 1971, apart from the realignment and the wider band? Is it at all viable and how long will it last? Where do we go from here? What are some options for international monetary reform and the chance of their realization? A central question will be the convertibility of the dollar.

What Has Changed?

Contrary to what has been widely predicted and confidently diagnosed—'the Bretton Woods system is finished,' 'the dollar standard is now history'—the international monetary system is pretty much what it was before August 1971. It is not surprising that the IMF as a bureaucratic institution survives. (International agencies never die. The best example is the Bank for International Settlements. It was officially declared dead and ordered to be interred in the Bretton Woods agreement; but there it is, alive and active.) Actually, the Fund functions as it did before. Exchange rates have been drastically realigned, the dollar sharply devalued[1] and most countries, the largest trading nations among them, have adopted a wider band.

The dollar is still by far the most important international reserve, official intervention and private transaction currency. It has lost some of its lustre, there is much talk about reducing its role in the international monetary system and it has been demonstrated that, contrary to what was widely assumed, the dollar can be devalued, although with great difficulties and under heavy pressure applied by the U.S. In fact, the gold-dollar standard has for the time being been

65

replaced by a pure dollar standard, as the *Deutsche Bundesbank* pointed out in its annual report for 1971.[2] Countries in surplus again buy dollars, adding to their reserves, to prevent their currencies from rising above the upper intervention point. Countries in deficit sell dollars from their reserves to keep their currencies from falling below the intervention point. And the U.S. again follows a passive policy, a policy of benign neglect with regard to the balance of payments, after the very active, if not aggressive, policy, adopted on 15 August 1971 had achieved its proximate goal: devaluation of the dollar and realignment of exchange rates.

Passive policy means, briefly, two things: first, that domestic monetary, fiscal and other general economic policies are guided by domestic policy objectives—price stability, employment, growth—and not by balance-of-payments considerations; second, that intervention in the exchange market and initiatives to change exchange rates are left to other countries. It does *not* mean lack of interest in the organization of the international monetary system, neglect of the interests of other countries or indifference to the dangers of inflation.

How Long Will the Calm Last?

Ever since the Smithsonian accord of 18 December 1971, doubts about its viability have been widespread. Advocates of exchange flexibility have freely predicted that new crises are inevitable. In our present world, a fixed-rate system cannot work smoothly, they think, and the wider band can stave off only minor disturbances. Advocates of a truly international currency system, too, are sceptical of the present arrangement; the dollar standard is no longer acceptable, they believe. And the framers of the December accord themselves regard it as an interim solution; part of the agreement was, indeed, that "discussion should be promptly undertaken . . . to consider reform of the international monetary system."

Difficulties arose, in fact, soon after the Smithsonian Agreement. At first, the dollar was near the upper end of the new band, presumably in anticipation of the widely-expected repatriation of funds to the U.S. When the back-flow did not materialize, the dollar fell later in January close to the lower intervention point and some foreign central banks had to buy dollars to prevent their currencies from rising above the permitted margin. In March, the dollar strengthened and there seems to have been a considerable back-flow of funds, partly the result of the shrinking interest differential, but probably largely attracted by the rising stock market, which, in turn, reflects the quickening pace of recovery.

U.S. monetary policy had been sharply criticized both at home and abroad for letting short-term interest rates fall to low levels and thereby discouraging the back-flow of dollars. To my mind, this criticism was not justified and its full implications are rarely spelled out. To be sure, the Federal Reserve could make money sufficiently tight to induce a return flow of funds. But that surely would slow up recovery of output and employment. The critics should make it clear whether they wish to suggest (a) that the United States should accept slower recovery and more unemployment for the sake of the balance of payments or (b) that there is a possibility of raising interest rates sufficiently without adversely affecting recovery and employment.

The first suggestion, which may indeed be entertained by some foreign critics, is simply unacceptable and unrealistic. No U.S. government—nor that of any other country—will consciously tolerate or create significantly more unemployment than may be needed anyway to curb inflation, solely for the purpose of improving the balance of payments. That it should be possible, on the other hand, to push up short-term interest rates sufficiently without adversely influencing recovery and employment is highly improbable. Some critics may have in mind what used to be called "operation twist": that is to say, that short-term interest rates should be pushed up and long-term rates pushed down. The idea was that lower long-term rates would favorably affect the internal situation, while higher short-term rates would improve international capital flows. But this theory is defective for two reasons. First, it is very difficult, if not impossible, to twist significantly the structure of interest rates and, second, even if it could be done, the differential effect of a twist on internal and external equilibrium is more than doubtful.

Alternatively, the critics may think of "operation mix": that is, to use fiscal policy for influencing the internal situation and monetary policy for improving the balance of payments. But quite apart from serious theoretical objections that could be raised about the effectiveness of "operation mix," the argument overlooks the fact that fiscal policy is already extremely expansionary, with an estimated record deficit for 1971-72 of over $30 billions. A still larger budget deficit would hardly strengthen confidence in the dollar.

What should we conclude from this? Since the members of the Group of Ten wanted to return to fixed exchange rates and refused to accept a larger devaluation of the dollar in terms of their currencies, they should get used to sailing in a boat with an elephant—if I may use Mr. Trudeau's colorful expression which Dr. Emminger has very aptly applied to the dollar. Under fixed exchanges, minor heaves of the giant American economy can produce large flows of dollars across the border.

But is the present arrangement, the dollar standard, at all tolerable? My own opinion is that, abstracting from political and prestige considerations and assuming for the moment that the United States is able to keep inflation under control, the dollar standard could work quite well without imposing hardships on other countries.[3] It is worthwhile to elaborate briefly, first, because the dollar standard is likely to remain with us for some time until alternative arrangements can be worked out; and, second, because many of its features would not be essentially changed after an SDR standard or something like it had been set up. Of course, the United States, as well as other countries, especially the members of the Group of Ten, would have to observe the rules of the game. These rules are not hard to formulate, or difficult or onerous to observe. Countries other than the United States, when in persistent deficit which they can no longer finance by depleting reserves or by ad hoc borrowing, should promptly depreciate their currencies or, better, let them float. Countries in persistent surplus, if they do not wish to add to their reserves or to let prices go up, should promptly appreciate their currencies or, better, let them float up.

The greatest, nay indispensable, American contribution to the working of the system is to curb inflation. But, even if the price rise in America is reduced to internally acceptable proportions, we cannot be sure that dollar balances abroad will not continue to grow. So long as the dollar remains the most important international reserve currency and SDR creation is not sufficiently stepped up, there will be an upward trend in official, as well as private, dollar balances held abroad. Even if normal increases in reserve needs are satisfied by increasing SDR allocations, the United States could again develop a deficit. Moreover, without anything wrong with the U.S. balance of payments, if any major currency, the Deutsche mark or the yen, seems to become ripe for revaluation, dollar balances, official and private, from all over the world will converge on the countries concerned. Thus, a Deutsche mark or yen crisis can easily take on the appearance of a dollar crisis.

I suggest that the United States should take a tolerant view if other countries accumulate dollars. Anyone who prefers to take dollars rather than real goods in exchange for part of his exports should be regarded as a benefactor and not as an evil-doer. The opposite view, which is prevalent in the United States and elsewhere, reflects a mercantilistic fallacy. But mercantilism often has a grain of truth. Let us try to separate truth from fallacy.

Pressure on Surplus Countries

It will be recalled that an important feature of the Keynes plan for monetary reform was that surplus countries should be subjected to pressures to do their share in the balance-of-payments adjustment. The ruling system, in Keynes's view, put the whole burden of adjustment upon the deficit countries. What Keynes was afraid of, with experience of the 1930s in mind, was deflation in the deficit countries. Ever since, with or without reference to Keynes, plans for international monetary reform have invariably contained proposals to apply pressure, or even sanctions, against surplus countries, as well as against deficit countries.

The great concern with surpluses seems to me largely anachronistic, for the simple reason that practically no country, certainly not the United States, is willing anymore to permit deflation and unemployment for the sake of the balance of payments. Needless to add, unemployment is still a very serious problem in the United States and elsewhere. But the reason is domestic dilemmas posed by the coexistence of unemployment and inflation. External dilemmas posed by the coexistence of balance-of-payment deficits and unemployment do, of course, occur, but they are no longer solved by deflation, but by currency devaluation or by imposition of controls. The question of controls will be taken up presently. But the problem of persistent surplus countries requires further discussion from the American standpoint. It is, after all, the dollar that is subject to large accumulation. As yet, no other currency qualifies for that role, although recently there have been complaints that some countries have switched reserves from the dollar to Swiss francs and Deutsche marks.[4]

Why should the United States object to the accumulation of liquid dollar balances abroad? Surplus countries have several options. They can let prices rise or upvalue their currencies or let them float or they can reduce trade barriers and remove capital export restrictions. Clearly, there are no American objections to any of these measures. They can impose controls or engage in "dirty floating"; to that I come presently. Or they can accumulate dollar balances. This option is supposed to have adverse effects and to present dangerous hazards to the American economy which cannot be tolerated.

A direct deflationary impact, through conversion of dollars into gold or other U.S. reserve assets, of which Keynes was so afraid, is no longer possible. An indirect deflationary effect of dollar accumulation abroad is, however, conceivable if it reflects a trade or current account deficit.

There exists, in fact, a vague and inarticulate but strong current of apprehension in American government circles which attributes the sub-optimal performance of the American economy at least in part to the deterioration of the trade balance. I find this theory unconvincing, because a three billion dollar deficit of the current balance can hardly be regarded as the dominant factor in a trillion dollar economy. At any rate, if it is true, as I think it is, that American general economic policies are determined by domestic policy objectives (growth, employment) and domestic policy constraints (inflation), the deflationary effect of a three billion short-fall of effective demand can and will be offset by monetary and fiscal measures, except for a possible temporary slippage. A thirty to forty billion budget deficit supported by appropriate monetary measures should be ample for that purpose.

It has been argued that letting liquid dollars accumulate abroad is risky, because foreign countries sooner or later will get tired of holding dollars and will start to unload, thereby creating harmful instability. To be sure, other countries will not allow dollars to accumulate ad infinitum. But they have no way to stop further accumulation or to reduce existing balances other than the options mentioned: inflate, appreciate or impose controls.

The most powerful argument against allowing accumulation of dollars is that it hurts particular American industries. An undervalued yen permits the Japanese to export more cars, textiles, TV sets, etc., than they would otherwise and this plays into the hands of American protectionists. There obviously is a tiny grain of truth in this argument: in fact, exactly as much—or as little—as in objections to free trade, capital imports or gifts from abroad on the ground that any of these may hurt particular industries and foster protectionism. I have argued elsewhere at greater length that only a small part of the damage done to particular American industries by imports can be attributed to the accumulation of dollars abroad or, expressed differently, to the temporary undervaluation of certain currencies.[5] Here I confine myself to saying that, for the American economy as a whole, since imports are a small fraction of GNP, the small part of imports attributable to dollar accumulations abroad can be only a tiny element.

Instead of inflating, appreciating or accumulating dollars, surplus countries may use controls, including "dirty floating." So far as commodity trade is concerned, since the ordinary import-restricting controls would aggravate the imbalance, the controls would have to be negative, so to speak; that is to say, import-stimulating and export-restricting, which can be described as "dirty appreciation" of the currency. But this policy is just as unpopular as "clean appreciation." Therefore, there is little danger that surplus countries will use "negative" controls on trade.

Dirty floating—by splitting the exchange market into a "free" (or loosely controlled) market for capital transactions and a pegged market for current transactions—as it is being practiced by Belgium and France, is clearly an inefficient and wasteful method of disguised appreciation of the currency. It leads to evasion, progressive bureaucratization of trade and hurts the countries that engage in these practices as much as, or more than, others. For the United States, it is no more than pin-pricks and the proper reaction, to mix a metaphor or two, is to let the dirty floaters stew in their own juice.

I conclude that, from the economic standpoint, the post-Smithsonian dollar standard is manageable and viable. In my opinion, it does not impose a burden on other countries, provided the United States keeps inflation under control. True, even under this assumption some countries, probably only a few, may find themselves with unwanted surpluses, either because their inflation control is better than in the United States or because international demand for their exports happens to be exceptionally favorable. Such countries then have the choice of floating (or appreciating) their currency or inflating their economy a little bit. I say "little" because under modern conditions with numerous actual and potential export and import commodities the balance of payments is quite elastic in the medium and long run with respect to differential inflation and exchange rate changes.

However, many will say that this is an idealized picture. The fact is that the dollar standard has become rather unpopular both in the United States and abroad. Many Americans see it as a burden and a source of international embarrassment and dispute. And abroad it is widely regarded as an "exorbitant privilege" of the United States (de Gaulle's words). In my opinion, both views greatly exaggerate. It is neither a heavy burden nor an exorbitant privilege, but it has been a great boon for world trade at large. Be that as it may, let me turn to the problem of reform of the system, aimed at reducing the special role of the dollar, making it more equal to other currencies.

There is no lack of more or less ambitious plans of replacing the dollar by SDRs, of pooling and consolidating international reserves in the IMF which would issue SDRs or some composite reserve units ("CRUs") or of confronting the dollar with a new currency—"Europa," "Eurofranc" or "Eurosterling"—of an integrated Europe. Only some general aspects of the problem can be taken up in a short paper. To put the problem in perspective, I first discuss the issue of dollar convertibility.

Dollar Convertibility

On 15 August 1971, the dollar was formally declared inconvertible into U.S. reserve assets. De facto, it had been inconvertible for quite some time for large drawings, although there had been some nibbling at the U.S. gold stock by small conversion.

Ever since the Smithsonian accord, it has become popular in Europe, not so much in Japan, to demand that steps be taken to make the dollar again convertible. It is fairly generally agreed that convertibility into gold is out and that some bilateral or multilateral funding or consolidation of outstanding official dollar balances (overhang) would have to be achieved before convertibility of the dollar into some ultimate reserve asset could be considered. Even if this were done, the large volume of liquid or semi-liquid dollar liabilities in private hands which could easily find their way into official balances would constitute a potential threat, at least so long as the current (or basic) balance of the United States is in deficit.

The popular proposal that convertibility be restricted to dollar balances currently acquired through a U.S. current (or basic) deficit is not a feasible solution. Surplus countries would ask for gold or SDRs, while deficit countries could not well be denied the right to finance their deficits by drawing down their existing dollar balances. Thus, U.S. reserves could be depleted, even if the overall balance of payments were in equilibrium. Elaborate machinery, involving, inter alia, statistical determination of overall and bilateral balances of payments, would be required to cope with this problem.

Enough has been said to confirm the widely-held view that convertibility of the dollar into U.S. reserve assets presupposes a major reconstruction of the international monetary system. To negotiate and carry out such a reform will inevitably take much time, probably years. It is of the utmost importance that, in the meantime, the international payments mechanism continues to function.

Asset versus Market Convertibility

Until now, world trade has suffered surprisingly little from the numerous currency crises of the last few years, including the dollar crisis of 1971. A factor contributing importantly to that happy result is that, in a deeper sense, the dollar has remained fully convertible all along. We must sharply distinguish between *asset* convertibility and *market* convertibility. In recent discussions, what people have in mind when they exhort the United States to take steps to make the dollar again convertible or, what comes to the same thing, to intervene actively in the exchange market in order to strengthen confidence in the dollar, is *asset* convertibility, convertibility into U.S. reserve assets. But it is *market* convertibility that is important for world trade.

Market convertibility means that anyone can use his dollars not only to buy, invest and disinvest in the United States, but also to convert his dollars into any other currency in the market at the prevailing rate. Foreigners, including foreign central banks, enjoy full market convertibility of their dollars; for Americans, there exist certain restrictions, so far as investments abroad are concerned.

It will be recalled that, in the late 1940s and 1950s, currency convertibility was the topic of a lively international debate. It was market convertibility that was at issue, in other words, the elimination of the numerous stringent controls inherited from the war which inhibited the expansion of the world economy. The present inconvertibility of the dollar "is not comparable to the inconvertibility of the currencies of other industrial countries in the 1950s," as a recent IMF document put it. At that time, the American government pressed for early restoration of convertibility, while the British government, stunned by the disastrous failure of the premature dash for convertibility in 1947, resisted. The currency realignment of 1949 paved the way for convertibility. In the later 1950s, more and more countries abolished controls and made their currencies convertible under Article VIII of the IMF charter. It was market convertibility that was indispensable for the subsequent rapid growth of world trade. Two things should be stressed. First, it is substantially full and unrestricted convertibility at uniform exchange rates that counts. In some more or less restricted sense, almost every currency is convertible, but some only via narrow black markets. Second, not only is market convertibility entirely compatible with changes in exchange rates and floating rates—thus, the floating Canadian dollar has been fully convertible all along—but market convertibility presupposes realistic exchange rates which in many cases only flexible rates can provide. On the other hand, split exchange markets, dual and multiple exchange rates and other devices of control are the very negation of true convertibility.

To repeat, the dollar is fully convertible in the market sense. For world trade, it is of the utmost importance to keep it convertible, until the dollar is replaced by SDRs or something else in a reconstructed international monetary system. However, it takes more than one country to keep a currency convertible. The United States should continue its policy of not restricting the market convertibility of the dollar. But other countries should refrain from reducing convertibility, and thereby damaging world trade, by splitting exchange markets, introducing dual rates and other types of exchange control, instead of devaluing or floating their currency when in deficit, or appreciating or floating their currency if they do not wish to inflate when in surplus. A few words will be said later about the desirability of depreciating the dollar in terms of gold and SDRs, if it became overvalued with respect to many other currencies.

Reconstruction of the System: to Reduce
the Special Role of the Dollar

If the dollar is to be made convertible—in this section, convertibility means *asset* convertibility, unless otherwise stated—the dollar overhang must be eliminated or sharply reduced by multilateral consolidation or pooling. On this, almost everybody seems to agree. But there are many important and complex questions of implementation on which expert opinion diverges widely and official consensus is nowhere in sight.

Should a pooling of reserves be compulsory or optional? If compulsory, provision must be made for working balances; how are these to be defined? How comprehensive is the scheme to be? Some plans—for example, Edward Bernstein's famous Reserve Settlement proposal—comprehend all types of reserves, including gold and SDRs; others envisage that gold and dollar reserves be pooled and exchanged for specially-issued SDRs. In these schemes, the United States would become the debtor of the Fund for the dollars surrendered by other countries, a gold guarantee would apply and presumably a lower interest rate be charged. A highly controversial question that surely will be raised with much urgency is the "link" between SDRs and development assistance to poor countries.

The United States, before accepting a reform involving asset convertibility of the dollar, would certainly require assurance or safeguards concerning the many billion more or less liquid dollar balances held abroad in private hands. Furthermore, the removal of the alleged "special privilege" of the inconvertible dollar would be conditional upon elimination of the corresponding "special handicaps" with respect to exchange rate changes. There are two of these. First, under present arrangements with a band of 2¼ percent on each side of parity, the exchange rate between any two currencies other than the dollar can change, under certain circumstances, by as much as 9 percent, while the exchange value of the dollar vis-à-vis any other currency can change by no more than 4½ percent.[6] Second, under present circumstances it is for the United States extremely difficult, until last year many people thought impossible, to change the par value of the dollar. The second is the more important and less tractable handicap.

The first handicap or "asymmetry" stems from the fact that the dollar is used by all countries as the intervention currency to keep the exchange value of their currency inside the range of permitted fluctuations. Under this arrangement, any currency can change by 4½ percent vis-à-vis the dollar if it moves from one end of the band to the other. Suppose now that for any reason—differential inflation or a change in international demand—currency A rises from the floor of the band to the ceiling and currency B falls from the ceiling to the floor; then they move by 9 percent vis-à-vis each other, while the dollar has moved by 4½ percent vis-à-vis each. For a country in deficit, a potential 9 percent devaluation vis-à-vis many currencies could be a great help. For the United States, the maximum possible help provided by the present band would be a depreciation of the dollar of only 4½ percent.

This could surely become a handicap for the United States if asset convertibility of the dollar were restored. But, so long as the dollar is inconvertible, it can be regarded as only a potential handicap, if one accepts the popular view that accumulation of dollar balances by other countries is a burden on the United States. I criticized this theory above as a mercantilistic fallacy, and I need not go through all that again.

This first asymmetry or handicap could be removed by making SDRs and gold (which now are rigidly linked) the "pivot" and intervention currency, instead of the dollar. All national currencies, including the dollar, would then stand in symmetrical relationship to the international unit, as was the case under the old gold standard. The dollar would be allowed to fluctuate vis-à-vis SDRs within a band of the same width of 4½ percent as all the other currencies. As a consequence, the maximum variability of the dollar vis-à-vis other currencies would then be the same as that of all other currencies: 9 percent with a band of 4½ percent.

The straightforward method of achieving that result and thus removing the first asymmetry would be to make SDRs negotiable instruments suitable for official intervention, as well as for private holding and trading. But that would require a change of the Fund's Articles of Agreement, basically not complicated but actually very difficult to negotiate.

Theoretically, the same result could be achieved, without a national or supranational intervention medium (dollar, SDRs or gold), by what has come to be known as "symmetric" or "multi-currency intervention." In that case, too, it would be necessary to give the dollar a band in which to fluctuate around the SDRs as the *numéraire*. The existing (asymmetric) dollar-based intervention system or a hypothetical SDR- (or gold-) based system is largely automatic, market-oriented and makes use of the existing efficient, highly competitive exchange markets to maintain consistent cross-rates through private arbitrage with a minimum of public intervention. In contrast, the symmetric multi-currency intervention system would have to rely on elaborate rules and detailed guidance and supervision by the Fund to achieve the same result: namely, to make the dollar equal to other currencies in one respect: to give it the same maximum variability vis-à-vis other currencies, 9 percent with the present band of 4½ percent. It is not worthwhile, however, to pursue this subject any further. For the great complexity of the multi-currency intervention system, in contrast to its very limited objective, makes it highly improbable that it will be tried in practice.[7]

The second asymmetry—the difficulty, or alleged impossibility, of changing the par value of the dollar—is altogether different in nature and a much more important matter than the first-mentioned asymmetry. This, too, would be a handicap for the United States were asset convertibility of the dollar to be restored. So long as the dollar is inconvertible, it can be regarded as a handicap only if the fallacious view is accepted that accumulation of dollar balances abroad is a burden for the United States.

This asymmetry is more deeply rooted than the first and cannot be removed by mechanical changes of the intervention system. Nor can substitution of SDRs for dollar reserves in an international consolidation scheme give the U.S. complete freedom to devalue the dollar or to let it float without fear that the move will be frustrated by widespread imitation, although it may perhaps make it a little easier.

Why did other countries not accept as large a devaluation of the dollar as the United States wanted, even in the form of a depreciation of the dollar in terms of gold? The major reason surely was that they were afriad of impairing the competitiveness of their industries vis-à-vis the United States or, what comes pretty much to the same, that they were reluctant to give up or reduce their trade surplus. (That it is inconsistent to complain about imported inflation and, at the same time, to cling to a trade surplus, as many did, is another matter.) The difficulty of devaluing the dollar is rooted in a basic asymmetry: namely, the large size of the American economy. If a small or medium-sized country devalues its currency, the rest of the world (apart from a few other small or medium-sized countries) can absorb the impact on their trade. If a large country devalues, there are bound to be repercussions on, and reactions by, many other countries. This asymmetry cannot be removed by monetary reform.

Exchange Flexibility

Many of these problems could be solved, or at least reduced to small proportions, by greater exchange flexibility. If most countries that are dissatisfied with the working of the dollar standard followed the Canadian example and let their currency float vis-à-vis the dollar, the dollar itself would in effect become flexible and the asymmetry, privilege or handicap would disappear, in substance if not in form. But there is no use elaborating on this because no such solution seems to be negotiable at this point.

I am afraid the same holds of the less ambitious and, to my mind, quite feasible scheme proposed by Professor John Williamson.[8] Williamson links, in a highly ingenious way, SDR creation and a "crawling peg" arrangement. It is true there is almost general agreement that there should be more frequent changes of exchange rates. But any generalized crawling peg or "gliding parity" arrangement, either of formula or individual decision type, binding or presumptive, would seem to be out of the question at the present time.

Nowadays, almost every official document and speech on monetary reform stresses the importance of prompt diagnosis of emerging payments disequilibria and speedy adjustment of exchange rates. This is a great advance over the state of the debate a few years ago, when mention of frequent changes in exchange rates was taboo in official utterances. But the discussion rarely faces up to the basic difficulty of the adjustable peg (par value) system: that more frequent but still discrete and fairly large changes of exchange rates may make things worse rather than better. Concretely, if the international value of a currency is changed, say, every ten years, there is probably enough time after each change for confidence to be restored. If the change comes on the average after, say, every two years, the interval is too short for "stability illusion" (analogous to money illusion) to be revived. Hence, destabilizing speculative capital flows may become larger rather than smaller. Full flexibility or gliding (or crawling) parities avoid this difficulty. The crucial problem is to determine how fast the glide or crawl has to be to avoid destabilizing effects.

The Dollar Standard Once More

Our discussion comes to the somewhat negative conclusion that it will be very difficult and take a long time to reform the international monetary system so as to make the dollar equal to other currencies and to eliminate the special privileges and handicaps allegedly inherent in the present arrangement. In the meantime, the world is on the dollar standard. To repeat, in my opinion, the dollar standard is not a bad or highly inequitable system, provided U.S. inflation does not get out of hand. But, whether this proposition is accepted or not, there should be agreement that it is of the utmost importance for the continuing growth of world trade and for world welfare that the free market convertibility of the dollar is preserved until something else can be put in its place. The market-convertible dollar is the indispenable lubricant of the wheels of world trade.

But what if U.S. inflation gets worse? Or what if my judgment—that, if U.S.

inflation remains moderate (by present world standards), not much inflation abroad would be required to maintain payments equilibrium—turns out to be too optimistic? One thing is certain: there would then be plenty of trouble, recrimination, more or less justified criticism of the United States and a tendency to form rival currency blocs in Europe and possibly elsewhere. But in some basic respects the situation would not be changed by excessive inflation in the United States. Thus, the only rational choice of surplus countries which do not want to accumulate more dollars and refuse to participate in U.S. inflation is (and would continue to be) to let their currency float up. But will they act rationally? Dirty appreciation or dirty floating is not a rational reaction. It would hurt the dirty floaters and everybody else more than the United States. To restrict imports and trade would be even more irrational; it would be tantamount to cutting off one's nose to spite one's face. These remarks result from straightforward economic analysis and are not intended to excuse or justify U.S. inflation or to play down the dangers of inflation.

If, as a consequence of excessive U.S. inflation, the dollar were to become overvalued with respect to many or most currencies, a depreciation of the dollar (in terms of gold and SDRs) might facilitate, politically, a realignment of parities, although it would not obviate other parity changes, because other currencies would not be uniformly undervalued. Basically, depreciation of the dollar is not a matter of great importance because, contrary to what is often assumed, it makes no difference, except from a political or national prestige standpoint, whether the dollar is depreciated or other currencies appreciated. "It is incorrect to equate a devaluation of the dollar [in terms of gold] with the contribution of the U.S. to the burden of adjustment." (Dr. Rinaldo Ossola, *Reflections on New Currency Solutions*, remarks made in London, 15 February 1972.) But, so long as the dollar is the world's foremost reserve, transaction and intervention currency and gold plays a role in the minds and expectations of many people, it is in the interest of world trade (no specific American interests are involved) not to tamper with the dollar price of gold for political and prestige reasons unless absolutely necessary.

There is one step that the United States could take which would make the dollar standard more acceptable and equitable, even in the case of excessive American inflation: To offer some sort of purchasing power guarantee to foreign official dollar holders. This proposal has been made by Professor Fellner.[9] The United States would offer to foreign official dollar holders the option to exchange their dollars for special bonds carrying a purchasing power guarantee and a correspondingly lower yield. These guaranteed bonds would be for official use only and could at any time be converted at par into ordinary bonds. The form of guarantee and the yield would have to be agreed upon. The most sensible type of guarantee would be in terms of a broadly-based price index of internationally-traded goods. The U.S. wholesale price index would be a good proxy. A gold guarantee inevitably would become more and more artificial as gold's monetary role diminished. An alternative might be to restrict the guarantee to recently-acquired dollar balances.

The first reaction of the official mind to a purchasing power guarantee, as in most other cases of new ideas, will be to shrink back and think of all sorts of reasons why it could and should not be done. One argument might be that giving a purchasing power guarantee to foreign central banks would be a dangerous precedent and would be difficult politically without giving domestic savers the same privilege. But the precedent may not be bad at all. In an age of inflation there is much to be said, and there is indeed increasing demand, for giving at least the small saver a means to protect himself from inflation.

A guarantee for official dollar holdings surely is no panacea, but it would help to strengthen the present system until something better has been put in its place.

Outlook and Concluding Remarks

I believe the chances are good that in the future, as in the past, the United States will succeed better than most countries in curbing inflation. Consumer prices have risen less in the United States than in the great majority of other countries over somewhat longish periods. But this in itself is not a sufficient proof, for so long as the world is on the dollar standard, inflation in the United States sets the pace for inflation in all the many countries that maintain fixed exchange rates and keep their currencies convertible. This follows from the fact that U.S. monetary policy is determined by domestic policy objectives and that the feedback via the balance of payments is negligible, because of the small size of the foreign trade sector in the American economy.

The price dominance of America is not generally understood, either in the United States or abroad, notwithstanding the frequent complaints about America "exporting inflation." At any rate, most complainers do not understand that the only effective protection against imported inflation is a floating exchange rate and they are, inconsistently, very reluctant to accept a deterioration of their trade balance.

That most countries had more inflation than the United States could have been a case of induced (imported) inflation. But if, in any country, prices rise persistently much faster than in the United States, one would suspect a stronger propensity to inflate. The suspicion is confirmed if a country, to maintain equilibrium, is forced to depreciate its currency from time to time against the dollar and, in between depreciations, to use controls on capital and similar devices. It is not difficult to find examples, even among the loudest complainers about the American export of inflation.

Suppose now that the United States does in fact curb inflation (and makes its policy more attractive by offering some kind of guarantee to foreign official dollar holders). There will then be enough time for the community of nations to negotiate a reform of the international monetary system. If many countries really wish to replace the dollar by SDRs, it could be done gradually, on a voluntary and experimental basis. A fraction of the outstanding official balances could be turned over to the Fund in exchange for SDRs. It would not be necessary at once to set up a rigid schedule with a firm terminal date for complete conversion of all dollar holdings (apart from working balances) into SDRs. That could be left for later negotiations.

It would go beyond the scope of the present paper to suggest alternative solutions for the final reform of the system. Let me add one last observation. At an international gathering earlier this year I was struck by the remark of a prominent German economist. He said that from the point of view of guarding against world inflation he preferred the dollar standard to the SDR standard. For the internal resistance to inflation in the United States was still strong, while an international body administering the SDRs might not be able to resist the strong inflationary pressures to which it would undoubtedly be subjected. This seems to me a refreshingly realistic evaluation of the inflationary dangers, especially if, as now seems likely, a link between SDR creation and development assistance will be forged. The framers of the reform of the international monetary system will be well advised to keep this danger in mind.

Notes

1. The magnitude of the effective overall devaluation of the dollar varies according to the method of calculation. At the end of 1971 the trade-weighted average effective devaluation since early May 1971 against *all* currencies, including those which were devalued against the dollar, was about 7 percent. In some official statements a figure of 12 percent was mentioned. That was vis-à-vis eight countries of the Group of Ten (excluding Canada). Because of the wider band the effective devaluation is apt to change a little from time to time. However, to speak of a roughly 8 percent devaluation cannot be far off the mark.

2. Dr. Edwin Stopper, the president of the Swiss National Bank, has expressed it as follows: "According to a widely held view on 15 August 1971 the dollar-gold exchange standard was put to rest. Actually it was not the existing monetary system that broke down, but the notion that it was based on the dollar-gold exchange standard. In reality it functioned, practically from the beginning, as a dollar standard" (speech, 28 April 1972).

3. The annual report of the DEUTSCHE BUNDESBANK has this to say: "There is a good chance that the position of the dollar as the key currency (LEITWÄHRUNG) will again become stronger, if the United States succeeds in regaining sufficient internal stability."

4. A diversification of reserves resulting in the widespread adoption of

multi-currency reserves would lead to a pyramiding of international liquidity which could become an inflationary factor in the world economy.

5. See my papers 'U.S. Balance of Payments Policy and the International Monetary System' in CONVERTIBILITY, MULTILATERALISM AND FREEDOM, Essays in honor of R. Kamitz, ed. by Wolfgang Schmitz, Vienna and New York, 1972, and A STRATEGY FOR U.S. BALANCE OF PAYMENTS POLICY by Gottfried Haberler and Tom Willett, American Enterprise Institute, Washington, D.C., 1971. For a quantitative appraisal, it must be kept in mind that only that part of dollar accumulation abroad that corresponds to the trade balance should be counted, not the huge speculative and interest-sensitive funds held abroad.

6. Since 24 April the six Common Market countries (later joined by the U.K., Denmark and Norway) have given up some of their flexibility by restricting movements in their exchange rates among themselves so that the maximum deviation is 4½ percent.

7. For an excellent analysis of the efficiency of the present dollar-based system, as compared with a multi-currency system, see Richard N. Cooper, "Eurodollars, Reserve Dollars, and Asymmetries in the International Monetary System," JOURNAL OF INTERNATIONAL ECONOMICS, Sept. 1972. Another danger of multi-currency intervention is that it would probably lead to the widespread adoption of multi-currency reserves. As mentioned earlier, this development would constitute an inflationary threat through the pyramiding of international liquidity. See also the criticisms of such an outcome by C. Fred Bergster, REFORMING THE DOLLAR: AN INTERNATIONAL MONETARY POLICY FOR THE UNITED STATES, Council on Foreign Relations Paper on International Affairs, No. 2, Sept. 1972, pp. 9-13.

8. THE CHOICE OF A PIVOT FOR PARITIES, Essays in International Finance, No. 90, November 1971, International Finance Section, Princeton University, Princeton, New Jersey.

9. William Fellner, "The Dollar's Place in the International System: Criteria for the Appraisal of Emerging Views," THE JOURNAL OF ECONOMIC LITERATURE, American Economic Association, Menasha, Wisconsin, September 1972.

5 The Case for Gold

Don D. Humphrey

The case for raising the price of gold is not overwhelming, but it is receiving less attention than it deserves. One reason is the stubborn refusal of the United States to recognize that the Bretton Woods system is unworkable with a gold shortage. A second reason may be that gold has found little support in academic circles since Sir Roy Harrod's long and unsuccessful advocacy,[1] though one must mention Milton Gilbert's notable essay of 1968 which I found more convincing.[2] Harrod, emphatically, makes the main point that gold leaves more room for national autonomy, while Gilbert's model shows why incremental monetary gold is the only means of financing surpluses in the international payments system without corresponding deficits, and without the sacrifice of sovereignty.

A further objection to raising the price of gold is that almost no one likes the gold lobby and most of us find it highly objectionable. If India, Bangladesh, Pakistan, and poorest Africa owned the gold mines, instead of South Africa and the U.S.S.R., I would suggest that the economic case for demonetization of gold would lose supporters and the case for raising the price would be more palatable. In a sense, the case for gold has been spoiled by its supporters—the gold lobby. And the French obsession with gold has not helped the case either.

The case for gold is largely political, the case against it largely economics. In this instance, optimal economics is second-best politics. The aversion of many economists to gold or, at least, their lack of interest probably reflects an occupational preoccupation with equilibrium and quest for freely fluctuating exchange rates. We relish Keynes' trenchant phrase, the "barbarous relic" (in reference to gold).[3] Despite suspension of convertibility and the floating of leading currencies (the shock of August 15-December 18, 1971), it soon became apparent that the world is not about to abandon fixed but adjustable exchange rates. At the official level, the earlier terms of reference of the Group of Ten on liquidity had excluded changing the gold price and flexible exchanges from consideration (the latter was considered later by the Fund).

Adequate increments of liquidity are indispensable to fixed rates and essential to a smooth process of adjustment. I shall argue later that the facility for Special Drawing Rights is a fair weather system and that SDRs cannot be made "as good as gold." The rest of the world resents an inconvertible dollar because conversion to gold is the only means that others have to express their dissatisfaction with dollar hegemony. At the same time, the greater convenience of dollars is almost universally recognized and, when convertible beyond doubt, the dollar is not only "as good as gold," it is better than gold in the sense of allowing foreign central banks the option of holding interest-bearing assets. Different reserve assets serve different purposes.

A dollar standard leaves the world under the rule of the Federal Reserve and, when the dollar is inconvertible, others have no way of influencing American balance-of-payments policy. A price increase with remonetization of incremental gold reserves offers wider latitude for national autonomy than the alternative of a world bank or any agreement delegating control of the world's money to international bureaucrats. Although a gold and convertible dollar system may be suboptimal, a return to Bretton Woods discipline may be more readily attainable than international agreement on a pure credit facility.[4]

The price of gold, that is, the gold value of national currencies and dollar convertibility are very much the concern of other nations, but the official price of gold is fixed by United States. Because the decision to raise the price of gold involves the issue of dollar hegemony versus national autonomy, it should be resolved by a consensus of leading nations rather than by a unilateral decision of the United States as has been the case. Whatever their attitude may be, other countries are unable to devalue relative to gold without altering the exchange rate, but they would follow the United States in a "uniform change of par values," which is Bretton Woods language for raising the official price of gold. Its architects were far sighted enough to recognize the possible necessity for this.

Bretton Woods

The Bretton Woods system of international money was based on gold, and foundered because of the gold shortage and the rigidity of exchange rates. According to the Fund's rules, conditional credits were available for temporary deficits and national currency would be used for market intervention. But the reserve-currency role was to be subordinate to gold and convertibility was a substitute for market intervention. The original conception was that nations would hold their reserves in gold. Owing, however, to inflation and the growth of world trade and investment, demand for international liquidity rose faster than supplies of new monetary gold. I shall attempt to show that the gold shortage, by shifting too much weight to the dollar, undermined the discipline of Bretton Woods and contributed to the reluctance to adjust. The system is unworkable without incremental additions to monetary stocks sufficient to satisfy the demand for gold by surplus countries and, at the same time, allow United States to acquire enough new gold to maintain convertibility. As outlined here, "the case for gold" means a major price increase to expand supplies enough to meet these conditions. But the price should not be raised so high as to produce larger balance-of-payments surpluses than the world can absorb without inflation. Alternatively, if gold supplies exceed monetary demand, authorities may satisfy their reserve requirements and allow the free-market price to fall below the official price of gold if this is found to be feasible.

Central bankers regard a surplus of foreign payments as a healthy condition— a normal target. Conversely, deficits are treated as something to be put right because they are not sustainable. This gives the system a mercantilistic tint which is derived from the recognition that trade and investment are expanding. To satisfy this demand, the global supply of liquidity must not be so tight that the target of surpluses, as a norm, forces the residual supplier i.e., the reserve-currency center, to lose liquidity continuously. Moreover, unless the world accepts an irredeemable paper standard, a gold component is needed in the incremental growth of reserves to avoid systemic disequilibrium. It is basic to a fixed-rate system that the discipline of adjustment be allowed to work, without a systemic shortage of liquidity, so that countries following reasonable balance-of-payments policies can maintain stable exchange rates.

The sum of global surpluses must equal the sum of the deficits, apart from gold or fiat money. Hence, in the absence of fiat money, the sum of all surpluses minus the sum of all deficits is equal to the increment of gold reserves. The function of the growth of reserves is not to finance deficits but to finance surpluses. When the new gold available was less than the surpluses that monetary authorities decided to accumulate, they could make up the short-fall by buying gold from United States stocks or by accumulating dollars. The surpluses could come only from the reserves of other countries or from deficits of United States. It follows that only new gold (or fiat money) can satisfy the demand for surpluses without creating corresponding deficits elsewhere in the system. The substitution of dollars for gold to finance surpluses increased United States liabilities to foreign central banks. The reason why raising the price of gold would relieve this systemic imbalance is that it would relieve the gold shortage that caused United States to lose liquidity in the first place.

Failure to distinguish between supply- and demand-determined deficits resulted in a strong feeling in Europe that somehow dollar deficits "reflected misbehavior on the part of United States—even when United States was clearly not having excess demand, when the margin of unemployed resources was unnecessarily large, and when it could not be convincingly shown by what combination of policy measures the United States could meet the demand to eliminate its deficit."[5] United States deficits on an official settlements basis reflecting only demand for reserves by foreign central banks are not a signal of misbehavior.

To be sure the United States, also, suffered deficits because of structural change and, in the end, because of excess demand. For these, we should have accepted the discipline of gold losses and, when necessary, adjusted the exchange rate like other countries.

The stage for crises was set when the gold shortage was compensated by reluctant accumulation of dollar reserves. The immediate actors were massive flows of capital across the exchanges. These were precipitated by interest rate differentials from different phases of the cycle and heavily reinforced by speculation that the disequilibrium exchange rates were no longer sustainable. The exchange rate rigidity was a choice of governments, not a defect of the system. In case of the dollar, however, the adjustment process was confounded by a liquidity problem, the fact dollars are an imperfect substitute for gold.

Theoretically, the growing substitution of credit money for commodity money is bound to undermine confidence in convertibility, if the stock of commodity money is fixed or growing too slowly to satisfy monetary demand. Surplus countries must be free to exercise the gold option and still leave the reserve-currency center able to acquire enough new gold to avoid serious risk of devaluation.

The success of any fixed-rate system depends on how promptly par values are adjusted, when necessary to avoid exchange controls or other restrictions on trade and investment which are harmful to others. The Fund Articles are designed to prevent borrowing without taking corrective measures to adjust and, in any event, adjustment was supposed to be inevitable for debtor nations when earned reserves and drawing rights were exhausted. The Bretton Woods design for liquidity with "adequate safeguards" was circumvented when United States borrowed extensively outside the Fund in order to protect its gold stock.[6]

Discipline

Discipline serves as a constraint on foreign payments in two ways. In the first, an external deficit reduces the nation's money supply and would start the adjustment process, unless counteracted by the monetary authority. Bretton Woods discipline is on the balance of payments itself. For the most part, both have worked well when permitted to operate. Of course, nations may postpone both disciplines so long as they can rely on their own reserves. This is why remonetization of new gold would provide for the growth of reserves without international surveillance.[7]

The discipline from loss of reserves works only if it is accepted as a guide for national monetary policy. Europeans were critical of the Federal Reserve for replacing, domestically, the liquidity that United States was losing through foreign deficits. Conversely, with respect to surplus countries, the money created by buying gold and dollars is inflationary, which is the sole discipline on the surplus country to adjust. Americans have been critical of surplus Europe for resisting adjustment while complaining about the inflationary effects of accumulating American dollars.

In this connection, it is useful to distinguish between supply-determined deficits, caused by excessive domestic liquidity, for which United States should take the Bretton Woods medicine, and demand-determined deficits, caused by the shortage of gold, for which there is no remedy except to raise the price of gold or print a new international money which will be generally accepted as an asset without liabilities.

With two major exceptions, balance-of-payments discipline for the more developed countries worked in a constructive way. The system broke down in the past decade because United States and Britain avoided Bretton Woods discipline by borrowing outside the system. For by-passing Bretton Woods and borrowing without its "adequate safeguards," Britain paid dearly in the loss of foreign assets and accumulation of new debt. (See the Bank of International Settlements, Annual Report, 1967-68.) The American effort to avoid gold losses paved the way for the system's collapse.

Instead of taking gold losses as a signal that gold was undervalued, the United States sought to hold onto its gold by borrowing and by a series of controls. Starting with Roosa bonds denominated in foreign currencies, then by expanding swaps and, then, under the General Arrangements to Borrow by the Group of Ten, the United States postponed devaluation and adjustment. Finally, in March 1968, six countries cooperated with United States to close the gold pool and stop further loss of official gold reserves. The Netherlands continued to ask for gold, Germany and Japan promised not to. The two-tier price of gold seems to be working, but remains a potentially disturbing element and a hindrance to the return of confidence.

While calling on the United States to accept payments discipline, other countries provided a possible means of escape by accepting guaranteed United States debts, by restraint in converting their dollars into gold, and by accepting the two-tier system. The United States should have taken the Bretton Woods path to devaluation, which others could have encouraged by using the gold option. Under the facade of convertibility, however, it was generally held that United States was powerless to adjust the exchanges because dollar devaluation would produce a uniform change in par values, as other nations would seek to avoid both loss of competitive position and the loss of purchasing power of their dollar reserves when converted into other currencies. In the crisis of events, this was proven wrong.

Adequate Gold Facilitates Adjustment

Although the exact form of adjustment is uncertain, the following may be indicative of the effects of larger gold supplies. The gold exports of producing countries are treated like other commodity exports. The enlarged import demand of South Africa, for example, would be expected to help British exports, and a stronger pound sterling would help the dollar. Similarly, if the

U.S.S.R.'s imports of wheat were sustained or enlarged with less credit from exporters, the foreign payments of United States and Canada would improve, as less export financing would be needed.

But even if the extra demand of gold-producing countries enlarged the surplus of surplus countries, in the first instance, deficit countries would gain in two ways from the repercussions. The extra surpluses resulting from additional exports to gold-producing countries are certain to add to inflationary pressure in the surplus countries, which would erode their current-account surplus. Interest rates would, also, tend to fall as surplus countries increased their capital exports and demand for capital imports declined in countries benefiting directly from the export of gold. In addition, the higher gold price would reduce private demand making more gold available to central banks.

Enlarging the surpluses of surplus countries with extra exports to gold-producing countries would make them less reluctant to adjust. Above all, the extra gold increment, by financing surpluses without deficits, would benefit the United States balance of payments. In short, deficit countries would benefit either directly from enlarged exports and easier money markets or, indirectly, from the fact that extra inflationary pressure in the surplus countries would facilitate adjustment.[8] Dollar liquidity is not a full substitute for gold with respect to adjustment, else why did the system break down? If liquidity is so tight that many nations are actively striving to protect their foreign balance, the burden of adjustment falls on the deficit country while adequate liquidity in the form of gold is likely to shift some of the pressure to adjust to surplus countries. The long-term shortage of gold contributed to a systemic reluctance to adjust. A concern for adequate liquidity is inseparable from adjustment which, incidentally, is not recognized by the SDR facility. (The price of gold was arbitrarily excluded from the Group of Ten's terms of reference, quite possibly at the insistence of the United States.)

Special Drawing Rights

If the SDR facility should develop into something like a gigantic network of swaps for medium-term credit, it can become a useful supplement to reserves. The attractiveness of the unconditional feature of SDRs, however, involves sacrificing the discipline to adjust, which means that the facility will require self-discipline in order to work well.

Allocation of SDRs does not of itself facilitate adjustment and the effect of their transfer remains problematical. The loss of SDRs puts no particular pressure on deficit countries to correct the disequilibrium and surplus countries may be reluctant to initiate steps to eliminate their surpluses, in view of the uncertainty about future allocations.

The precise nature of liabilities under the SDR facility remains unclear. The unique aspect of international liquidity provided by gold is that it can be used to expand reserve assets without creating corresponding liabilities. There is no agreement to duplicate this feature of gold with SDRs; fiduciary assets become either a liability of debtors or the scheme will involve printing money on an international scale. Drafting the SDR Articles involved papering over disagreement on this point.[9]

Suppose that deficit countries transfer SDRs to settle their debts, without correcting their policies. If this continues beyond a temporary period, the deficit countries will have acquired real resources in exchange for an interest-bearing, gold-guaranteed obligation. Though initially dormant, the SDR liability may become active. If a nation opts out, or in case of a general liquidation of the facility, presumably, outstanding obligations would be converted into fixed-maturity debts.

Now the architects of the SDR facility proclaimed that it was not to be used to settle persistent deficits. If this should happen, the countries losing real resources in exchange for SDRs may become annoyed at the misuse of the facility. They could seek to tighten the reconstitution requirement; reduce the "holding limits," stop further allocations or opt out of the system. Each of these possible actions limits the utility of SDRs as a substitute for gold and implies Gresham's Law effects regarding their attractiveness relative to alternative reserve assets. In the actual transfer of SDRs, United States has been the largest receiver, except the IMF itself. Someone has called this "negative banking."

SDRs are flawed by an absolute gold-value guarantee and, if the price of gold is raised, creditor nations will gain at the expense of debtors to the system. As a result, conservative nations may be reluctant to use their allocation except as a last resort, while those who are eager to dispose of their SDRs may store up trouble. In the instance of ordinary Fund positions, the gold guarantee is applicable at the discretion of the Board of Governors, depending on circumstances.

Some are eager to "link" the issue of SDRs to distribution of development aid, which is flatly contradictory to the original objective and is regarded by others as a threat to the entire scheme. It is scarcely a good omen for future international agreement on a generally accepted fiduciary asset, if those opposed to "linking" should be outvoted.

In considering the composition of reserves which may be held a long time, sovereign states cannot afford to ignore contingencies just because they may seem improbable at the time. Fiduciary reserve assets have been blocked in war and in political disputes short of war. Gold, on the other hand, is at the disposition of its holder in foul weather and fair. Different purposes are best served by different reserve assets and while fiduciary assets may be optimal in terms of controlling supply, they are suboptimal for the purpose of serving other objectives.

The analytical tool for dealing with fair weather and foul on the international front is an uncertainty matrix. Conservative nations, holding all their reserves in gold, would seem to be assuming that about "everything which can go wrong will go wrong," which seems to others an unnecessarily costly strategy. The record of different national motivations and objectives in holding reserves will be cited. It establishes a basis for believing that there are demands for more than a single type of reserve asset, despite the problem of Gresham's Law.[10] It is a safe bet that few central banks would choose to hold all of their reserves in Special Drawing Rights or similar assets. As for current proposals to liquidate official gold stocks (at $38 an ounce) in exchange for SDRs, some nations may feel that this would be like asking them to give up their armor and trust their security to the United Nations.

A reserve money that is entirely dependent on international agreements for its issue and acceptability is a fair-weather system. Since allocations are uncertain and the acceptability of SDRs may be limited in times of serious political conflict, one cannot imagine that a fiduciary asset which is necessarily political would be considered as safe and as dependable as gold.

Gold Shortage

It has been said that gold supplies are subject to unpredictable shifts in production, the vagaries of Soviet sales and private speculation. In fact, however, gold production and industrial demand showed a fairly smooth trend for fifteen years. The Soviets held onto their gold for the same reason that central banks have, namely, the undervaluation of gold. The several bouts of speculation are a symptom of the shortage, not its cause.

Data on gold supplies should have made the liquidity shortage evident at an early date, if it had been sufficiently emphasized that newly-minded gold was the only means of financing external surpluses without corresponding deficits. Only reserve-currency expansion, based on the extra large concentration of gold in initial U.S. stocks, enabled the system to work as well as it did.

That there has been a gold shortage was belatedly recognized several years before the crises of 1968 and 1971. The initial Report of the Deputies of the Group of Ten (August 1, 1964) recognized that the flow of new gold into official reserves "cannot be relied on to meet fully the liquidity needs of the future." Official net purchases of gold averaged $575 million in the period 1961-65. In that period, Europe was accumulating dollars, reluctantly, and would have preferred more gold.

The gold price remained fixed at the prewar level of $35 an ounce until December 1971, when it was raised to $38 an ounce. The mounting costs of mining from the inflation of the Second World War and after resulted in a shortage of supply to meet the official demand for incremental liquidity in an expanding world economy. The fixed price of gold encouraged the substitution of gold for other metals. Industrial demand is also growing from rising real incomes. As regards hoarding, inflation reduces the purchasing power of an ounce of gold when the market price is tied to the official price. Hence, larger hoards were needed in order to maintain gold's purchasing power relative to other resources. The enlarged private demand from both price and income effects was bound to encourage speculation that monetary authorities would not be able to hold market prices down to the official level. The ill-fated gold pool dissipated official reserves in an unsuccessful effort to do so until abandoned in March 1968, when the two-tier system was started.

A large price increase would expand monetary gold supplies largely by the mark-up of stocks, but also by: (a) reducing the quantity taken by private demand; and (b) stimulating production of marginal mines; and spurring exploration for new mines. The once-over price increase would be expected to discourage speculative diversion of supply, though the effect on long-term hoarding in expectation of inflation seems more uncertain.

The Case Against Gold

The case against gold is that a large price increase would be costly, inefficient, inflationary, unfair to less developed countries, and give aid and comfort to the gold lobby. We now consider each of these objections.

Credit money is cheaper than gold and supply is more amenable to rational control by experts. Because of its greater efficiency, credit money has displaced gold in national monetary systems as governments grew more sophisticated. It can be argued that demonetization of gold, internationally, is a logical extension of what has already taken place at the national level. Recall, however, that legislation was necessary to suppress the private holding of gold and remove it from circulation. Internationally, no comparable power exists and proposals to demonetize gold stocks are not realistic, although they attract the attention of experts.

While the case against gold on grounds of economic efficiency has merit, it is deceptively simple without a searching examination of the political dimension: deceptive, because it ignores the *uncertainty* inherent in the nature of agreements among sovereign states. Today nations agree, tomorrow the same states disagree. A world of sovereign states is a universe of anarchy moderated by transient agreements, shifting coalitions, and national rivalries. Nations opt out of solemn agreements and denounce treaties. While there may be an element of myth in the color of gold, its acceptability is beyond question. A condition for the monetization of new gold, however, is that the official price must be raised above the long-term market price so that its monetary value determines its market value unless the market price is allowed to float. Nonetheless, gold's fall-back value as a commodity is a basic attraction which gold substitutes lack.

By contrast, uncertainty as to the future supply and acceptability of SDRs in troubled times make them second- or third-best. (Parenthetically, it seems to me that the dollar is more serviceable than Special Drawing Rights, precisely because it is "convertible" into a vast range of commodities, services, and investments.)

The economic efficiency argument against gold is overstated when pure credit and commodity standards are compared, because there is no question of returning to a pure gold standard or moving to a pure credit standard. The more acceptable system allows the widest possible latitude between holding barren gold and interest-bearing assets. The magnitude of the cost of monetizing incremental gold supplies can hardly be a serious obstacle, when divided among many nations which have the option of holding interest-bearing assets.

Assuming that the United States undertakes to buy all gold offered at the official price, a more serious question is that of finding the "right" price, i.e., a price which remains above its free-market, commodity value without becoming inflationary. Since we do not rely on gold alone for reserves, interest-bearing assets provide an elastic substitute. Moreover, if the market price were not supported by the United States or the IMF, the amount of monetized gold would just satisfy the demand for gold reserves and "excess" supplies would be absorbed by lower market prices. Thus, the economic inefficiency of a pure commodity standard with respect to both real costs and management of supply is quite substantially reduced by credit substitutes, without sacrificing the gold option.

On the positive side, the anonymity of gold puts control solely in the hands of its holder. A state choosing gold over interest-bearing reserve assets is saying, in effect, that the real cost is a hedge against the risk of holding substitutes, and provides independence in a crisis. In the *political* economy of a world of sovereign nations, it is by no means self-evident that a gold component of international reserves is suboptimal. In short, alternatives to expansion of gold reserves involve an unnecessary sacrifice of national prerogatives and deny nations an independent hedge against the risk that SDRs may not always be generally acceptable.

One is struck by the diversity among nations with respect to the tradeoff between gold and other reserve assets. A large number of central banks, mainly capital importing countries have held a low gold component because they regard their exchange rate as generally tied to that of the reserve currency. Hence, they gave little weight to the risk of balance-sheet losses on exchange rate adjustment. These nations regard some of their reserves as "overborrowing" and the interest rate on their reserves as partial compensation for the interest they pay. At the extreme, for many years, Sweden held virtually all of its reserves in dollars as a deliberate calculation of compound interest returns against missing the windfall gain from a possible increase of gold prices. Other central banks are given little chance to make money and the interest they earn on reserves affords a degree of independence from government.

On the opposite side, a small number of European banks held virtually all of their reserves in gold to avoid the risk of balance-sheet losses which some suffered when sterling was depreciated in 1931. It was mainly to avoid the risk of appreciation of their own currency against gold which motivated these countries. Safety in this respect was given greater weight than the "loss" of interest.

"A few central banks have always considered it an obligation to take at least part of any increase in reserves in gold so that the 'discipline of gold' should be a reality for the United States. Others did the same thing to maintain the principle of convertibility, even after it was no longer feasible to convert all their dollars."[11]

Finally, consider the "war chest" motive. In troubled times foreign-exchange balances may be blocked. "The war-chest motive is sometimes disparaged by writers who look upon gold as anachronistic, but it is evident that every major country gives it some weight in its reserve policy."[12]

As regards the dollar's future as a reserve currency, let the United States take a strictly neutral position. It was not American policy, but the general utility of the dollar that made it the leading reserve currency in the first place. Our error was to defend the dollar against gold losses by borrowing with special guarantees.[13] Considering the vast foreign investment of the United States in addition to our domestic wealth, if other countries did not find United States credit worthy without a gold guarantee, this should have been taken as a warning signal of the need for raising the price of gold owing to a systemic liquidity shortage. It seems unnecessary, if not impossible to prevent the whole world from acquiring liquid dollar assets. But some may prefer not to, and we should have no regrets at being freed of the cost of interest charges in our foreign payments.

Inflation

Part of the standard case against raising the price of gold is that it would be inflationary which seems to assume that the increase in liquidity would of necessity be excessive. Marking up the value of gold stocks should not be confused with money created by surplus countries for the purpose of buying newly-mined gold. If excessive, the latter may be inflationary. But why would leading gold-holding countries—United States, Germany, France, Switzerland, or the Netherlands—go on a spending spree just because of bookkeeping profits? The nations holding some nine-tenths of the world's gold reserves have generally given as much priority to fiscal discipline as was politically feasible and, when unable to resolve conflicting objectives without inflation, they have not been noticeably deterred by want of windfall profits. One may doubt that the marking up of stocks would cause widespread fiscal irresponsibility. There may be exceptions, but that is their problem and not an international one.

Less developed countries hold no more than a small fraction of official gold stocks and the record of many on inflation is as good as that of the developed countries. The irresponsible spenders among them do not have enough gold to inflate the world economy. A glance at the statistical magnitudes leaves this point without much weight.

The distinction between stock and increment is important here, for it is by making the supply of new gold adequate to meet official demands that the price effect will relax balance-of-payments rivalry and avoid controls. Herein lies a problem: external surpluses are inflationary and a nation with large and persistent surpluses would have to adjust or take the consequences. Admittedly the question of where to fix the price is a serious one. The official price should remain fixed for, say 15-20 years, yet not be so far above a free-market price as to create excessive liquidity. The United States needs an enlarged gold stock to restore convertibility. Thereafter, the increment of monetary gold needed for liquidity depends on the world capacity to absorb external surpluses without serious inflation.

A Reverse Two-Tier Plan?

As an alternative to maintaining the market price at the official level, a reverse two-tier plan may be worth consideration. If the market price were allowed to find its own level below the official price, it would be necessary to prevent nations from buying gold merely for resale to the United States. This may be avoidable if, as at present, only the IMF were allowed to monetize new gold. Surplus nations could freely add to their gold reserves, but only by buying from the United States or the IMF at the official price. Accumulated dollar reserves need not be made immediately convertible except at the discretion of the United States. In effect, the plan would serve as a variable tax on gold production at the official price—the tax declining slowly over the long run as the market price of gold rose toward the official price.

The United States would have the obligation to buy enough gold, from time to time, through the IMF to insure current-account convertibility without a doubt. However, the United States would not necessarily be obliged to maintain massive gold stocks at all times, as long as market conditions permitted adequate liquidity—"adequate" meaning sufficient newly-mined gold to satisfy current demand for gold reserves. In any event, full convertibility of the dollar does not have to be reestablished at one stroke, but may be limited to current-account convertibility, initially, with conversion of the "overhang" at the discretion of the United States.

Just as at present, no nation would buy or sell monetary gold in the market. The feasibility of a reverse two-tier plan depends on whether policing by the IMF would be a serious problem. The present temptation is to sell official gold for its higher market value; under the reverse plan, the temptation would be to buy market gold for circulation at its higher value as a reserve asset. It is not evident why policing the one should be more troublesome than the other.

Of course, the case for gold does not depend on two-tier pricing. If feasible, however, the reverse of the present system has several advantages. First, it would avoid the inflationary implications of excess liquidity, if the gold price should be set too high. It allows a margin for error. Second, the cost of monetizing gold would be minimized and the extra foreign exchange earned by gold-producing countries would be less. Third, the industrial use of gold would be less restricted. Fourth, the long-term trend of market prices would be toward the official price, instead of away from it as at present. The rising trend of industrial demand for gold would insure that the market price would, eventually, reach the official price. Fifth, dishoarding of private gold stocks would probably be moderated.

Opinions differ as to the effect of a higher price on gold hoarders. Some writers expect hoarders to sell out. But considering the fact that the great bulk of private hoards is held (until recently at least) as a hedge against inflation and that dishoarding has been quite modest in countries that devalued their currency, it is not evident that dishoarding would be large enough to cause worldwide inflation. In any event, governments have the power to tax gold sales if dishoarding should become a problem. Uncertainty in this respect may be an additional reason for not guaranteeing the market price.

In sum, it is the increment of gold and not the stock which may be inflationary, but there is no convincing reason why surplus nations should accumulate official reserves to the extent of causing worldwide inflation. To guarantee the market price may not be necessary. The extra import demand of South Africa and the U.S.S.R. would not be great enough in relation to world supplies to create serious inflation. The charge that raising the gold price would create worldwide inflation involves the unjustified assumption that a higher price would necessarily create excessive international liquidity.

Less Developed Countries

Increasing the gold price, it is said, would be unfair to less developed countries which hold relatively less gold reserves. A share of the windfall gain on gold stocks could be redistributed to the poorer countries. However, the countries holding most of their reserves in gold may argue that the countries holding relatively more dollars have already been compensated by the interest they earned. The question of aid for development is really independent of international monetary reform and the main point is that the less developed world would benefit from a system that avoided restrictions on trade and investment for balance-of-payments reasons.

Preoccupation with profits on stocks of gold diverts attention from the fact that less developed countries would benefit from the favorable effects of incremental additions to gold reserves on capital markets. Competitive raising of interest rates to protect the foreign balance has resulted in tight money markets in the lending countries. Both reserve centers imposed direct controls on foreign borrowing. Although less developed countries are excluded from U.S. mandatory restrictions on borrowing, this measure forced international companies to borrow abroad, which raised the cost of borrowing in the Eurodollar and European markets. As a result, the borrowing and lending rates of the World Bank and International Development Association were raised substantially. The Third World has also suffered from the reduction and tying of development aid for balance-of-payment reasons. An increase in the price of gold would benefit less developed countries by increasing the availability of capital and reducing the cost of borrowing. They would also gain if restrictions on trade could be removed as a result of more adequate international liquidity. Dollar liquidity is not equivalent to gold liquidity because U.S. deficits have led to controls which are detrimental to the development of poor countries. In short, the gold shortage has resulted in controls and tight money and an increase in the gold price would, without doubt, benefit less developed countries.

The Gold Lobby

Why reward the speculators, South Africa and the U.S.S.R. by raising the price of gold? This is the wrong question. The right question is: "Are adequate gold reserves worth the cost, given the fact that the alternative means a sacrifice of sovereignty?" The anti-gold lobby seems to give no weight to the consideration that each nation which buys gold for reserves must believe that it is worth the cost. United States, regularly, bought precious metals from the U.S.S.R., even when most trade was banned. The Soviets did not block sales because we used their rare metals to make war planes. Roy Harrod found it "very obscure why an operation, which gives U.S.S.R. a certain present but simultaneously gives the free world a much larger one, is said to benefit the U.S.S.R."

I would not have the United States press the purchase of gold on anyone, but I would be more comfortable if we stopped foreclosing the option for everyone. The view suggested here would not compel anyone to buy South African gold, but would allow each nation to decide for itself when its gold ratio is "adequate" and whether adequacy is worth the cost. However, a necessary condition for realization of the gold option is that the official price must be above the long-term market price, and this should be decided by a consensus of leading nations.

It is not self-evident whether the present price of monetary gold strengthens the forces of oppression within gold-producing countries or contributes to liberalization.[14] As regards South Africa, Harrod argued that the benefits would go, first, to the mining companies "which on the whole have a very enlightened leadership" and, second, to the Bantu mine workers who "save most of their earnings, and when they return home with their money, they take a more commercial view of agriculture . . . Nothing could do so much to improve the racial relations in South Africa as rendering the underprivileged more economically viable and therefore, better able to stand up for themselves."[15]

It is evident that Europe is not about to abandon gold but, to the contrary, many nations would like higher gold ratios in their reserves. Given the fact that the United States refused to pave the way for adequate gold liquidity by raising the price, active members of the gold pool would seem to have had little choice in the March 1968 crisis. Either they supported the United States in creation of a two-tier system or the continued diversion of U.S. gold stocks into private hoards would have forced suspension of convertibility. Note that the purpose of that decision was to preserve official gold stocks and that demonetization of newly-mined gold was a by-product. Had it been known that convertibility was going to be suspended, in any event, would that crisis-dictated decision have been made? (There were only seven nations involved.)

Pressure from others, later on, forced the United States to agree that the Fund buy South African gold under certain conditions. The primacy of gold was also reaffirmed by the absolute gold-value guarantee in the SDRs facility.

The American position on the gold price may have kept some allies, Germany, for example, from open opposition to us. Changing the American posture to one of willing accommodation is likely to affect the attitude of others on the role of gold.

The American Position

The American position doubtless reflects reluctance to let down those who hold large dollar reserves and, conversely, to reward France and others, holding a high ratio of gold, with windfall profits. But this leaves out of account the relevant fact that holders of dollars have been compensated with interest and compound interest is a powerful force. By steadily refusing to guarantee holders of dollars against devaluation, United States, in effect, served notice of the possibility. Moreover, everyone is well aware that Bretton Woods expressly provides for changing the price of gold.

Past statements by American officials on this question cannot be binding on the future and should not preclude the United States from respecting the views of other nations and cooperating with them on the future of gold reserves. Dollar holders will not actually lose anything; they miss a windfall gain which is offset by compound interest and, if the interest already earned is not as much as the windfall, it will be if they continue to hold dollar reserves. This, plus the fact that United States would act only in response to a consensus, should leave us less vulnerable to cricitism. On the other hand, to prevent, unilaterally, the possible monetization of newly-mined gold may seem a more questionable use of power. Moreover, many countries without large gold stocks would benefit from the dismantling of controls. To rule out a major change in the price of gold is to rule out a system that provides liquidity and adjustment, without sacrifice of national autonomy.

The fact that congressional action is needed to change the gold price has been advanced as one reason for the reluctance of American officials to open the issue, since this would encourage speculation. But since the gold rush of 1972-73 has already produced high market prices, this no longer seems important. Moreover, the Congress was cooperative with the Smithsonian Agreement. Nonetheless, it would facilitate a negotiated settlement if the Congress delegated this power to the Executive Branch.

The issue between adequate gold liquidity and the alternative of international credit or fiat money involves a determination of the proper and acceptable line between national autonomy and world institutions, which poses two questions. What is the optimal form of an international community and what is attainable? International agreement on an alternative to gold will be extremely difficult to reach, may take a very long time, and is likely to involve compromise which is suboptimal. Meanwhile, the hegemony of the dollar is more strongly entrenched than before August 15, 1971. Raising the price in order to monetize newly-mined gold is a simple means of restoring Bretton Woods—a satisfactory system that is known to work when given a chance, but which was made unworkable by the shortage of gold.

Notes

1. "One of the most endearing and enlivening—though occasionally exasperating characteristics of Roy Harrod's distinguished public career as a running commentator on current issues of economic policy has been his Oxonian capacity cheerfully to espouse causes which his professional colleagues have been virtually unanimous in regarding as hopelessly lost, if downright hopeless."

Harry Johnson in ESSAYS IN HONOUR OF SIR ROY HARROD, INDUCTION, GROWTH AND TRADE, eds., W.A. Eltis, M.F.G. Scott, and J.N. Wilfe, p. 266.

Harrod's chapter on gold in REFORMING WORLD MONEY is his most extensive contribution, presenting many points in the same form as his earlier publications.

2. Milton Gilbert, THE GOLD-DOLLAR SYSTEM: CONDITIONS OF EQUILIBRIUM AND THE PRICE OF GOLD Princeton Essay in International Finance, No. 70. I have drawn extensively on Gilbert.

3. In his early work (1945), George Halm wrote of the Keynes plan:

Gold is not essential, has no important function to fulfill and only distorts the admirably simple structure of the Keynesian scheme. . . .

Thus the Keynes plan allows gold to expand the quantity of international money but not to contract it . . . .no purpose whatever is served. . . .

Why, then, is gold included . . . ? Sec. VI-26 gives the following reasons:

1. 'Gold still possesses great psychological value which is not diminished by current events; the desire to possess a gold reserve against unforeseen contingencies is likely to remain.
2. 'Gold also has the merit of providing in point of form (whatever the underlying realities may be) an uncontroversial standard of value for international purposes, for which it would not yet be easy to find a serviceable substitute.
3. 'Moreover, by supplying an automatic means for settling some part of the favorable balances of creditor countries, the current gold production of the world and the remnant of gold reserves held outside the United States may still have a useful part to play.'

Halm found the first point "meaningless in the context of the Keynes Plan" unless he was concerned that some important countries might not join or "would play an independent gold standard game outside the Union." After disparaging Keynes' other points, Halm concludes, "This mortifying attempt to rescue the role of gold in a plan which is supremely independent of gold is the weakest part of the Keynesian scheme." INTERNATIONAL MONETARY COOPERATION, pp. 147-48.

The following is a personal letter from Keynes to Halm dated June 22, 1945.

I feel moved to write a line to say how much I have appreciated your "International Monetary Cooperation." It seems to me decidedly the clearest and most objective analysis available of the evolution and provisions of the Bretton Woods plans.

There are only a few points where I should have myself liked to see a slightly different development. I mention three of them below:

1. In discussing the question of why it is advisable to retain a provision for gold, the main point is, of course, that no scheme which did not make such a provision would have the smallest chance of acceptance, either in America, which has gold reserves, or in Western Europe, which has gold reserves, or in the Argentine, which has gold reserves, or in Russia, which has gold production. In short, there is no option.
2. I feel there might have been rather more detail about those difficult gold-recapture provisions, which are largely Bernstein's work. Intellectually they are quite interesting, but extremely difficult to understand at a first reading or by someone who does not appreciate beforehand what they are driving at. A popular exposition of what it all boils down to would, I think, have helped general understanding.
3. As in most discussions, the Bank for Reconstruction gets off with very brief comments. The poor thing has suffered through turning out to be so dreadfully non-controversial. This is leading, one fears, to a considerable under-estimate of its importance. For immediate purposes it is more essential to get the Bank for Reconstruction going quickly than the Fund.

4. For the sake of brevity, SDRs are included under the term "credit." The extent to which they become "debts" is an unresolved question that is discussed later.

5. Gilbert, op. cit., p. 14.

6. Britain also borrowed extensively outside the system.

7. Unlike gold, the future supply of SDRs is wholly dependent on continued international accord. As presently constituted, the facility has no provision for adjustment.

8. Some writers argue that increasing the price of gold would be seriously inflationary and "would in no way help the complex and delicate process of adjustment." It is "unduly optimistic, if not utterly naive" to suppose that a rise in United States gold stocks would benefit external payments. This confuses the mark-up on stocks with the gold increment. It is the latter, not the former, which facilitates adjustment. (Miroslav A. Kriz, GOLD: BARBAROUS RELIC OR USEFUL INSTRUMENT?, Princeton Essay in International Finance, No. 60. p. 27.)

9. Machlup deals with this issue in the final chapter of REMAKING THE INTERNATIONAL MONETARY SYSTEM.

10. When the IMF recently offered a choice of gold or SDRs in exchange for national currencies, eleven countries took gold and three chose SDRs. IMF's delayed reporting prevents official identification. However, IMF purchases from Canada, Italy, and Finland coincide with the SDRs paid out. Purchases, presumably for gold, include Germany, Japan, Holland, Belgium, Austria, Australia, Norway, Mexico, Venezuela, Brazil, and Kuwait.

11. Gilbert, op. cit. pp. 6-7.

12. Ibid, p. 7.

13. Robert Triffin distinguishes "traditional" i.e., voluntarily-held, foreign-exchange reserves from negotiated reserves i.e., Roosa bonds, swaps, guaranteed loans, IMF claims and sterling acquired to rescue the pound. He estimates that for the North Atlantic Area, January 1964-June 1968, negotiated reserves more than tripled, rising by $8.8 billion, while traditional reserves declined by $3.5 billion. (A Paper for the SECOND PACIFIC TRADE AND DEVELOPMENT CONFERENCE, Honolulu, January 1969.)

14. The attempt to punish South Africa by demonetizing gold poses a possible threat that some may try to block acceptance of SDRs from countries whose social or political policy they oppose.

15. On reading this, I confess to having a sense that Harrod was pressing his case too hard. But Harry Johnson points out that unless the gains were counteracted by government policy, "the remarks quoted penetrate to the heart of a proper economic analysis, which would indicate that side-payments may be well worth while if they increase one's own benefit from the game, and that if one believes in economic discrimination as an implement of policy it is important to determine who bears the burden of discrimination." (Harry Johnson, ESSAYS IN HONOUR OF SIR ROY HARROD, p. 283.)

6

Convertibility for the Dollar and International Monetary Reform

C. Fred Bergsten

What is "Convertibility?"

The U.S. dollar remains convertible into all other foreign currencies. Private money markets throughout the world remain willing to sell other currencies for dollars. Virtually all central banks continue to buy dollars in exchange for their own currencies in order to keep their parities from appreciating at all or, in the case of those countries whose exchange rates are floating, from appreciating too rapidly. The dollar thus continues to play a major role in private international finance and as a reserve asset in the portfolios of foreign central banks. It is "inconvertible" in only one very special sense: it cannot be exchanged by foreign monetary authorities into the reserve assets of the United States (which consist primarily of gold and Special Drawing Rights).

The United States is not the only country which does not now stand ready to convert its own currency into its national reserves, as called for by the Articles of Agreement of the International Monetary Fund. The same is true for any country whose exchange rate is floating, such as the U.K. and Canada for some time—and the currencies of both, like the dollar, are convertible into other national currencies in the exchange markets. Indeed, almost any currency will almost always be "convertible" in the private markets (including black markets) at *some* (usually a fluctuating) price. The dollar would itself be a freely fluctuating currency now if it were U.S. policy which determined the outcome, since the U.S. is intervening very little (if at all) in the exchange markets.

Prior to the widespread adoption of floating rates in March 1973, however, the case of the dollar was unique in that it alone combined inconvertibility into national reserves *and a fixed exchange rate.* If a majority of the other major countries return to pegging their currencies to some par value (or "central rate") declared to the International Monetary Fund, or even if they adhere to some *de facto* peg through "duty floating," this situation would recur. (If freely floating rates become permanent for most countries, convertibility of currencies into national reserves will become a dead issue; this paper assumes that it will not.) We shall henceforth refer to this unusual phenomenon as "market convertibility."[1]

Such a situation could not now arise for any currency other than the dollar. All other countries actively use their reserves when they seek to maintain fixed exchange rates,[2] selling their reserves (buying their own currencies) to keep their rates from depreciating and adding to their reserves (selling their own currencies) to keep their rates from appreciating. If they stopped doing so, their exchange rates would float outside the agreed margins around their fixed parities.

Most of this intervention, throughout the postwar period and still today, has been affected through their buying and selling dollars. There was thus no need for the United States to intervene actively in the exchange markets, with U.S. reserves, to maintain a relatively fixed exchange rate for the dollar. Other countries did so for the United States in the course of maintaining their own exchange rates against the dollar. Thus a relatively fixed exchange rate for the dollar is compatible with U.S. abstention from the foreign-exchange market because of the intervention currency role of the dollar.

One result of this system was that virtually all foreign countries held sizable working balances in dollars,[3] while the United States held virtually no working balances in foreign currencies.

A second result was that the system functioned smoothly. There can be only $N-1$ exchange rates in a world of N currencies. If all N countries sought to achieve an independent exchange rate, the system would be overdetermined and could not work. United States abstention from the exchange markets, however, meant that only $N-1$ countries were seeking to achieve the $N-1$ exchange rates. There were no important problems of coordination, and the market itself readily produced a consistent set of exchange rates.

A third result was that other countries controlled the exchange rate of the dollar. Other countries intervened actively in the exchange markets, while the United States remained passive. The United States could change the official price of gold, but not the prices at which other countries bought and sold dollars— which set the exchange rate between the dollar and their currencies, and was a major determinant of international trade and capital flows. The Nixon Administration feared that other important countries would use this leverage to abort any U.S. effort to achieve a sizable devaluation of the dollar, so decided in August 1971 and again in February 1973 to negotiate exchange-rate realignments rather than simply announce unilateral changes of parity like other countries always have.

So the United States has traditionally abstained from using its reserves in the exchange markets. From 1934 until August 15, 1971, however, the United States declared itself ready to convert any dollars held by foreign monetary authorities into U.S. gold.[4] The postwar monetary system negotiated at Bretton Woods authorized this U.S. policy as a means by which a country could fulfill its "convertibility" obligation, as an alternative to active exchange-market intervention, and thus provided the legal foundation for the key currency role of the dollar just described.[5] One can therefore characterize U.S. postwar policy (until August 1971) as one of "passive convertibility," as contrasted with the "active convertibility" of all other countries.

There áre thus three relevant types of convertibility:

1. *active convertibility* of national currencies into the reserves of their countries of issue, sanctioned by the Bretton Woods system and maintained by most countries today.
2. *passive convertibility* of national currencies into the reserves of their countries of issue, sanctioned by the Bretton Woods system and maintained by the United States until August 15, 1971.
3. *"market convertibility,"* as defined above, in which a currency is convertible into other national currencies at a fixed rate (within the prescribed margins) in the exchange markets but neither actively nor passively into the reserves of the country which issues it. This was the situation of the United States prior to March 1973.[6]

Why Convertibility? The Background

It is universally agreed that currencies must be convertible *into each other* to facilitate an optimum flow of trade and other international transactions. Currency inconvertibility requires the use of comprehensive foreign exchange controls, was a major impediment to international flows in the early postwar period, and remains a serious barrier to trade with the Communist countries and numerous less developed countries.

However, we have already noted that almost any currency can almost always be converted into almost any other currency at *some* price. The objective of convertibility is thus more accurately stated as minimizing the instability of the price at which conversion is assured.[7]

Until recently, there was a widespread consensus that "convertibility" thus required "fixed exchange rates"—as called for by the Articles of Agreement of the IMF. Many have tended to equate the interconvertibility of currencies with convertibility of each into national reserves, because the latter technique was used to preserve the fixed exchange rates at which the former took place.

Now there is a growing view, in both official and private circles, that exchange rates cannot remain truly fixed without spawning a proliferation of controls over international transactions, and that they will be more stable if permitted—even encouraged—to fluctuate more readily. The history of the postwar monetary system, in which the "fixed-rate" regime amounted in practice to "jumping parities fixed *until further notice*," strongly supports this view. For the purposes of this paper, the key question is: which of the three types of convertibility, for both the United States and other countries, will provide maximum support for a stable and effective international monetary system? (We again assume away the fourth possibility of *no* convertibility for any currency into national monetary reserves, i.e., freely floating exchange rates.)

At least until the middle 1960s, the postwar monetary system rested fairly successfully on the dollar. Virtually all countries maintained their exchange rates by intervening in the dollar market for their currencies. Most countries held a growing share of their reserves in dollars. The dollar provided most of the growth in both private and public international liquidity. Much more importantly, other countries were able to achieve the payments surpluses they desired because the United States was willing to run payments deficits. Foreign balance-of-payments targets, as well as exchange rates, were thus reconciled largely by the abstention from the game of the Nth country—the United States.

In such a system, it is fair to ask why the dollar needed to be convertible into U.S. assets at all. There were, however, solid economic, political, and psychological reasons.

The objective of the system was to preserve fixed exchange rates. This in turn required countries to pursue policies which enabled them to preserve their parities. The ability of other countries to convert their dollars into U.S. reserves provided an avenue—*the only avenue*—for them to signal that, in their view, U.S. policy was not conducive to doing so.

Such signals had no effect on U.S. policy at least through 1957, while U.S. reserves remained far higher than any foreseeable need to use them. Once U.S. reserves began to decline sharply, however, it had to regard reserve losses as significantly undermining its capacity to continue to play by the rules of the Bretton Woods system.

Thus the major U.S. balance-of-payments programs of the 1960s, each composed essentially of new restrictions over U.S. international transactions, followed a period of significant gold losses: in early 1961 after the short-lived breakout of the London gold price, in early 1965 after France launched its "gold war" against the dollar, in early 1968 after the massive run on the private gold market (which at that time led directly to U.S. gold losses through the operations of the gold pool). It has also been argued by close observers that the gold losses of the early 1960s were decisive in keeping U.S. interest rates higher than was desirable on purely domestic grounds, that the losses of 1967-68 were decisive in inducing key congressmen (such as Wilbur Mills) to finally support the income tax surcharge in 1968, and that the threat of massive gold losses played a major role in inducing President Nixon to finally adopt an incomes policy in August 1971. So the system of dollar convertibility has clearly had an important impact on U.S. domestic and foreign economic policy—providing pressure for "discipline" over U.S. internal policy in some cases, inducing the adoption of controls over international transactions in others.

The gold convertibility of the dollar also played an important role in its acceptability to foreign monetary authorities.[8] Some central banks held dollars solely because they bore interest, were convenient to use, represented a claim on goods anywhere in the world, and were based on the world's strongest economy. But a number of conservative central banks valued the U.S. convertibility pledge, in addition, if only because they could use it to refute internal charges that they were "mindlessly financing the United States." Their views were particularly important in a fixed-rate system, because they were often the major surplus countries from whom the United States needed financing for its deficits. Gold convertibility was even important to the role of the dollar in private international finance, because the private sector had confidence that their own central banks would always be willing to buy dollars at a fixed rate. Thus it significantly helped the United States finance its balance-of-payments deficits by contributing to its ability to build up dollar liabilities to foreigners—one of the benefits of convertibility to the United States which offset the pressures on it to take actions to maintain its fixed gold parity.

Finally, the convertibility obligation provided an appearance of symmetry between the United States and other countries in a world which was highly asymmetrical. After the other major currencies became convertible in the late 1950s and early 1960s, inconvertibility for the dollar could have meant only one of two things. It would probably have meant a fixed-rate system in which the United States had the ability to finance any level of deficits through the dollar—since there was no conceivable alternative monetary base to the dollar—with no adjustment responsibilities. Such a situation would have been politically intolerable for other countries, particularly since there was very little they could have done about it—except take very destructive steps, such as the adoption of more controls and a retreat to inconvertibility for their own currencies. Alternatively, it could have meant abandonment of fixed exchange rates—which, at that time, would have been completely unacceptable to all other countries. The broad U.S. foreign policy goal of maintaining a world economic structure which promoted harmony among the non-Communist nations thus played a major role in the U.S. decision to maintain a convertible dollar, just as it had in the much earlier U.S. push to create the IMF system itself.

So dollar convertibility played a major role in the postwar monetary system. As the 1960s progressed, however, the two declined together. Dollar convertibility became increasingly nominal, as U.S. liquid liabilities grew far beyond the level of U.S. reserves into which they could in principle be converted. The system was racked by repeated crises, proliferating controls, and growing exchange rate disequilibria. The need for fundamental reform became increasingly clear.

Why Convertibility? The Future

The role of dollar convertibility in any new monetary system depends on the nature of that system.[9] It is not an objective in itself, as many Europeans (and even some Americans) implied when they suggested immediately after the Smithsonian that "the restoration of convertibility" should be accorded top priority, with other issues to be decided subsequently. Such a view in reality represented a desire to return to the system which had just been discredited, on the rather naive (or mischievous) view that the only problem had been the misalignment of exchange rates which was hoped to have been corrected at the Smithsonian—but which lasted only fourteen months.

There are three reasons why Bretton Woods-style convertibility for the dollar could not work now. First, the "dollar overhang" of $60-80 billion—the legacy of the past reserve currency role of the dollar—continues to swamp U.S. reserves of about $12 billion. Large amounts of these dollars could flow back into private hands if the current U.S. balance-of-payments position improves,[10] and large amounts are in countries perfectly willing to hold them—especially if their doing so will *keep* the United States from trying to eliminate its deficits! But enough countries are unhappy with their dollars that the United States might immediately face requests for major conversions and hence have to revert quickly to inconvertibility. The risk that this could occur would undermine from the start the stability of any system which included both the overhang and a resumption of dollar convertibility. Collapse of the contemporary sterling overhang in six weeks (after the United States had tried to get Britain to negotiate a funding operation for it) ruined Britain's attempt to restore convertibility in 1947, and we must not repeat that error now.

In addition, the existence of the overhang would mean that the United States might not acquire reserve assets when it runs payments surpluses in the future, because other countries could simply pay for their corresponding deficits by running down their dollar balances. The United States could not then agree to finance its payments deficits with reserve assets, because it could be losing reserves over time even if its annual surpluses and deficits balanced out. The United States could run out of reserves altogether even though it was, over time, in payments balance!

The private overhang could add to the magnitude of these problems. Foreign monetary authorities may be unwilling to hold dollars which they receive from the private sector, especially if they doubt that the private sector will repurchase the dollars in the near future. So definitive arrangements for both the official and private overhangs are needed to permit a restoration of dollar convertibility.[11]

Second, U.S. reserves of $12 billion are now quite small even in terms of *current* deficits which the United States might run. They are smaller in relation to annual imports, for example, than those of any other major country except the United Kingdom and Sweden.

In 1971 and 1972, the U.S. basic deficit, which includes trade in goods and services and long-term capital movements and is the best existing measure of our underlying position, exceeded $9 billion. The official settlements deficit, which adds short-term capital flows as well, was almost $30 billion in 1971 and over $10 billion in 1972. The size of these numbers should not be regarded as abnormal for any period of time as short as a year, since they represent differences between gross flows totaling hundreds of billions of dollars which can change radically in response to relatively small changes in the national economies (or exchange rates between economies) which underlie them.

Third, and closely related, the improvements made recently in the adjustment process do not yet assure that national payments imbalances will be attacked more effectively in the future. Better adjustment, by other countries and by the United States, would permit the United States to restore convertibility on a smaller reserve base. At present, however, the outlook encompasses the possibility of continued frequent, sizable, and persistent imbalances.

In my view, the United States could thus prudently agree to restore convertibility of dollars acquired by other countries as a result of U.S. basic deficits only if four conditions were met: elimination of the dollar overhang, a sizable increase in U.S. reserves, new means for handling the huge flows of liquid capital which will continue to permeate the system,[12] and a dramatic improvement in the adjustment process.[13] But should it do so even under these conditions?

The national interest of the United States calls for two basic changes in the monetary system: an improvement in the adjustment process, and a new basis for world liquidity. The adjustment process must be sharply improved, so that the United States can avoid disequilibrium exchange rates—which lead to a deterioration in its trade balance, costing jobs at home and undermining domestic political support for the preservation of a liberal trade policy.[14] This improvement must come primarily through adequate flexibility of exchange rates. Domestic deflation (beyond that needed for purely internal reasons) would simply be too costly to the U.S. economy, because the foreign sector represents such a small share thereof. Direct controls over trade flows (import surcharges and/or export subsidies) are ineffective; they are absorbed by private traders if applied for temporary periods, and are certain to trigger retaliation and emulation by others if intended to be permanent. Capital controls are ineffective unless made so comprehensive that they stifle desirable economic activity. Surplus countries could of course reduce their import barriers and controls over capital exports, but it is unrealistic to expect much adjustment from such measures.

The United States has a particular interest in being able to initiate adjustment since one can never count on other countries to take the necessary steps. Since exchange rate changes are the only economically effective means of external adjustment that is politically acceptable in the United States, their embodiment in the monetary system is very much in the U.S. national interest. Adequate steps by others, and unimpeded U.S. initiatives, can be assured only by international agreement on a set of guidelines which will indicate when adjustment should take place—and when it must be allowed to take place— backed up by international sanctions against countries which fail to comply.

Such guidelines could be implemented either through discrete parity changes within a parity ("fixed rate") regime or through permission/denial for market intervention by monetary authorities within a no-parity ("dirty float") regime.

One barrier to exchange rate flexibility, and especially to initiatives by the United States to change the dollar rate, is the widespread role of the dollar in the international monetary system. The intervention role of the dollar means that other countries set the exchange rate of the dollar, as outlined in the first section of this paper. This was revealed clearly in August 1971 when the United States had to *negotiate* a dollar devaluation—and when France kept its rate (for commercial purposes) unchanged for four months despite U.S. pleas, the suspension of convertibility, and the import surcharge. Countries holding dollars in their reserves are also reluctant to revalue their dollar parities because of the reduction in the value of their assets which will result, and the United States may—as in the past—not wish to cut the value of others' holdings by its own actions. This problem would be particularly acute if exchange rates were to fluctuate more freely and more frequently, since the reserves of all dollar holders would then become much more unstable than they were in the "fixed-rate" regime of the past. More generally, the international roles of the dollar have in the past tended to promote U.S. immobilism on exchange rate issues, because of the standoff between those who wanted adjustment via the rate and those who opposed rate changes because they might undermine the capacity of the dollar to provide continued financing for U.S. deficits.

So the second major change in the system, which is necessary to achieve the needed improvement in the adjustment process, is a sharp reduction in the reserve currency role of the dollar. Fortunately, it can readily be replaced by Special Drawing Rights as the central element in official reserves. Annual creation of SDRs can provide the needed growth in official reserves, just as a special issue of SDRs can be used to consolidate the dollar overhang. Substitution of SDRs for dollars would have a number of desirable effects on both the liquidity mechanism and confidence in the system as a whole, in addition to facilitating the needed improvement in the adjustment process.

These two basic changes in the system will require fundamental concessions from other countries. They will have to agree to subject their exchange rates to international rules, and to sanctions available to the international community to back them up, as already officially proposed by the United States—though some (Japan, Germany) know it will mean broader pressure on them to let their rates appreciate periodically. They will have to agree to place Special Drawing Rights at the center of the monetary system—which will require some (especially France) to give up their hopes for restoring gold. They will have to agree to create enough SDRs annually to really meet world liquidity needs—though some (Germany, Switzerland, the Low Countries) may be more conservatively inclined. They will have to agree to a consolidation of the dollar overhang on terms which are generous to the United States. They will have to agree to a marked expansion of the swap network to recycle liquid capital movements.

More fundamentally, they will have to get used to the new notion that the United States, too, has balance-of-payments and trade-balance goals which will make it much harder for them to realize their own goals. They will have to let the United States adjust, rather than continuing the comfortable (if sometimes irritating) route of financing U.S. deficits as in the past. They will have to exercise increased responsibilities for management of the system, since the United States no longer has either the economic strength nor the internal political consensus to maintain an economic umbrella over the system as in the past.

It is inconceivable that the United States could successfully negotiate all these changes in the system without agreeing to resume convertibility of the dollar into U.S. reserve assets. A world which is asked to move toward symmetrical treatment of the United States can hardly be expected to accede without symmetrical adoption of responsibilities by the United States, as called for in its obligations under the Articles of Agreement of the IMF. There is in fact a widespread foreign desire to achieve total symmetry between the dollar and other currencies; U.S. insistence on continued dollar inconvertibility would imply total asymmetry instead. Thus a restoration of dollar convertibility appears to be a sine qua non for international agreement in the monetary area.

The alternative to a reformed system of greater exchange rate flexibility under international rules, based on SDRs with dollar convertibility, is a continuation of the status quo: proliferating controls and unregulated, competitive exchange rate changes (perhaps through dirty floats) based on an increasing variety of competing reserve assets, including an inconvertible dollar.[15] Such a "system" appears to some to be attractive from a U.S. standpoint, because no external pressure can be placed on U.S. policy through conversion of foreign dollar balances.[16] Unfortunately for the United States, however, there are two sides to the coin. In a system with no agreed adjustment rules, other countries can use their dollars to block U.S. efforts to adjust its exchange rate—and they would be particularly likely to do so if the United States insisted on staying inconvertible.

This is particularly true under the regime of dirty floats adopted by most of the major countries in early 1973, since their activities under such regimes undergo no international surveillance at present. Even before then, however, a number of countries had already adopted two-tiered exchange rates, which maximize their competitive position in international trade while making U.S. foreign investment more costly. Under French "leadership," the entire Common Market could make such a system an integral part of its new monetary union unless global monetary reform provides a better alternative. Other countries could adopt direct controls over U.S. investment inflows. They could even refuse to accept more dollars, which would severely undermine the use of the dollar for private transactions (as well as its reserve currency role) by forcing its depreciation in the exchange markets and eliminating the traditional "purchaser of last resort." Even without such steps by others, crises would be frequent because of the inadequacies of the system. Needless to say, such economic conflict would adversely affect political relationships which are vital to U.S. security concerns. No countries would have been economically strong enough or politically independent enough to contemplate such steps a decade ago, but the expanded European Community and Japan can do so now.

An inconvertible dollar world would thus jeopardize major U.S. national interests. It would also jeopardize the national interests of other countries, perhaps to an even greater degree. So the likelihood that such a world represents the real alternative—as implied in Secretary Shultz's speech to the IMF in September 1972—should help galvanize cooperative reform. Indeed, U.S. agreement to restore dollar convertibility is perhaps its major lever in the reform negotiations—which is why the Administration has been right to avoid any steps toward "partial" or "interim" convertibility prior to achieving agreement from other countries on what the United States wants from these negotiations.

What of the costs to the United States under such a restoration of dollar convertibility? The new international guidelines would call on other countries to appreciate their currencies or take other steps to eliminate their surpluses, or permit the dollar to depreciate, when the United States was in payments deficit. Under the proposals of Secretary Shultz, there could apparently be no pressure on the United States to restrain its domestic economy—the guidelines would always permit a U.S. devaluation if the United States was in deficit. My own view is that the United States (and other countries) should devalue only when an external deficit coincides with significant internal unemployment. This would leave open the possibility that foreign dollar conversions would place the United States under pressure to restrain its domestic economy when inflation rather than unemployment was the key domestic problem. In such instances, however, restraint would be desirable for purely internal U.S. reasons anyway—so the dollar conversions would help provide a *needed* dose of domestic "discipline," as they did in 1968 (and perhaps in 1971, depending on one's view of the desirability of the Nixon wage-price restraints). In short, the United States has to risk being forced to adjust by others—though only when it should do so anyway—in order to be assured that it will be able to adjust when it wants to.

Professor William Fellner, in a recent article on a related subject, agrees that a resumption of dollar convertibility would require giving the United States "extra-large" contingency reserves, the need for which would, however, be mitigated by greater exchange rate flexibility. However, he opposes returning to dollar convertibility, suggesting that the United States instead meet foreign concerns by guaranteeing the purchasing power of dollars held by foreign monetary authorities.[17]

Professor Fellner argues that dollar convertibility would not help solve any of the problems facing the monetary system, and fears that it could actually impede the functioning of a reformed system by reviving the notion that the United States could be forced by a "reserve squeeze" to deflate its domestic economy. He regards this as both impossible to achieve and undesirable if it were achieved. Hence dollar convertibility would perpetuate a delusion which would divert attention, and policy action, away from the needed increase in flexibility of exchange rates and undermine the needed improvement in the adjustment process.

It is undoubtedly true that, as Professor Fellner fears, some surplus countries will always try to avoid having to initiate adjustment by pressuring some deficit country to do so. And it is true that dollar convertibility could encourage them to include the United States in such efforts. As noted above, however, such pressure might on some occasions actually help the United States do what it should do anyway. But, more broadly, this possibility strongly reinforces the need for the United States to insist—as a condition of its resumption of convertibility—on firm guidelines which indicate when surplus countries must initiate adjustment, and vigilant implementation of those guidelines (including the use of sanctions against offenders) after they are agreed. A system operating effectively under such rules is in fact the only way to obviate the risk cited by Professor Fellner.[18]

Active of Passive Convertibility?

I have advocated that the United States resume converting dollars into U.S. reserve assets under a reformed international monetary system which satisfied U.S. national interests. A remaining question is whether such convertibility should be carried out in the passive manner of the past, or through active U.S. intervention in the exchange markets a la all other countries.

The distinction between active and passive market intervention should not be confused with the distinction between an active and passive parity policy. I have argued above that the United States should actively change its parity, against some "ultimate" *numeraire* (preferably SDR). But it could do so while remaining entirely passive in the exchange markets. The choice between the two types of intervention policy rests on additional considerations.

A passive U.S. intervention policy was entirely consistent with the dollar-based system of the past, and supported U.S. interests. United States abstention from the markets assured that the N currencies would be linked consistently through $N-1$ exchange rates without any need for active coordination. The United States let other countries set the "exchange rate of the dollar" because it preferred financing to adjustment. The dollar as intervention currency could fluctuate only one-half as much against any other currency as could two other currencies against each other,[19] so was likely to be more stable in the exchange markets (even assuming no parity changes) than any other currency and thus the most attractive currency for foreigners to hold (all other things equal). The total margins were so narrow that the United States gave up very little by accepting this limitation on its own flexibility. The system required the monetary authorities of other countries to explicitly take the onus of actively seeking conversions into U.S. reserve assets if they wanted to get rid of their dollars, which many were reluctant to do for political reasons as well as for fear of being blamed for contributing to systemic instability; all other countries, by contrast, lost reserves through the impersonal play of market intervention. The British could only suspect "the gnomes of Zurich," but the United States could explicitly finger the Bundesbank.

An active U.S. intervention policy might be more consistent, however, with a reformed system which sought effective adjustment (including adjustment initiated by the United States) instead of lots of financing (mainly through the dollar). The United States may no longer be willing to let other countries set the exchange rate of the dollar: within the widened margins which must be part of any new parity-based regime—at least the 4 1/2 percent which prevailed after the Smithsonian Agreement, compared with 1 1/2 percent in practice before then, and preferably much more—the United States would gain a great deal of added adjustment potential, and freedom for its internal monetary policy, if the dollar could flex as much as any other currency. The reduced U.S. zeal for dollar financing of deficits reduces the importance to the United States of forcing other countries to take active initiatives to trigger conversions, and the importance of this procedure would be eliminated completely if the United States agreed to full asset settlement of its deficits as part of the new system. From the U.S. standpoint, the potential for improved adjustment may be worth more than the reduced potential for financing. Indeed, the proposals of Secretary Shultz at the IMF meeting suggest that the present Administration has reached such a conclusion.

An active U.S. intervention policy would call for significant technical changes in the exchange rate mechanism, however. Additional currencies would have to start playing significant intervention currency roles, as the United States began intervening with them. This would in turn require new rules to avoid destabilizing shifts among holdings of them. Active coordination would now be needed, at least among the major countries, to avoid conflicting market intervention.

It is clear that such a system would be less efficient and more cumbersome than the single-currency system of the past. World trade and investment can be financed more cheaply via a single currency. The cost to multinational firms of holding liquid balances can be minimized by holding them in a single currency.[20] Indeed, it is impossible to completely eliminate the "asymmetry" through which the dollar plays a far greater international role than any other currency (even if it were desirable to do so).

However, other currencies will naturally be financing an increasing share of world transactions as the economies on which they are based become more equal to that of the United States. It appears that all parties favor an effort to move toward a multicurrency intervention system—the United States because it would get better adjustment, the others because they would get greater symmetry between their currencies and the dollar. And new modes of coordination among the key countries will have to be part of any new adjustment process anyway, either to oversee market intervention in a world of floating rates or to prompt needed parity shifts in a regime of "stable but adjustable" parities. From the United States standpoint, the best outcome would be a sufficiently firm agreement on new adjustment rules so that a continuation of the intervention currency role would not deflect any needed changes in the exchange rate of the dollar.

Conclusion

A resumption by the United States of convertibility of the dollar into U.S. reserve assets must be seen in the context of the fundamental reform of the international monetary system which is needed. Such convertibility would be redundant in a system of freely fluctuating exchange rates. In any return to a parity-based regime (perhaps implemented by "dirty floats"), the United States can prudently restore convertibility only if basic changes are made to improve the adjustment mechanism, eliminate the problem of the dollar overhang, assure adequate amounts of world reserves through the SDR mechanism, and deal effectively with liquid capital movements. Such changes, which are very much in the national interest of the United States, can be negotiated only if the United States agrees to restore convertibility as part of the package. Thus the United States should agree to do so as part of a negotiated reform package. It should continue to resist agreeing to any interim or partial convertibility in the meantime, which would reduce its bargaining leverage. The choice between the active and passive methods for implementing U.S. convertibility in the new regime depends on whether the other major countries decide that it is worthwhile to give up the economic benefits of relying on a single currency to achieve greater symmetry with the dollar.

Notes

1. The IMF has never reached a legal decision as to whether a country must maintain a fixed exchange rate to qualify as a "convertible currency" under its Article VIII. See J. Keith Horsefield, THE INTERNATIONAL MONETARY FUND 1945-65, Vol. I, p. 480. In practice, a number of countries have of course floated their exchange rates without losing "Article VIII status."

2. Within margins on either side of their parities, which were widened from ±1 percent permitted by the Article of Agreement of the IMF to ±2 1/4 percent in the Smithsonian Agreement of December 1971.

3. Excepting only the members of the sterling area and French franc zone, which followed the same process with sterling and francs instead of dollars. In turn, the U.K. and France defended their parities in the dollar market.

4. With the institution of the two-tiered gold system in March 1968, the United States excluded from that policy any dollars acquired by foreign monetary authorities from selling their gold into the private gold markets.

5. The IMF Articles require that a member country maintain convertibility of its currency only for current account transactions. This distinction is virtually impossible to implement in practice, and has not been used by any Fund member—although almost all have availed themselves of the corollary permission to apply controls to capital transactions while generally abstaining in recent years from controls on current account transactions.

6. Numerous other distinctions can be made: nonresident vs. resident convertibility, current account vs. total convertibility, etc. The discussion in the text is limited to the distinctions which are most relevant for broad policy. For more detailed discussion see Gottfried Haberler, CURRENCY CONVERTIBIL-ITY (Washington, D.C.: American Enterprise Institute, 1954).

7. This consideration has dominated the discussion of convertibility in the IMF throughout its history. See, e.g., Margaret G. de Vries and J. Keith Horsefield, THE INTERNATIONAL MONETARY FUND 1945-1965, Vol. II, pp. 75-76. Convertibility would of course fail to enhance the flow of inter-national economic transactions if it could be achieved only by applying controls which directly limited those very transactions themselves, e.g., through mis-guided efforts to preserve "fixed" exchange rates.

8. It must always be remembered that the dollar was the *only* major currency which was convertible until 1958 (except for the Canadian dollar, whose exchange rate floated freely after 1950).

9. Haberler, op. cit., p. 23, made precisely the same point in 1954 when he argued that the Europeans should restore convertibility of their currencies (into other currencies, of course) only if they adopted flexible exchange rates to assure that the convertibility could be maintained.

10. Incidentally, I foresee a smaller reflow of this type than do many others because I observe a sharp rise in the use of several European currencies for private international purposes and expect it to continue, buttressed by the efforts of the Europeans to create an internal monetary union.

11. There are several proposals for how to do so. The most popular is the creation of a special issue of SDRs into which foreign monetary authorities could convert unwanted dollars. The United States would then pay interest on the dollars to the IMF, to enable it to pay interest on the new SDRs. The United States might also amortize the dollars over a long period of time, although there are strong arguments against its doing so. This scheme would change the composition, but not the level, of world reserves. It is opposed by some who fear that the SDR is too new to be created in such sizable amounts at this time. This objection could be met by creating a new IMF debt instrument into which the dollars could be converted, instead of SDRs, as proposed by the Monetary Committee of the Atlantic Council, TO MODERNIZE THE INTERNATIONAL MONETARY SYSTEM, September 18, 1973, pp. 22-24. A wholly different approach is for bilateral funding of the overhang through the conversion of liquid dollar reserves into nonmarketable Treasury securities, but the maturities usually mentioned are far too short to provide a real solution to the problem.

It is doubtful that all countries will agree to consolidate all of their dollars. Thus any such new arrangement must be optional, and will leave some overhang outstanding. In all probability, those dollars will have to remain inconvertible into U.S. reserves even if all foreign dollars created by new U.S. deficits are made convertible. This creates significant but solvable technical problems. (See C. Fred Bergsten, REFORMING THE DOLLAR: AN INTERNATIONAL MONETARY POLICY FOR THE UNITED STATES, Council on Foreign Relations Paper on International Affairs, No. 2, September 1972, pp. 64-68.)

The private overhang could be handled along with the official overhang by making dollars now held by private foreigners eligible for similar conversion into SDRs (or new IMF instruments, or nonmarketable Treasury securities) if they moved into official reserves. If the shifts were viewed as temporary, they could properly be handled by swaps among the central banks as in the past.

12. I would prefer that any renewed convertibility of the dollar (and other currencies) be limited to deficits in the U.S. basic balance, with short-term capital flows recycled through an expanded swap network. Convertibility could also encompass all international transactions and be based on deficits in the official settlements balance, however, in which case U.S. (and everybody's) reserves would have to be much bigger; but I would regard it a mistake to focus on the official settlements balance because this would call for exchange rates to change, and/or huge reserve movements to take place, as a result of liquid and often reversible capital flows.

13. Which does not call for freely flexible exchange rates, in which convertibility of the dollar (or any other currency) into U.S. reserve assets (or the reserves of any other country) would be redundant. My specific proposals for each aspect of reform can be found in my REFORMING THE DOLLAR: AN INTERNATIONAL MONETARY POLICY FOR THE UNITED STATES, pp. 48-88, which is drawn from my forthcoming book THE INTERNATIONAL ROLES OF THE DOLLAR AND US INTERNATIONAL MONETARY POLICY (Praeger Publishers, for the Council on Foreign Relations, forthcoming 1973).

14. A significant part of the AFL-CIO pressure for the Burke-Hartke bill can be traced directly to the job losses resulting from the increasing overvaluation of the dollar in the late 1960s.

15. Some observers have referred to the "system" which has existed since the U.S. suspension of convertibility as a "pure dollar standard." This is wrong, however, because of the rapid growth in the international use of several other national currencies (primarily the DM but also the Swiss franc, guilder, and yen) as both reserve assets and private transactions currencies. The present "system" thus looks increasingly like a "multiple reserve currency standard," probably the least stable alternative which has been seriously studied.

16. Chapter 10 of my forthcoming book (cited in Note 13) analyzes in detail the three possible ways the United States could seek a dollar standard: by *force majeure*, as at present; by offering gold-value guarantees on all

foreign dollar reserves, which would mollify those countries (probably a majority) which cared only about the valuation of their reserves but not those (a small but powerful minority) which also cared about the U.S. policies which produced U.S. deficits; or by undertaking policies which would make the dollar the most attractive asset in the exchange markets, which however could levy enormous costs on the U.S. economy. Only the first is mentioned in the text, because it now appears by far the most likely candidate of the three.

17. As noted in footnote 16, however, guarantees would meet only the asset-valuation concern of foreign dollar holders; they would not meet foreign concern over U.S. policies. See William Fellner, "The Dollar's Place in the International System: Suggested Criteria for the Appraisal of Emerging Views," JOURNAL OF ECONOMIC LITERATURE 10, 3 (September 1972); 735-56. He does not indicate explicitly whether his analysis relates to convertibility on the official settlements or basic (or some other) balance, but his context makes it clear that he assumes the former.

18. Professor Fellner makes several other interesting points in his article. He argues that there is no need for the United States to initiate exchange rate changes, because "equiproportionate disequilibrium of the other countries relative to the United States—with balance among them—would be very rare"; hence it would usually make more sense for other countries to initiate parity realignments. I have argued elsewhere (op. cit., p. 40), to the contrary, that both U.S. adjustment interests, and systemic interests in a better adjustment process, would be served by the United States becoming a *frequent* initiator of parity changes. This is because such changes are far easier to implement here than in other countries, given their far smaller impact on the domestic economy, and because (for the reasons stated in the text, p. 105) they are by far the most efficient way for us to achieve adjustment of our balance of payments. Professor Fellner may be right about the rarity of equiproportionate U.S. disequilibria, but they have occurred twice in the recent past and the same phenomenon holds true (if to a lesser extent) for all countries. It is true that an active U.S. parity policy would force other countries to make adjustments among themselves, as indeed happened in the fall of 1971, but a passive U.S. parity policy would risk continued inaction by everybody even under a new set of rules and intentions.

Professor Fellner also notes the problem of deciding whether shifts of foreign-held dollars from private into official hands are temporary or permanent, and hence whether they should be recycled, on the one hand, or should trigger asset settlement and/or adjustment on the other. This is a real problem only if the new system is based on the official settlements balance, however, and adds to my case for focusing instead on the basic balance.

19. Each nonintervention currency was allowed to fluctuate by one percent on either side of its intervention currency. Thus two nonintervention currencies, each fluctuating by one percent against the dollar *in opposite directions*, could fluctuate by two percent against each other. The dollar could never be farther than one percent from any other currency.

20. Henry Wallich, "The Monetary Crisis of 1971—the Lessons to be Learned," The Per Jacobsson Lecture of 1972, p. 14.

7 Stateless Money

Fritz Machlup

German students of economics in the first half of this century and students of German monetary theory of that period were forced to waste their time on the "State Theory of Money," as expounded by Georg Friedrich Knapp in a book published in 1905 (4th German edition 1923, English edition 1924). The essence of this theory is that all money is created by the nation-state and that its acceptance as means of payment is assured by force of law and by the tax authority of the government. There was much quibbling about the meanings of creation, issuance, proclamation, acceptability, acceptation, acceptance, validity, valuableness, face value, value, and purchasing power of money. Many German students of monetary theory were fascinated by the State Theory, perhaps because they were predisposed to recognize the great power of the nation-state in all areas of human activity. They would have been flabbergasted by the title of this essay: "Stateless Money."

The Nation-State: "Sole Creator of Money"

Of course, when Knapp spoke of money he did not think of the intangible kind of money that now constitutes the bulk of the money stock in the financially most advanced countries. For him money was represented either by a metal coin or by a paper note. As a matter of fact, his State Theory was factually wrong even at the time he wrote, for there was a silver coin circulating freely and accepted by everyone in the Near East, Middle East, and Northern Africa: the Maria Theresia Thaler, issued by the Austrian Mint. It was money without any governmental proclamation, legal enforcement, or official benediction.

The world has moved far away from the monetary institutions of a time when writers had to argue whether or not bank notes were money and when they had hardly begun to extend this argument to demand deposit liabilities of commercial banks. Nowadays few students of money and banking are taken aback if we talk about money that is neither issued nor validated by a governmental agency, does not have the quality of legal tender, cannot be used to pay taxes, and is not counted by statisticians when they measure the country's stock of money.

115

Xeno-Currencies

The stateless money about which I am going to talk is the Euro-dollar together with all other Xeno-currencies. It was in an article published in September 1970 (in the *Banca Nazionale del Lavoro Quarterly Review*) that I first used the expression "stateless money" to refer to Euro-dollar deposits. Xeno-currencies are deposit liabilities of commercial banks, denominated in currencies other than that of the country in which they are located. Most of these—in fact, all of those that are included in the statistics compiled by the Bank for International Settlements—are owned by nonresidents. Thus, three different nationalities may be involved: that of the issuer (bank), that of the holder (depositor), and that of the currency (denomination). This is why I have referred to these liquid assets as stateless money. Of course, their moneyness has still to be shown, even if their statelessness is recognized.

Before I attempt this, however, it may be helpful to get an idea of the order of magnitude involved. The total dollar value of deposit liabilities to nonbanks (plus those to banks outside the reporting areas) in dollars and in other foreign currencies owed by banks all over the world other than the United States was estimated to have been $63 billion in April 1971; of this amount, $50 billion was denominated in U.S. dollars and $13 billion in other currencies. Sixty billion dollars were held in banks located in Europe and $3 billion in banks in the rest of the world. The matrix in Figure 7-1 presents this breakdown in a clearer perspective.

In order to get an impression of the significance of the figures in Figure 7-1,

Denominated in	Europe	Non-Europe Non-U.S.	All Non-U.S. World
U.S. Dollars	47	3	50
Non-Dollar Xeno-Currencies	13	Negl	13
All Xeno-Currencies	60	3	63

Figure 7-1. Deposit Liabilities in Xeno-Currencies of Banks Outside the United States (interbank deposits within reporting areas eliminated) as of April 1971 (in billions of U.S. $)

one will want to see them compared with the money stocks of a few selected countries. The officially reported stocks (as of March 1971) of money in the narrower sense (M_1), including only demand deposit liabilities of commercial banks, were (in terms of U.S. dollars) $42 billion in the United Kingdom, $42 billion in France, $27 billion in Germany, and $213 billion in the United States. It is more reasonable, however, to make the comparisons with stocks of money in a wider sense (M_2), which include such other bank deposit balances as are commonly regarded as cash assets by their holders. The figures given in *International Financial Statistics* for money plus quasi-money may be used for this purpose (except that for the United Kingdom this information is not available). The totals were $64 billion in France, $98 billion in Germany, and $456 billion in the United States. From all these comparisons it may be concluded that the volume of Xeno-currencies is not negligible.

The Moneyness of Xeno-Currencies

Economists have never fully agreed on the degree of moneyness that an asset must have to be recognized as part of the stock of money. Although they do not draw the same lines in the spectrum of "liquidity" of assets, most of them speak of money and money substitutes, money and other circulating media, money and quasi-money, money and near-money, or money and partial money.

Since most kinds of money are legally liabilities of the issuer, the first two questions that are usually asked about a debt with a high degree of liquidity are (1) whether the debt is strictly "payable on demand" and (2) whether its holder receives interest on his claim. The second question became relevant only because in certain countries, including the United States, the legislators prohibited the payment of interest on demand deposits. They probably were befuddled by the scholastic prejudice against charging interest and by a strong belief that it would be socially beneficial to restrict competition among banks. If it were not for such prohibitions (or, alternatively, cartel arrangements among banks) interest would be paid on all bank accounts including demand deposits, and the supposed criterion of moneyness—that no interest is paid to the holder of the claim—would have to be dropped. (If support to this assertion is needed, I may refer to the writings of Milton Friedman, Sir John Hicks, Harry Johnson, Robert Mundell, Paul Samuelson, and James Tobin.)

The first question, whether the debt is payable on demand, would be of doubtful significance even if its meaning were clear, which it is not. From a strictly legal point of view, "payable on demand" would imply a legal obligation of the bank and a legal right of the depositor. The difficulty arises regarding the opposite, that is, bank deposits "not payable on demand." Does this mean that the banks are "not required" or "not permitted" to pay on demand? And how can either the obligation or the prohibition be enforced? In the case of time deposits with commercial banks (and even savings deposits) the banks in most countries are not legally required to pay on demand but are permitted to do so if they wish—and they cannot afford not to wish if there is any competition at all. In the United States savings deposits are not transferable to third parties by the depositor's order, but many banks go around this prohibition by providing cashier's checks on the depositors' demand. (I am indebted to Lester Chandler for helpful advice on all these distinctions.)

As a result of the practices just described, bank deposit balances not payable on demand but only at specified dates or after due notice may, nevertheless, be regarded by the holders as just as liquid as any of their demand deposits or any other cash. Even where a capricious law forbids banks to pay time deposit liabilities before maturity, or without the agreed waiting period after notice of withdrawal, the moneyness of the claims may be secured by the banks' practice of lending to the depositor at any time or, as in the case of certificates of deposits, by making them negotiable. Money-market instruments of this and various other types are widely regarded as cash assets.

The logical question to ask is whether the usability or actual use of an asset as a means of payment is an essential requisite of moneyness. This is clearly a matter of definition. There is no doubt that the "demand for money" to satisfy the precautionary and speculative motives is a demand for more or less liquid assets that can function as store of value but need not always be means of payment. If the transactions cost of exchanging certain non-means-of-payment into means of payment is small and if the probability of loss in the case of conversion without prior notice is low or zero, these liquid assets can meet the demand for money and therefore *are* money (or "partial money") for all practical purposes. Monetary theory has too long remained too fussy regarding the function of money as means of payment. If theory and policy are chiefly concerned with determinants of effective demand, they cannot afford to minimize the role of the non-means-of-payment among the liquid assets held by the community.

Euro-dollars and other Xeno-currencies are bank-deposit balances with maturities from call (day-to-day) to twelve months or even longer. No one can know whether most holders of twelve-month deposits consider them exclusively as investments (alternatives to corporate bonds and AA stocks) or as liquid balances (alternatives to demand deposits). Survey research might yield answers, but no such research has as yet been undertaken. However, for deposits of shorter maturities, such as one month or three months, there is little doubt that the holders regard them as cash assets; the few whom I have asked about it have said so without hesitation or qualification and, I believe, may be taken as representative of the group.

The Status of Statelessness Once More

Money issued by a governmental agency or commercial bank in Country X, denominated in the currency of Country X, and held by a resident of Country X

is without question included in that country's "money supply." If one of these three conditions is not satisfied, the inclusion may be questioned but is sometimes approved; if two of the three conditions are not fulfilled, the inclusion is generally denied.

Federal Reserve Notes, issued by any of the twelve Federal Reserve Banks, circulate widely in several parts of the world. They are the only means of payment (for amounts of one dollar or more) in the Republic of Liberia and perhaps also in some other small countries; and substantial amounts of dollar notes are in the hands of hotel clerks, money changers, and banks all over the world. The amounts of U.S. paper currency held outside the United States are unknown, though rough estimates have probably been made by the authorities. In any case, banknotes outside the country are usually included in the statistics of its money stock.

In the financially most developed countries, however, banknotes and other paper currency are far less important than deposit liabilities of commercial banks. The question whether the banks' demand-deposit liabilities to nonresidents should be counted in the domestic money stock has sometimes been raised, but the answer was usually affirmative.

Thus, with regard to both banknotes and bank deposits, the fact that their holders are nonresidents is not considered a disqualification of these money assets for inclusion in the national money supply. Being issued and owed by a resident institution and being denominated in national currency is regarded as sufficient for their recognition as part of the country's money supply.

We consider next the status of demand deposits owed by resident banks and owned by resident depositors but denominated in foreign currency. Under foreign-exchange restrictions of many countries such deposits would be against the law, prohibited by regulations, or subject to cumbersome restrictions. The case is, nevertheless, not entirely imaginary, for there still exist a few free countries in the world or, at least, some where regulations are liberal enough to permit such bank accounts. I do not know, however, whether the banks that have deposit liabilities to residents on accounts denominated in foreign-currency report these balances along with other data to the monetary or statistical authorities. I can think of reasons both for including them in and for excluding them from the published figures for the country's supply of money or quasi-money.

The third combination where two conditions are satisfied seems somewhat odd: residents of Country X holding balances denominated in currency of Country X with banks located in Country Y. I presume that the authorities of Country X will not include such "claims against foreign banks" in their own money-supply statistic. (We know, for example, that dollar balances held by American residents on deposit with banks in Europe are not counted in the money stock of the United States. Likewise, D-mark balances held by German residents on deposit with banks in London are not included in the money stock of Western Germany.) However, the case is not so cut and dried as it seems. Think of an army of occupation in Country X; the authorities of the occupying power, Y, may issue the currency of Country X to the residents of X; the fact that the issuing agency is foreign need not interfere with the recognition of this currency as part of the money supply of Country X.

There are also three combinations where only one of the three conditions is satisfied. There is no need, however, to review them systematically, for no country would recognize such "one-third money" as part of *its* money supply. We must raise the question, however, whether any economic argument can be found that would support the inclusion of such stateless money in the money supply of any particular country.

Why One Wants to Know the Money Supply

The question whether some particular assets should or should not be counted in a country's money supply can be answered only if one has decided why one wants to have the information about the money supply. Why do we want to know a country's money stock and its changes?

Those who believe that the quantity of money and its changes do not matter may find such information irrelevant. There are still plenty of people, however, who believe that these magnitudes do matter. These curious people need not be "monetarists" or "quantity theorists"; there are also less committed economists who know that changes in the quantity of money may make a difference with regard to a number of variables in the economic system. Among these variables may be the rates of investment, consumption, production, employment, commodity-price levels, interest rates, securities prices, and other not unimportant things in which economists, government officials, politicians, businessmen, labor leaders, investors, and other human beings may be more or less intensely interested.

Behind all the economic variables that may be affected by changes in the quantity of money or quasi-money is the rather simple (and probably unquestionable) notion that an increase in that quantity is likely to affect the demand for commodities, services, labor, durable assets, and securities. In simple models of a closed economy there is no demand for foreign things and no foreign demand for domestic things. For a world of several countries one usually assumes that additions to the quantity of money in Country X will increase demand for things domestic as well as foreign. The origin of that new money in X is not unimportant, and the assumption that it is money of Country X, held by residents of X is significant in the processes of "portfolio adjustment," "asset selection," and "effective-demand expansion" that are engendered by the monetary expansion. But what if the new money is not issued in X, or not held by X-residents, or not denominated in X-currency? As I wrote recently in a paper (delivered at a conference of the American Enterprise Institute) about Euro-dollar deposits, "we do not know whether these deposits are substitutes for the money of the country of the issuing bank, for the money of the country in which the holder resides, or for the money in which they are denominated."

In an abstract theoretical model, one would probably find it most useful to focus on the residence of the *holder* of the cash asset and on the question whether he is the first recipient of the asset or one who has received it at a later (perhaps final) point in the process of adjustment initiated by its creation. In an analysis of empirical records, however, information on initial and subsequent holders of Xeno-currencies is unobtainable and information on the residence of the holders, if it were available, would be of no avail. For one could not know whether depositors were holding the Xeno-currencies with a view to spending them as soon as possible or as a result of an adjustment of their portfolio to keep them as precautionary or speculative balances with a satisfactory yield. In no case can one presume with any confidence that these balances will be spent in the country in which the depositor resides, or in the country in which the bank is located, or in the country in whose currency they are denominated. They may at any time swell the demand for the goods, services, resources, or securities of any country.

This statement could, in a sense, be made also for cash assets that are recognized as parts of the country's money supply. The difference in this respect between national and stateless money lies chiefly in the degree of intercon-vertibility and mobility. The stateless money is more cosmopolitan, more international, footloose and *wanderlustig.* The holder of a Euro-dollar is only one easy foreign-exchange transaction away from command over any other currency that he may want.

Commodity Prices and Interest Rates

No good economist will disregard changes in the quantity of money and near-money when he attempts to explain sustained changes in the levels of commodity prices and interest rates. And no good central banker will disregard the rate of monetary expansion when he attempts to influence movements of price levels and interest rates. Analysts as well as practitioners, therefore, would make serious mistakes if they omitted from their definitions of money and from their estimations of the money supply cash assets that affect the people's spending, lending, and investing behavior. Such omissions occur when the definitions of money and near-money are too narrow and the estimations of the relevant magnitudes therefore incomplete. One cause of narrowness is the limitation to means of payment and the implied exclusion of cash assets held for every-ready conversion into transactions money. Another cause of narrowness is the limitation to near-moneys that, metaphorically speaking, show a national flag, with the consequence that international and stateless near-moneys are excluded from the monetary statistics of all countries.

Euro-Dollar Transactions

This essay on Euro-dollars and other Xeno-currencies as stateless money has treated only one aspect of Xeno-currency transactions: the use of Xeno-currency deposits held by nonbank depositors. In order to guard against misunderstandings by readers who are better acquainted with other aspects of the Euro-dollar system and therefore may be bewildered by the emphasis of my discussion, I should repeat another point, made in my paper for the conference of the American Enterprise Institute: "The Euro-dollar system can theoretically be subdivided into three subsystems: a money market in which banks are transactors on both sides, lending and borrowing liquid balances which they regard as cash reserves; a credit market in which nonbanks (individuals, partnerships, and corporations, but chiefly corporations) are lending to banks and borrowing from banks; and a deposit system in which nonbanks hold liquid balances which they regard as part of their cash position. The three subsystems interact in the unintended provision of additional liquidity."

Chiefly the third of these subsystems, and only tangentially the second, have been involved in the discussion of stateless money. This distinction may help those of my readers who have thought of the Euro-dollar system only as a market and not as a pool of cash balances.

Part II:
International Trade

The Next World Trade Negotiations

Bernard Norwood

I. The Agreement to Get Agreement

In early 1972, a few weeks after most of the world's trading nations took the final steps to put into effect concessions negotiated in 1967, the United States, Japan, and the European Community announced that they would "initiate and actively support multilateral and comprehensive negotiations . . . beginning in 1973 . . . with a view to the expansion and the ever greater liberalization of world trade. . . ."[1]

This agreement to turn to multilateral trade liberalization in the coming year, along with agreement on other immediate measures to relieve some trade problems, broke a pervasive anxiety that retaliatory restriction would follow the import levies imposed by the United States in mid-August 1971 to staunch the outward flight of gold and other monetary reserves.

Having decided that they should negotiate, *what* were they to negotiate? The joint declarations gave some clues: a progressive dismantling of obstacles to trade; the improvement of the international framework for the conduct of world trade. Also, the negotiations would be "conducted on the basis of mutual advantage and mutual commitment with overall reciprocity"; they would cover agricultural and industrial trade; and they would involve "active participation of as many countries as possible." The European Community included a statement that "commodity agreements" are one means to achieve the general objective, but the United States countered by saying, "such agreements do not offer a useful approach."

The several countries having committed themselves to negotiate, and having expressed a few well-rounded objectives, the U.S. government was at sea—and announced it. In Tokyo in May, William Eberle, President Nixon's Special Representative for Trade Negotiations, said he was "searching for some guiding principles with which to strengthen the framework of multi-national negotiations."[2] A short time later, he envisioned "fashioning" a "trade charter, setting

From early 1963 through the end of the Kennedy Round of trade negotiations in mid-1967, the author served President Kennedy's and President Johnson's Special Representatives for Trade Negotiations as senior adviser, negotiator, and frequent alternate. Presently he is Adviser in the Division of International Finance of the Board of Governors of the Federal Reserve System. The views expressed in this article are his own and do not necessarily represent the views of any official U.S. agency.

forth a set of principles establishing the common ground on which govern-ments can negotiate."[3]

For the leading trading powers to commit themselves to a major multilateral trade negotiation sometime in the following year without deciding on objectives more specific than "liberalization," "mutual advantage," "overall reciprocity," and broad trade and country coverage may seem bewildering. In previous trade negotiations, the principles and procedures were substantially agreed upon before countries finally committed themselves to negotiate. That countries have gone ahead boldly in contrast to precedent is a reflection of the extraordinary strains of the international trade and monetary scene.

II. The Setting

A. The Stretch and Strain of the International Rules

Increasingly over the last dozen years or so, members of the GATT (General Agreement on Tariffs and Trade) and the International Monetary Fund have acted counter to the established rules of trade conduct. Trade difficulties have been eased by waiving the GATT rules—temporarily and under stated condi-tions—and by offering negotiations to reduce tariffs and other obstacles to exports. In the monetary field, however, where exchange rates tended to be rigid, tensions were not so readily relieved. Occasionally, countries "floated away" from their obligations temporarily.

The United States, which had never imagined it could ever be a balance-of-payments "deficit" country, became perplexed and then worried by emerging signs of underlying weakness in the 1960s. Some government officials became concerned as the United States prepared to enter the largest trade negotiation ever held, the Sixth Round of Trade Negotiations under the General Agreement on Tariffs and Trade, known as the Kennedy Round. The large U.S. surplus of exports over imports shrank in 1965. At first attributed to domestic inflation and considered a natural and short-lived phenomenon, then stimulated by commencement of significant military expenditures in Southeast Asia, the trend continued. Shortly before the mid-1967 end of the trade negotiations, the United States became worried that the phenomenon might not soon vanish. This hardened the U.S. resolve not to grant any "nonreciprocal" concessions, that is, any concessions that would increase its imports more than the concessions by other countries would increase its exports. It was especially concerned that this not happen to the bilateral balance with Japan, and the United States began to pull back many tariff concessions offers in the hands of some other countries.

As the swing from export surplus to import surplus continued over the years following that final agreement, and as domestic inflation and unemployment became prime economic problems, President Nixon on August 15, 1971, launched a panoply of economic restrictions and incentives under a New Economic Policy (NEP). For trade, the most conspicuous feature was a 10 percent surcharge on imports of most dutiable goods.[4] Less noticed at the time of announcement was a 10 percent investment tax credit that discriminated against imported machinery and equipment. These and other trade and tax measures plus the ending of the convertibility of the dollar into gold and other reserve assets were taken for what the Administration regarded, and for what was widely accepted, as a compelling need to protect a seriously worsening balance of payments.[5] Some of the measures, it was instantly charged, flew in the face of U.S. obligations under the GATT. Worse still, critics pointed out that the import surcharge was levied while the previous trade liberalization agreement was still warm—the last of the five annual stages of Kennedy Round tariff cuts not being due to go into effect until four and a half months later, on January 1, 1972.

The NEP trade measures were intended to do two things: halt a rapid deterioration in the trade balance, and assist U.S. industry to become more competitive against foreign goods. Also, the measures directly and indirectly affecting trade, together with the move away from convertibility, would dramatize the need to realign exchange rates and reform the international monetary system.

As dramatic as the August 15 surprise package was, a no less remarkable aspect of the episode was the lack of retaliation in the following days or months. The U.S. government had good reason to fear that other governments would impose penalty duties against imports from the United States, since they had quickly declared that the U.S. measures violated GATT obligations. But foreign governments knew that retaliatory steps would result in new and possibly longer lasting restrictions and discrimination, rather than a removal of the U.S. measures. Retaliation would also threaten whatever chances there were of solving the problems responsible for the U.S. action. Other countries may also have feared that the United States did not have a better alternative to halt a deterioration that had been developing for years. Moreover, they had abundant evidence of rising protectionist sympathies in the Congress. Finally, they were told, and may have been anxious to believe, that the surcharge would be temporary.

B. The Underlying Deterioration in U.S. Trade Balance

The traditional U.S. surplus of merchandise exports over merchandise imports reached its peak in 1964. From that peak of $6.8 billion,[6] it shrank to a tenth that amount in 1968, increased slightly in 1970, and then turned into a deficit of $2.7 billion in 1971.

The multilateral Smithsonian Agreement of mid-December 1971 brought about a realignment of exchange rates and the rescission by the United States of the import surcharge and of U.S. government plans to make its investment tax credit discriminatory against imported goods. The exchange rate changes, among other things, were expected to correct the overvaluation of the U.S. dollar and thereby improve the trade balance. By late in the following year, however, the trade balance was still worsening—apparently running toward a 1972 deficit of about $6 to $7 billion. The wait for signs of the salutary effect on U.S. trade expected from the 9 percent dollar devaluation was agonizing.[7]

The devaluation and examination of the first few ensuing months of U.S. trade figures were followed by warnings that perverse effects should be expected, that an improvement would occur, but that the full beneficial effects would take two to three years to appear and, indeed, that perverse effect could be expected in the months immediately following the realignment.[8] By late 1972, no significant cut in imports had clearly shown up although the average dollar price of imported finished manufactures (as measured crudely by unit values) had increased. That increase was only about one-third of the devaluation of the dollar in terms of the currencies of the principal industrial countries, and some of this rise reflected a continuation of the pre-realignment trend. By late 1972, the total dollar value of U.S. exports was somewhat higher than what would have been expected in the absence of the devaluation. However, the increase was moderate, and the data in individual export markets were too incomplete to support firm conclusions about the effect of the currency realignment.

C. Trade Diversion from EC Enlargement

Prospects for U.S. trade with the enlarged European Community (EC) will be unsettled for some time—probably not becoming clear until well into, or even after, the forthcoming world trade negotiations. Estimates of the relative importance of the negative and positive effects of EC enlargement on U.S. exports have varied widely.

U.S. exports to European countries will probably suffer over the coming years as tariffs and other trade restrictions are removed between the original six members of the European Community, on the one hand, and the U.K., Denmark, and Ireland, on the other hand. The adverse trade effects arising for the United States as the result of the accession of the latter three countries will be offset to an undetermined extent by an increase in the level of economic activity of the enlarged European Community. Similar negative and positive trade effects will confront the United States as a result of the free trade area to be established between the enlarged EC, on the one hand, and the European neutrals—Austria, Sweden, Switzerland, and Finland (and, presumably, Norway) —on the other hand.

As figures for the first decade of the European Economic Community's development show, the most difficult area for United States trade will probably be in agriculture. Although it once was believed that the U.K. would exert a liberalizing influence on the Community's agricultural policies, the completion of the negotiations for U.K. accession and the U.K.'s desire to be a cooperative new member have removed whatever basis there was for that wishful thinking.

Much of the review and negotiation over the effects of the enlargement of the EC on trade of other countries will have taken place before the multilateral trade negotiations. Under the GATT, the EC and the acceding states, starting in 1972, are undergoing an examination to ensure that the new common tariff is not more restrictive than the average of the old "national" tariffs, and they must renegotiate any individual rate increases that may be incidental to the adoption of the common external tariff by the individual acceding states. Although the prospect of trade diversion is posed also by the association of the EC and the neutrals, no GATT requirement for renegotiation exists. These countries and the EC will be removing duties and other trade restrictions among themselves, which may cause some diversion of their purchases away from U.S. goods, but will not be altering their tariffs against imports from third countries.

Assuming that a settlement satisfactory to third countries is reached in the GATT review and renegotiation of concessions, the United States will have good reason to seek further concessions to offset the adverse effects of trade diversion. The enlarged EC can be expected to argue that the increase in total foreign trade—within the Community and between the Community and third countries—that should arise from the further step in the economic integration of Europe will be adequate to compensate the United States for any adverse diversionary effects. Taking account of the growth of economic activity and foreign trade in the EEC in its first ten years, the EC will probably be able to make a strong case. But it is not likely to be reassuring on all products of interest to the United States, especially on agricultural products. It is these uncertainties that will carry over from the GATT procedures on EC enlargement into the major trade negotiations.[9]

D. The Parties at Interest

A negotiation starting in 1973 will see more countries than ever before in the series of GATT-sponsored multilateral negotiations at the conference site but fewer countries than ever before seriously bargaining. As in the last big round, the developing countries, which have organized themselves in an UNCTAD framework, will be present and involved, as will be the middle-category countries, such as Canada and the EFTA countries. However, the key partici- pants—those prepared to give as well as to receive concessions and to accept the most ambitious rules—will have been reduced from four (the United States,

Japan, the European Community, and the United Kingdom) to three, the U.K. being assimilated to the EC. Many assumptions based on the experience of the last round will have to be assessed against this significant change in negotiating interests.

III. What the United States Must Go After in the Trade Negotiations

A. The Goal and the Balance of Agreement

The United States government will under any circumstances that can reasonably be anticipated over the next several years want to stem and, if possible, reverse the deterioration in its trade balance, increase its total foreign trade, and remove current and incipient trade disputes with other countries. To achieve these goals, the United States will want to cut foreign tariffs, reduce or eliminate foreign quantitative restriction as well as less tangible foreign administrative restraints on imports and foreign export incentives, and reduce foreign discrimination against its exports.

Redress of the trade balance may prove to be a conspicuous goal for two reasons. First, the presently large and unfamiliar trade deficit is widely regarded as bad, and its reduction or eradication can be presented to the country as an easily accepted objective. Second, the other goals—welfare benefits of lower cost imports and of a growing total foreign trade and the foreign relations benefits of the resolution of trade disputes—may seem to be less well understood. "Redress," at a minimum, could be halting the widening of the gap between rapidly growing imports and slowly growing exports. "Redress," at a maximum, could be the restoration of an export surplus.

Is it feasible, or advisable, to reverse the present trade imbalance? If the gap continues at approximately 15 percent, about what it was running in late 1972, exports would have increased that much faster than imports just to keep the gap from growing. To narrow the gap would require a still greater rate of export expansion over import growth. Many other countries are also hoping to strengthen their balance of payments by an improvement in their trade balance. Which are the countries that are prepared to enjoy the economic benefits of an expanding import surplus or a shrinking export surplus?

A more important, even if seemingly less critical, objective in the negotiation will be an increase in total U.S. trade, both exports and imports. This has been the traditional negotiating objective, at least for the United States, and it is no less relevant today. Even if the U.S. trade balance were not improved, the United States would be reaping widespread benefits from trade liberalization. It is the fear that liberalization will aggravate the trade imbalance and thereby draw more attention to employment, industrial adjustment, and the balance of payments that may lead the government to play down the fundamental benefits from increasing the efficiency of the allocation of productive resources and raising the standard of living of the people. This fear exists even though trade liberalization would contribute to anti-inflationary measures in this country.

The effects of any trade negotiation will be slow in coming about. The agreement will not be concluded until possibly years from the initial formal urgings pronounced in early 1972. The concessions, in line with practice established in the last few multilateral agreements, will probably be staged into place over several years.

In earlier bilateral and multilateral trade negotiations, the United States quantified and then compared the tariff concessions obtained and those granted. Largely because of data limitations, the balance sheet was based on crude calculations—generally a tabulation of individual percentage cuts multiplied by trade covered in the latest year for which data were available. In recent years, the state of the art has been advanced by assiduous theoretical work and by the increased use of the computer. However, the conceptual and the practical problems of measuring the future trade effects of tariff cuts compel governments to seek quantitative evaluations (generally described as "seat-of-the-pants" judgments) from commodity analysts and to produce the grossly simplified tabulations that are understood, if not respected, by legislatures and the public.

Whatever "back of the envelope" quantification negotiators use in drawing up offers and demands and finally in justifying their bargaining skill, governments will weigh many factors. In addition to estimates of the trade-creating effects of the concessions over the coming years, weight will be given to the cost of adjustment of domestic industry to increased imports, to the elimination of festering trade problems, and to progress in inducing a negotiating partner to enter into another agreement in a different economic, political, or national security area.

B. Tariffs

The heart of the negotiations. Tariffs will be the principal subject of the negotiation.

Many believe that little can be gained from further tariff cuts; they argue that tariffs no longer constitute a substantial impedient to trade. For example, the average levels of industrial tariffs for the United States, Canada, the EC, the U.K., and Japan range from 8.1 to 12.6 percent.[10]

However, tariffs still severely restrict trade in many commodities. These same countries have contended in negotiations that certain 5 percent rates of other countries are protectionist. Also, some rates are applied on a preferential basis and thereby divert imports from one supplying country to another, favored country.

In addition, many importing countries, finding that high tariffs run counter to domestic anti-inflationary programs, are anxious to find an acceptable means of tariff reduction. Unilateral reduction might subject a government to some criticism, whereas negotiations of a trade agreement can achieve the desired reduction without political repercussions and in fact might even be used to buy concessions from other countries.[11]

Moreover, whatever may be said about the greater need to negotiate on nontariff trade barriers, governments will find—as they have in the past—that the emphasis will shift to tariffs if for no other reason than that tariffs are politically and technically more susceptible to negotiation.

The tariff negotiation formula. Insofar as tariffs are concerned, the negotiations should aim principally at the reduction by 50 percent of each participant's *average* level of duties on all (dutiable) products, except those in an agreed, common list of agricultural products that are generally subject principally to nontariff trade restraints. Cuts could range selectively between zero and 100 percent. Duties covered by the reduction rule should be the most-favored-nation (MFN) rates in effect on January 1, 1972, the date on which the last of the five annual Kennedy Round concessions went into force. The average of the individual rates should be weighted by MFN imports in 1970 from all the countries participating in the negotiations. To overcome statistical problems, variations could be made in the formula.[12]

Most agricultural imports (by number although not necessarily by trade volume) are not subject to quotas or other special limits; they are subject in most countries to regular tariffs (or are duty-free) and should be treated in the trade liberalization exercise as nonagricultural products (for convenience, "industrial products") would be treated.

Agricultural products that, in any major importing country, are subject to special import devices should be excluded from the 50 percent rule, but not from negotiations. First, the nontariff devices used to control their importation (whether as an alternative to, or as a redundant accompaniment of, a tariff) are not susceptible to the arithmetic of the formula. Second, a negotiation on the import treatment of such products must treat the nontariff import restraints, which means treating, in turn, domestic agricultural programs to which the special import measures are generally related. The most important of these devices, and of the agricultural programs of which they are a part, are the European Community's variable levies under the Common Agricultural Policy (CAP). However, the European Community has heretofore been adamant in resisting negotiations on the levies and the CAP. Furthermore, the American president has been unable in recent negotiations to offer effective concessions on agricultural products covered by farm support programs. Agricultural products subject to variable levies in the EC (principally grains, poultry, and dairy products) and agricultural products subject to other nontariff barriers in other major countries intending to negotiate (butter and cheese in the United States) may have to be examined and negotiated separately from industrial commodities.

The average 50 percent goal would result in substantial reductions, while permitting a wide margin of selectivity to the participating countries in packaging their final concessions.[13] Many duties could be eliminated, but the plan would not achieve the objective of free trade in industrial goods that has been urged increasingly in recent years.[14]

There is one overriding reason for a target that falls short of the elimination of duties on all industrial products: the nine members of the enlarged European Community (EC) and the several states appended to it in a free-trade area relationship cannot be expected, in 1973 or soon thereafter, to agree on an ultimate dismantling of their industrial tariffs against third countries.

The member states will contend that their industries will have enough new competition to face as internal tariffs are removed over a transitional period of five years. Some of them will also argue that complete elimination of duties between the EC and the rest of the world will remove the "cement" that holds the Community together, namely, the common external tariff (and the individual tariffs of the appended states) applicable to the outside world. That there are counterarguments to these points—that there could be limited selectivity of concessions and safeguards for domestic industry and that ties of economic and political integration stronger than tariffs will keep the Community cemented together—in no way lessens the judgment that the Europeans are not going to agree in 1973 or soon thereafter to embark on a dismantlement of their industrial tariffs.

Agreement is more likely to be reached on selective cuts. It is important that the tariff reduction formula depart from the "linear" or across-the-board formula that, after a long gestation, was utilized in the last major round of trade negotiations.[15] The experience of that conference made some key participants wary of committing themselves again to a linear cut. As the Kennedy Round came to a close, the United States found that its offer of a 50 percent linear cut would result in marked imbalances when concessions were evaluated on a country-by-country basis. Consequently, as permitted under the Kennedy Round rules on last minute adjustments to ensure whatever balance a participant deemed necessary, the United States met with the Japanese and then with some other participants to pull back fully or partially many of its tariff offers.[16]

Although the U.S. acted because of what it could regard, under conference rules, as an unacceptable imbalance of concessions, participants that suddenly saw some of their anticipated benefits snatched away probably vowed themselves to be more selective in the future and less willing to accept a linear tariff-cutting rule.

It might be alleged that the proposed formula would be cumbersome, because it would require some item-by-item bargaining. But, the across-the-board technique, for the multilateral negotiation concluded in 1967 had more selectivity than is often assumed. Having had experience with the "linear" technique, countries would demand in a future negotiations qualifications at least as serious as were finally developed in the last one.

U.S. legislative authority. One issue that will have to be settled before negotiations can begin is that of domestic legal authority, that is, the authority of the president to give effect to any tariff concessions that he might negotiate. In the past, enactment of limitations on the tariff reduction authority Congress has given to the president has limited the scope of the bargaining with other countries. The Trade Expansion Act of 1972 (TEA), which provided Presidents Kennedy and Johnson with the authority to proclaim tariff concessions and, as a practical matter, provided them with the authority to negotiate, gave the president a "basic" authority to reduce U.S. duties by 50 percent but also permitted him to make 100 percent reductions, that is, to eliminate duties, in some circumstances. Pre-TEA authority never provided for 100 percent cuts, and the percentage reduction possibilities were more circumscribed by conditions than was the TEA authority.[17] In deciding whether to delegate the necessary powers, the Congress is likely to fasten its attention on two policy issues—on the protection of certain U.S. industries from increased foreign competition and on the kind of reciprocity to be secured from other countries.

On the first issue, already familiar safeguards relating both to the negotiation of an agreement and to the administration of the concessions make it unnecessary to limit the depth of individual cuts, as was generally the case in the past. It would be far wiser to preserve the ability of the negotiators to be selective in making cuts in U.S. duties, to phase reductions into force progressively over a period of years, and to make available assistance to workers and firms to adjust to new import competition than to utilize, even as a partial safeguard, an arbitrary, percentage limit on the president's authority to reduce individual rates.

To preclude the possibility of eliminating duties would cause effort to be wasted and opportunities for mutually beneficial trade liberalization to be missed. It would miss opportunities, since some countries have rates that are high solely because they have never negotiated with the countries that have been the principal suppliers of the articles covered by those rates. Moreover, authority for a full removal of rates, rather than only fractional cuts, would eliminate the nuisance rates.

Post-negotiations safeguards for domestic industry that may suffer from increased import competition—especially if it is concession induced—will be demanded by many U.S. economic interests. The contention will be that the present remedies, including a possibly liberalized adjustment assistance program, will be deemed inadequate. The ultimate safeguard is the import quota. The Japanese in late 1972 redoubled efforts they have made from time to time to limit strictly, although with healthy annual increases for some commodities, exports of a great many products. The question will arise, and may be brought to the negotiating table, of getting international agreement on the "voluntary" export restraints. A "market disruption" formula was gingerly discussed among some governments before the last major multilateral negotiation got underway. It was abandoned, in part because it was considered too selective (aimed solely at Japan), departed significantly from the principle of nondiscriminatory treatment, and would probably prove unnecessary. This time, any internationally agreed safeguard device would have to conform to a standard of nondiscrimination, even though only one country today might appear to be the target.[18] But the countries today most interested in obtaining its protection are the ones most in need of sharply increasing their sales into other countries' markets and will also have to think of their own vulnerability to the protective device.

The second issue—reciprocity—will be difficult, but no more so than in the past. Recognizing a desire of some participants to see some degree of balance in the tariff portion of the final trade agreement, the problem of measuring the trade benefits of cuts of as much as 100 percent will be the same as the problems of measuring cuts that are no greater than 50, 15, 20, or some other percentage.

Most, if not all, participants will want to assure themselves that they are achieving reciprocity by weighing all elements of the agreement—tariffs and nontariff concessions. Any participant believing it is not getting a beneficial settlement on industrial products can pull back selected offers of tariff concessions, or can change offers of concessions on other issues of special importance to it.

Disparities. The issue of tariff "disparities" is almost sure to come up in the new negotiation. Considerable attention centered on the issue in the Kennedy Round, and many negotiators convinced themselves by their own argumentation that disparities, reduced in that negotiation, must be wiped out in future negotiations. In addition, a negotiating rule, such as the one suggested above, that permits substantial selectivity in both the items to be covered and in the depth of the duty cuts may heighten the fear that peaks and valleys of a country's tariff will be accentuated rather than reduced.

The tariff disparity issue could be a troublesome element in a negotiation with the European Community (EC). The common external tariff of the EC, which was originally developed through a process of averaging the tariffs of member states, has a more even rate structure than that of the United States. The American tariff varies widely from item to item. The EEC negotiators in the Kennedy Round argued that a 50 percent across-the-board cut in all U.S. and all EEC duties would reduce U.S. protection less than EEC protection. They declared that cuts in the high duties in the U.S. jagged tariff would still leave those rates protective and that cuts in low U.S. rates would reduce already ineffective rates, whereas cuts in the medium rates in the EC's more uniform tariff would decrease their protective effect.

An enormous input of skilled labor went into the Kennedy Round effort to settle on a formula of "automatic" application to even out the peaks and valleys—at least to lop off the peaks.[19]

In the forthcoming negotiation, the absence of a formula for across-the-board tariff cutting should lessen the concern that the same negotiating credit will be given for a particular percentage cut in moderate and in high duties. A negotiating rule that allows for selectivity should not resurrect the intellectually stimulating but expensive debating on evening out peaks and valleys. Pressures by the EC on the United States for a reduction in any high rates that seem inordinately and unjustifiably restrictive can be left to qualitative assessment and to finely focused bargaining.

C. Agriculture

Agriculture will be included in the negotiation if for no other reason than that it would be politically impossible for large agricultural producing states to seem to acquiesce in foreign protective policies. However, serious difficulties stand in the way of obtaining agricultural concessions. The techniques of protection for the most important agricultural products, as well as for many of the lesser products, are substantially different from those applied to industrial products. For the United States, liberalizing trade in the agricultural sector means essentially liberalizing trade under the EC's Common Agricultural Policy (CAP). As that policy is now applied, rises and declines in the prices in world market of wheat, other grains, and vegetable and animal products related to grains are automatically offset by variations in Community import levies. The levies protect administratively determined domestic market prices, and third countries are made to be residual suppliers. Any new price advantage those outside suppliers might achieve—by a drop in their offer prices or a rise in the EC prices—is offset by an increase in the variable levies.

In the early days of the Community, the United States and other agricultural exporters gave much thought to challenging the legality under the GATT of the variable levy system, but decided instead to seek other, practical solutions for their agricultural exports to the Common Market. In the meantime, the Community established the CAP firmly, extending it to products other than grains and tying the system together in a web of interproduct relationships—the levies for chickens being determined by the amount of feed the chickens would eat and thus by the levies based on grain imports.

The United States must therefore come up with offers to entice the enlarged EC into modifying its protective system. Neither the administrative complexity nor the inflationary impact of the CAP on the Community is likely to induce the

Community to change its policy. Governments have a great capacity to sustain programs that burden the general, inarticulate populace, and the EC has not yet shown signs of being an exception.

The United States should not condition its acceptance of the entire trade agreement, however, on concessions on the CAP. Such insistence could bring about a collapse of the negotiations in other fields. Experience provides numerous examples of the dangers. The Dillon Round floundered and almost failed when the EEC resisted meaningful tariff concessions on agriculture. The negotiation dragged out painfully on this issue—it was officially designated as the 1960-61 GATT Tariff Conference, but was concluded on July 16, 1962—and was brought to an end only after President Kennedy sent a special emissary to the Brussels headquarters of the EEC, circumventing the U.S. and EEC delegations then at loggerheads in Geneva, to work out a final bargain on farm products. Similarly the Kennedy Round, brought to a close in mid-1967 after several years of bargaining and of seeming stalemates, almost foundered on the inability of the key countries to settle on agriculture.

However, there is no reason to exclude any agricultural item from the negotiation. Although the items subject to the EC's CAP would be among the most troublesome, the conference rules should not prejudice the possibility of getting agreement on prices—secured by the EC in the Grain Arrangement in 1967—or on such other elements of the CAP as would not represent an abrupt "dismantling" of that system. Agreement by the EC to alter its system substantially now would be out of the question but should not be ruled out if accomplished over many years and with compensatory benefits to the Community.

The United States might overcome the habitual resistance to bargaining on agricultural import protection techniques, including those of the CAP. It might do so by shifting the bargaining focus from specific forms of protection to the concept underlying agricultural protectionism around the world—border protection.

If the agreement can be reached among the key countries to negotiate on the agricultural border protection, regardless of which devices are used for that protection, liberalization of U.S. exports might be achieved. This approach would have far-reaching implications. First, domestic farm programs, which in various ways subsidize farm production or nonproduction in the United States, as well as in other countries, would have to be limited. Farm support programs would be deprived of import protection. Second, the United States would have to be willing to negotiate on its own agricultural border protection programs, thus making its agricultural import restraints (the Section 22 quotas or "fees" that have applied to a handful of products) subject to internationally agreed limitation or prohibition. This could have the effect of substantially constraining the domestic support programs that those special import restraints protect.

The EC should be asked to reduce the CAP variable levies and gradually over, say, ten years to supplant the threshold prices that trigger the levies with agreed fixed tariffs. Similarly, the United States might be asked to increase progressively its Section 22 agricultural import quotas until they become nonrestrictive and are abolished. This elimination of border restriction would force the United States either to buy up farm products and pay a possibly intolerable storage bill or to adjust its domestic programs to eliminate special incentives intended for domestic producers.

Both the EC and the United States should find it possible to adjust to the removal of the variable levy (actually of the ilk of the American Selling Price arbitrary customs valuation instrument) and of the Section 22 import quotas. The transition could be accomplished by lowering prices or compensating farmers by direct payments. The EC is already using the direct payment device to pay its tobacco farmers and, despite a present antipathy to extending that method to producers of other products, could consider such an extension in the grain and livestock sectors.

Agriculture border protection is not confined to a package of import restraints; it encompasses export subsidies, as well. Countries limiting their protection might resort to the well-established technique of selling "surpluses" in external markets with the aid of subsidies. The GATT contracting parties have been rather lax in regard to the same practice for farm products. If the United States is to attack foreign border protection against its agricultural exports, it must be prepared to accept, in common with other countries, limits on its own direct or indirect agricultural export subsidy programs.[20]

D. NTBs and Other Nontariff Distortions of Trade

Nontariff trade barriers (NTBs)—import quotas, other less visible restraints on the sale of imported goods, export subsidies, and other devices that distort trade—will be among the main objects of negotiations. First, they limit trade, and trade liberalization is an objective of the negotiation; second, it is alleged that they have not been properly recognized and treated in earlier negotiations and therefore must be attacked afresh.

Many times over the years, the GATT contracting parties have resolved that "something must be done about NTBs." For example, the Kennedy Round was designated officially the GATT Sixth Round of *Trade* Negotiations, not Tariff Negotiations, in order to stress that NTBs would be given prominence.[21]

The Kennedy Round attack on NTBs was launched early but bogged down immediately and stayed bogged down until late in the conference. Ultimately, agreements were reached on eliminating the arbitrary U.S. system of customs valuation—the so-called American Selling Price (ASP) system—that applied to benzenoid chemicals and to a few other products. In addition to this nontariff barrier, or "para-tariff" barrier, settlement were: agreements taking the form of

A "code" of antidumping practices; commitments by some countries to limit the "road taxes" that bore exceptionally heavily on bit American cars; and removal of other odds and ends of that ilk, such as a Canadian requirement limiting sales of imported goods in bushel-size baskets.

However, attempts to get agreements on other NTBs failed.[22] Notable among those that were debated but that were not embodied in any settlements published at the end of the conference were "border taxes" (levies imposed on imported goods to compensate for internal taxes borne by competing domestic goods and remissions, by reason of exportation of internal taxes).

Considerable work has taken place over the last several years, primarily within the GATT framework, to prepare the way for agreements on NTB liberalization. Progress has been achieved in some areas; among the potential agreements is one on the harmonization of technical standards that is designed to narrow the freedom of countries to use engineering and safety standards as arbitrary restraints on imports.

Governments will be aruging mostly about the hard core of NTB problems, plus new ones tied to scientific, engineering, and environmental developments—typified by automobile antipollution requirements. Some of the most difficult were settled in the Kennedy Round but were reopened when the U.S. Senate angrily objected to their having been negotiated without clear prior authorization by the Congress. Because of these objections, other countries may want to come back to the code of antidumping practices, which called for no implementing U.S. legislation but only the exercise of administrative discretion, at least to clarify its status in the United States. The agreement for the United States to abandon the ASP system of customs valuation in exchange for tariff and NTB concessions from other countries was concluded in the face of a hostile Senate resolution. It has not received the required congressional approval and thereby remains a potentially lively issue.

Despite these unsuccessful past experiences, agreement on some NTBs may be successfully negotiated.

First, the Senate Finance Committee has asked the U.S. Tariff Commission to complete, by the fall of 1973, a study of possible U.S. adoption of a new system of customs valuation. The Brussels system has widespread acceptance throughout the world and will serve as a basis for reconsidering the U.S. system and possible alternatives. Although the Brussels system differs from the U.S. system most conspicuously in that import valuation is essentially on a c.i.f., rather than f.o.b., basis, it also differs in not permitting arbitrary valuation of imports, such as the ASP system does. The Brussels system also differs from the U.S. system in being less complex. The U.S. system gives customs officials a cascade of *nine* alternative methods of valuing imports for duty purposes. To adopt the Brussels valuation system, the ASP system would have to be dropped. Also to switch to the Brussels system, the United States would have to renegotiate each of thousands of individual tariff rates in order to ensure that the conversion did not involve an unintended increase in the incidence of individual rates bound against increase in the GATT.[23]

Second, the lowering of tariff levels achieved in past negotiations has pointed up the relatively increased importance of NTBs. So many countries now share this view and so much background material has been prepared that most of the participants in a negotiation are committed to serious consideration of the NTB problem. No country has yet committed itself to make concessions. But the first step of getting countries to the table has already been achieved.

Third, the United States has shown that it can also play the game. With the adoption of the DISC legislation in 1971—the statute under which U.S. exporters can set up Domestic International Sales Corporations in order to defer income taxes indefinitely on their export earnings—the United States has adopted a counterpart to foreign government remissions of internal taxes on the occasion of the export of goods. Some GATT members have raised the question of the DISC's GATT legality—whether income taxes, rather than only excise and sales taxes, can be remitted without running afoul of the GATT prohibition against certain export subsidies on manufactured goods. But that cloudy question may only be settled by negotiation, which could be aimed at a general restraint on the use of tax remission schemes. If not settled, the legal question might be made moot by a new restraint on the part of foreign governments under threat of more ambitious U.S. use of the tax incentive technique.

A special headache for governments in negotiating on nontariff distortions comes from figuring out how to quantify liberalization and how to measure reciprocity. As the past hodgepodge of results shows, some agreements on particular devices may be self-contained; on others, tariff and nontariff concessions might be packaged together (as in the 1967 "ASP Agreement" on tariff valuation rules relating to certain benzenoid chemicals, on tariff cuts on benzenoid and other chemicals, and on effective discrimination in applying "road taxes").

E. The Trade and Monetary Negotiations Link

The international economic crises of the last few years, especially the one that led to the temporary application of U.S. import surcharges in mid-August 1971 and to the Smithsonian arrangements in mid-December of that year, have made the relationship between trade and monetary actions clearer than ever before. In the past, the two areas were abnormally compartmentalized. They were treated to a very great extent in separate international forums—the IMF and GATT—and generally by different ministries in most governments. Given the events of 1971, there is a heightened sensitivity to the need for closer coordination, if not common action, between the two areas.

Insofar as the trade negotiations are concerned, two fundamental issues must be addressed by the negotiators. The first is whether those negotiations should be linked with negotiations for monetary reform. The second is whether the balance-of-payments adjustment mechanism in the trade field can be improved—either working alone or in conjunction with monetary measures.

Governments will feel their way cautiously to decide what the relationship between the trade and monetary negotiations should be. Some governments may want to avoid anything more definite than the blandness of expected statements about linking "satisfactory progress" in one field to "satisfactory progress" in the other. Without prejudice to the possible substantive links, an institutional relationship could be established—such as having some body common to the IMF and the GATT report in one of those organizations on progress in the other and stand ready to solicit technical assistance from one to aid the other.

Governments may be less cautious in searching for some way of making the GATT more "relevant" to today's demands for balance-of-payments adjustment in the trade field. Since its inception in 1948, the GATT has permitted only one trade measure to countries suffering balance-of-payments difficulties, namely, to impose import quotas. Increasingly, in recent years, GATT contracting parties have resorted to import surcharges to limit their expenditures on imports. Following its use in the 1950s by Peru, developed countries resorted to it—in the 1960s particularly Canada, Denmark, France, and the United Kingdom, and, as part of the President's New Economic Policy, in August 1971, the United States. In his address to the September 1972 annual meeting of the International Monetary Fund and the World Bank, U.S. Secretary of the Treasury George P. Shultz proposed temporary, across-the-board surcharges.[24]

The choice in writing into the GATT an exception to the basic prohibitions against quantitative restrictions and against duties in excess of those in the schedules of concessions to permit emergency action to protect a deteriorating balance of payments was deliberate. The theory was that a quota is easily identifiable and therefore is more likely to be removed at the end of an emergency than would a supplemental tariff. Also, quotas can be precise in limiting expenditures on imports, whereas the precise effect of import surcharges cannot be predicted.

Surcharges have become preferred to quotas for a variety of reasons. Most important, it appears, surcharges do not require the development and administration of a new import control program. They can be applied quickly and with little additional burden to customs administration.

Also, although their application contravenes the GATT, the contracting parties have explicitly or tacitly consented to surcharges on condition that they be removed as quickly as possible or by a specified deadline.

Amending the GATT to permit import surcharges as an alternative to, or as substitute for, import quotas for balance-of-payments protection would regularize the hitherto illegal use of a trade measure and could put pressure on countries with unjustifiably large surpluses to take corrective action.

Whether the amendment would ever be adopted (the amendment procedure being exasperatingly slow at best) and whether it would provide pressure on the surplus country would depend largely on some important elements. Secretary Shultz' speech left these details unspoken.

While it is the GATT that would be amended to permit deficit countries to impose temporary surcharges, would it be the IMF that would decide whether deficit countries, individually or collectively, could impose those import restraints? If so, the device would stand as a weapon of collective self-defense to be used after an international judgment was made of the failure of adequate unilateral remedial action by the surplus country and the probable benefit of collective international action.

Would the import surcharge be applied by deficit countries to all their imports and at a uniform rate—which is the implication of Secretary Shultz' statement that any trade controls for balance of payments reasons "be in the form of surcharges or across-the-board taxes"? Imposition of surcharges at a uniform rate might be considered analogous to the change in exchange rates—a preferred device for balance-of-payments adjustment—but confined only to the trade account. But countries imposing surcharges have found it necessary to differentiate among imports for economic or domestic legal reasons. Generally, they find it practically impossible to apply the regular rate—or any rate—to "essentials," to raw materials that are important for export industries, to goods whose prices adversely impact the consumers' market basket, or to traditionally duty-free merchandise.

Would the surcharge be applied only to the recalcitrant surplus country or countries or to all supplying countries? In a world of foreign exchange convertibility, does discrimination in balance-of-payments adjustment make sense? In a situation in which growing concern is expressed about growing preferences (at least by the EC in favor of African and Mediterranean countries), does stand-by authority for trade discrimination make sense?

Today one tends to think of Japan as the possible prime target of surcharges. By the time any IMF and GATT system came into force, would the potential target be the United States?

IV. Conclusions

Motivation. The major United States task in getting trade negotiations underway in 1973 will be in stimulating interest among its major trading partners or at least putting them in a position in which they will find their disinterest too awkward to maintain. The newly enlarged, nine-member European Community understandably will not want to be bothered by negotiations with the United States and other third countries while it is passing through another Community transitional period. However, the EC attitude is neither new nor better justified than it was during the earlier days of European integration. The Dillon Round came just as the Community was taking the first steps in what was then planned as a twelve to fifteen year transitional period; the Kennedy Round was carried out toward the end of that period. The technical complications were mastered, and the economic adjustments of the two sets of trade liberalization—the Community's own integration steps and the liberalization toward outside countries—presented no insuperable problems.

Part of the stimulus will have to be a call for a common effort to a common problem; part will have to be an offer of interesting U.S. trade concessions.

The U.S. trade deficit. In considering what it will seek and what it will offer, the United States should not lose sight of the most fundamental advantages of trade liberalization by concentrating on the use of the negotiation to alter its imbalance of imports over exports. Insofar as the trade balance is concerned, it will be sufficient to stem the recent rapid deterioration and not to turn the deficit into a surplus. Even to suggest—consciously or unintentionally—that the latter outcome was the U.S. goal would drive other prospective participants from the conference hall.

The centerpiece of the negotiation. Whatever may be said either carelessly or validly about tariff negotiations being old-hat and perhaps not worth the bother, and about NTBs being the thing of the day, the centerpiece of the trade negotiation is bound to be further tariff reduction.

Tariff reduction remains important today because tariffs still have important trade effects. Also, tariff cuts are needed to limit the adverse effects of any trade diversion that will occur as new countries join the EC or affiliate with it in some free-trade on preferential trade arrangement. More important—although perhaps less rational—tariffs are simply more susceptible to negotiation and to liberalization than are nontariff devices that influence trade.

Also, tariff bargaining will be taking place outside the trade conference, and those peripheral negotiations might stimulate an interest in more comprehensive tariff bargaining. First, apart from the contemplated trade conference, the EC must negotiate with third countries over the increases in individual duties of the Six and of the three acceding countries as a new Common External Tariff (CXT) is formed out of the old CXT and of the other individual tariffs. Second, the United States may decide to adopt the Brussels Tariff Nomenclature and move toward the Brussels system of customs valuation and would have to renegotiate its existing concessions to bring them into line with the new system.

A useful basis for the tariff negotiation would be to establish an average weighted 50 percent reduction target, with countries free to be selective in their offers—offering cuts from zero to 100 percent. The 50 percent rule should apply to all articles, except those agricultural imports that are subject primarily to variable levies, quotas, or other nontariff barriers. The technique should achieve a critical requirement of opening the negotiation with a maximum offer by each country, leaving it to them to cut back as necessary to achieve whatever they would require as satisfactorily reciprocal concessions. The linear technique of the Kennedy Round, although successful for that conference, is not likely to prove acceptable for the next negotiation without drastic qualification. It would be far wiser to formulate a different, reasonable, and acceptable procedure at the outset of the negotiation than to adopt a technique that itself would require extensive bargaining.

NTBs. While tariff cutting will be the focal point, NTBs may be accented as the special feature of the negotiations. Certainly, they must be included in a substantial way. But progress will be meager, and participants should not build up false expectations. The United States, as it prepares to attack other countries' NTBs must be aware that other countries' lists of NTB complaints against the United States is of comparable length. It must be prepared to defend or negotiate on those complaints if it has any hope of making a dent in the NTBs of other countries.

Agriculture. Farm products must be covered. The insistence of a tie between agriculture and industry in the negotiations should, however, not be allowed to become so comprehensive or rigid as to make concessions on industrial trade a hostage to concessions on the CAP. If the United States is not content to settle for concessions only on the farm products now subject to fixed duties, but insists on concessions on the EC's CAP, it may jeopardize the entire conference.

There is no reason, however, to set aside CAP items at the outset of the conference. The EC—in the 1967 World Grains Arrangement—negotiated concessions on prices, and it might find it feasible and profitable to do so again. Furthermore, setting aside the CAP items might lead to setting aside all of agriculture—because much of the world's agricultural production and trade is subject to governmental policies other than tariffs. Deferral to another negotiation confined to agricultural concessions from the EC in the future, since the United States would have little to offer the enlarged EC.

Countries in that arrangement do not export important agricultural products to the United States (except Scotch whiskey, which happens to be classified as agricultural in the scientifically devised Brussels Tariff Nomenclature, and cheeses, which are subject to U.S. quotas that are supposed to protect a dairy support program).

Negotiations for a fundamental transformation in the CAP could be undertaken if they called for adjustments over a long period—on the order of 10 years—and, more important, if they were part of a program under which the United States and the other key participants put up all their agricultural border protection for concession. Those concessions would call for a progressive lowering of border restraints against imports and of stimuli for exports, regardless of the techniques used, and would force governments unilaterally over the years to change or eliminate domestic farm programs that underlie so much of the official ordering of world farm trade.

The miscellaneous and peripheral issues. A trade negotiation should have room for the seemingly endless trade issues that are certain to be proposed for inclusion at the outset and as the conference moves along. But the hopeless cases should be weeded out.

A large reservoir of issues—EC preference to Mediterranean countries, "reverse preferences" by developing countries (generally African) to certain industrialized countries (generally the EC), the U.S.-Canadian Automotive Agreement, East-West trade—can provide the pieces for conjuring up settlements in which the many countries with greatly diverse interests can find "mutual benefit."

If the conference drags, and only the most uncontrollably optimistic would anticipate otherwise, delegations can be kept together by working on subsidiary problems while governments maneuver to unstick the big issues.

The link between the trade and monetary negotiations. The substantive and procedural relationships between negotiations on international monetary reform and on trade matters must be worked out as those two activities move along. Clearly, special attention will have to be given to import surcharges, whether in the monetary sphere or trade sphere or both. However, it would be unwise to try to fix the relationships between the two sets of negotiating activities before rather definite lines of settlement on monetary reform emerge.

Domestic authority. The United States will be wasting its time in leading countries to the bargaining table if it is unable to give them reasonable assurance that a final agreement will be carried out. In the light of numerous trade negotiations with the United States since 1934, other governments are familiar with U.S. domestic political realities in regard to trade agreements. They know that without specific authority from the Congress, or some form of prior approval from the Congress, the success of the agreements reached will be endangered. The United States cannot expect other countries to table offers until the U.S. Congress has given the president authority to put negotiated tariffs into effect and has given a sound indication that nontariff barrier settlements brought home by the president will be approved.

Notes

1. U.S.-European Community declaration, issued in Washington and Brussels, February 11, 1972. The U.S.-Japanese declaration, with virtually identical language to that quoted, was issued on February 9. Department of the Treasury press release, February 11, 1972 (texts of both declarations).

2. Press release 161 of the Office of Special Representative for Trade Negotiations, Executive Office of the President, Washington.

3. Eberle at Rutgers University, New Brunswick, N.J., June 7, 1972. STR Press release 165.

4. Some dutiable imports, most importantly automobiles, were subjected to a less than 10 percent surcharge or to none at all. Dutiable imports were subjected to lesser surcharges if the full surcharge would have resulted in total duties in excess of the "column 2" rates in the U.S. tariffs schedules, those rates being essentially the Smoot-Hawley rates of 1930. Also, imports under quota were not subjected to the surcharges.

5. For other motives for the NEP, see C. Fred Bergsten, "The New Economics and U.S. Foreign Policy," FOREIGN AFFAIRS 51, 2 (January 1972): 199.

6. On a balance-of-payments basis, which differs slightly from the Census basis for determining the trade balance.

7. Devaluation of the dollar, measured in terms of new par values and "central rates," amount to 9 percent weighted by the import trade of other industrialized countries.

8. For example, Arthur F. Burns, Chairman, Board of Governors of the Federal Reserve System, before the Joint Economic Committee, U.S. Congress, July 26, 1972. Federal Reserve BULLETIN, August 1972, pp. 696-700.

9. Another uncertainty will be the extent of the development of the EC policy of granting preferential treatment to the Mediterranean, African, and possibly other countries. This policy will surely provide the basis for debate on nondiscrimination; that is, on the concept of most favored-nation treatment.

10. Averages weighted by own trade and further weighted by trade of EC, United States, Canada, Japan, U.K., Sweden, Denmark, Norway, Finland, Switzerland, and Austria. Imports in 1967, except 1968 for Canada. Duties reflecting Kennedy Round concessions. See BASIC DOCUMENTATION FOR TARIFF STUDY, GATT, Geneva, July 1970.

11. In recent years, the U.S. Congress has suspended several duties—for example, on minerals in raw form—and authorized the president to make the duty-free treatment permanent in trade negotiations. Among others, PL 89-204, 79 Stat.839, approved September 27, 1965, on certain nickel items.

12. For example, a country's duties might be weighted by the imports in the respective products for an agreed base year, into all OECD countries, rather than into all countries in the negotiation period. Also, if a large number of the participants, say, the developing countries, do not accept the 50 percent tariff reduction rule, the weighting might be confined to the import trade of those participants accepting the rule. With regard to the base year selected for data purposes, 1970 may be the latest year for which data would be available for most or all participants' trade at the outset of the conference. It may be necessary to use earlier years' data for some countries. It may also be feasible to

agree, if the negotiation is long, on shifting to a later year. If the base year is 1972 or later, it would permit the use of data covering trade influenced by the full Kennedy Round cuts; 1970 would reflect only partial effects of that conference.

13. Participants would surely withhold some tariffs completely, reduce others less than 50 percent, and they would therefore have to offset those less-than-target reductions by greater cuts on some products, virtually ensuring that some rates would be eliminated.

The margin of selectivity could be reduced by setting the 50 percent goal for categories of commodities—say, for raw materials for semi-manufactures, and for finished goods—rather than for all dutiable imports collectively.

14. For example, the Commission on International Trade and Investment Policy (Williams Commission). See its 1971 report to the President, U.S. Government Printing Office. Also, U.S. presentation to GATT ministerial-level session, November 10, 1972. NEW YORK TIMES, November 11, 1972.

15. The linear or across-the-board formula called for the reduction, by 50 percent, of all industrial tariffs, with a bare minimum of exceptions that would be subject to confrontation and justification. The rule was accepted by the United States, the United Kingdom, the European Economic Community, the EFTA countries, and Japan. See the author's "The Kennedy Round: A Try at Linear Trade Negotiations," THE JOURNAL OF LAW AND ECONOMICS 12, 2 (October 1969): 297-319.

16. Each withdrawal of a U.S. concession on which Japan was the principal supplier meant some loss of potential trade benefit to the European Community, the U.K., Australia, or almost any other country, each of which would have enjoyed the concession as a result of the most-favored-nation application of each country's tariff. The countries that found themselves suddenly deprived of certain concessions from the United States found it almost impossible to withdraw concessions that would impact the United States, because to do so they would also withhold the same concessions from other, secondary suppliers, which, in turn. . . . And so it would go. The United States had a strong defense in that the negotiating rules expressly preserved the right of a country to engage in such a final balancing act. Also, the United States had subjected its offers to fewer exceptions than its negotiating partners as a whole. Moreover, most participants in that negotiation made no effort to adopt the linear rule. The withdrawal process commenced so late in the conference that other countries' offsetting withdrawals, which threatened a thorough unraveling of the agreement, were limited.

17. The Reciprocal Trade Agreement Act, originally adopted in 1934, permitted the president to proclaim negotiated reductions of U.S. tariff rates by as much as 50 percent and set forth detailed procedural requirements. The basic 50 percent authority was extended several times (and re-based, in 1945, on rates then reflecting earlier concessions), and the procedural requirements were

expanded and tightened. The authority was renewed in the 1950s, first at 15 percent and then at 20 percent.

18. Japan or any other country that would consider itself a likely target would insist on a nondiscriminatory standard.

19. The resulting settlement of the disparities issue was a general acceptance of the main line of the argument, a small but otherwise undefined credit by the United States to the EEC in a bilateral balancing session, and a final haggling on concessions such as a 20 percent cut on the U.S. duty of 9/10 of one percent on hyacinth bulbs.

20. An important unresolved problem may jeopardize any advance in agricultural negotiations. In 1962, when the United States and the EEC could not agree on new agricultural concessions, the United States accepted an I.O.U. in a formal Standstill Agreement. Rights to new concessions preserved by that Agreement were not cashed in during the Kennedy Round. They could be carried over indefinitely, but the United States government may not find that course of action easy to accept.

21. As further examples, the GATT "Review Session" of 1954-55 was devoted exclusively to a rewriting of all the GATT provisions other than the tariff schedules. Also, the conference that led to the GATT itself reached agreement on a comprehensive, although heavily qualified, commitment to outlaw the use of the import quota and other nontariff restrictions—whether those devices were applied to articles subject to tariff concessions or not. Furthermore, much of the bargaining at other regular sessions and at lesser meetings has also been devoted to NTBs.

22. On the contrary, overwhelming success was achieved: in *extending* the life of some NTBs, specifically, import quotas on cotton textiles through the prolongation of the Cotton Textile Arrangement; and in avoiding attack of U.S. import quotas on petroleum imports—which covered over a billion dollars' worth of trade—since Venezuela, the dominant supplying country to the United States, was not a participant in the conference.

23. There would be two elements calling for respecifying rates in order to prevent an unintended increase in the restrictive effect of the tariff. First, each ad valorem rate would have to be reduced, since it would in the future be applied not only to the value of the good in the exporting country but to that value plus the cost of transportation to the United States. A 10 percent duty on the f.o.b. basis might have to be respecified as 9 percent on a c.i.f. basis. Second, having done that, some further reduction might be necessary to prevent the incidence of the new duty from increasing for distant countries. For example, Canada might come out all right with a 9 percent rate but Australia might suffer an increase at that new rate because of the relatively high freight charges to which it would apply and might demand an 8 percent rate to avoid any increase in tariff effect. That 8 percent rate would then become the new most-favored nation rate.

24. Press release No. 21, IMF/IBRD/IFC/IDA, Washington, September 26, 1972.

Deadweight Loss in International Trade from the Profit Motive?

Paul A. Samuelson

The theoretical models of international trade, from Ricardo to the latest textbooks of mainstream economics, usually ignore profit rates—and their alleged tendency to be higher in the capital-poor underdeveloped world than in the advanced nations. Can the existence of profit differentials negate the verities of the theory of comparative advantage?

When I began to investigate this highly-relevant question, I had not enjoyed the opportunity of reading the interesting Marxian analysis by Dr. A. Emmanuel, entitled *Unequal Exchange.*[1] The present finding does not have a direct bearing on the Emmanuel thesis that equalization of the profit rate, by capital mobility from the low-interest advanced world to the capital-poor less developed nations, represents *unequal* exchange—and helps to explain both the lowness of real wages in the poor regions and how those wages can be raised by substantial percentages. So I leave to another occasion an audit of unequal exchange,[2] and tackle head on the vital question of whether the existence of profit vitiates efficient international trade.

Before Profit

Suppose Asia, with ten times the population of America, can produce only about the same amounts of food and clothing as America. But suppose the ratio of labor costs of food to clothing is 2-to-1 in Asia as against 1-to-2 in America. Suppose everyone everywhere spends half his income on food and half on clothing.

Then on the understanding that labor is the only factor of production and that profit rates are zero in both countries so that all time-phasings of labor inputs can be ignored, we can state the following properties of competitive equilibrium:

1. Asia will specialize on clothing in which she has Ricardian comparative advantage. America will specialize on food. Asian food imports will equal in value America's clothing imports; on our special demand assumptions, half of the GNP will be in the foreign trade sectors.

I owe thanks to the National Science Foundation for financial aid.

2. Despite the fact that America ends up ten times better off in per capita real incomes, people in both regions gain from this competitive trade: trade brings gains to the typical Asian and also to the typical American. (It is not very meaningful to ask, Which gains most in trade?)

Worldwide, more of both food and clothing is produced as a result of the geographical specialization and trade. Figure 9-1 shows world production possibilities in the steady state, FEC, with specialization. Compare the post-trade equilibrium at E with the autarky total of world production at A. Specialization permits, in this example, a 33 1/3 percent increase in every output and in average world productivity.[3]

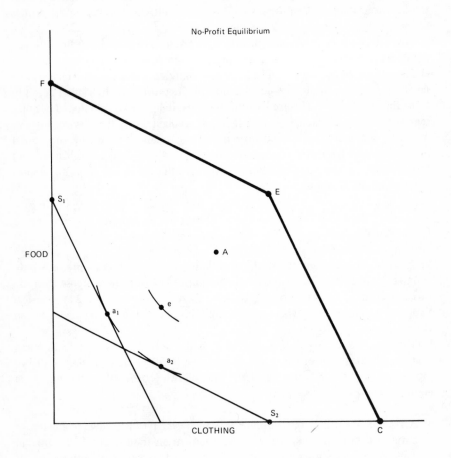

Figure 9-1. Deadweight Loss in International Trade from the Profit Motive

Effect of Positive Profit Differentials

All the above is elementary Ricardian comparative advantage. Being elementary, it ignores the time-phasing of labor inputs and the effects of that on relative unit costs of production when the competitive profit rate is positive, $r>0$. Now, as Marxian and non-Marxian economists recognize, steady-state autarky price ratios will differ from ratios of embodied-labor costs, the degree of the differences depending upon the height of the rate of profit.

Let us suppose that there will be balanced trade between continents, but no borrowing or lending. Let us concentrate on equilibria that will be observed under steady states, when productions, consumptions, wages, and prices never change. Suppose for whatever reason—it could be greater Ramsey-Böhm systematic time preference—the profit rate is higher in Asia than in America. And suppose that clothing production is more roundabout than that of food in both countries, in the unambiguous sense that the domestic cost ratios of clothing to food increase uniformly with respect to increases in the profit rate r.

Then, under autarky, America's clothing-food price ratio would be raised a bit above 2/1 by our low, positive r. Under autarky, Asia's clothing-food price ratio would be raised very much above 1/2 by the high r there. If the profit differential is large enough both before and after trade—remember that no lending is permitted that could serve to erode that differential or wipe it out—Asia may be *forced to specialize in food for which we have seen she was unfit in terms of socially necessary labor costs.* America will be *forced to specialize in clothing, for which she had a comparative disadvantage at zero profits.*

Figure 9-2 shows final world equilibrium at E', with 50 percent less production than at E, the zero-profit equilibrium. Consumption standards are shown for America and Asia, at e' where both are worse off than at the e point enjoyed in Figure 9-1's zero-profit equilibrium. Actually the citizens of both continents are worse off in this positive-profit free-trade equilibrium than they would have been under autarky (either with or without positive profits). Apparently the existence of positive profit rates has not only wiped out all the gains from trade, it has even produced losses of production from a false and distorted geographical pattern of specilization. The reader must not think that any capitalists gain what the workers lose: actually, if production had been as at E, and allocated among the continents in any reasonable way, there would be enough extra to give capitalists more real profit income than they are getting at the actual competitive equilibrium of A and still to leave enough left over to make every worker in the world better off. Indeed, prohibitive tariffs, while they cannot undo the loss of E's beneficial geographical specialization, can at least undo the harm of the "perverse specialization" created by the profit differentials and free trade.

One is tempted to conclude, therefore, the following:

Positive profit rates—more particularly positive profit differentials—create deadweight losses of production, consumption, and welfare even when there is no

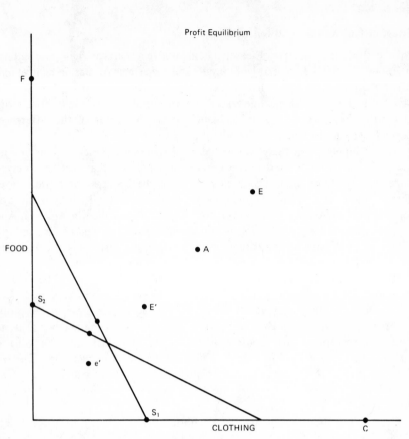

Figure 9-2. Deadweight Loss in International Trade from the Profit Motive

monopoly, no externalities, no political or imperialistic exactions, and no using up of exhaustible resources, and so forth.

A formulation like the above, if it has not yet appeared in the writings of socialist critics, some day will.[4] Therefore, it is important to appraise it unflinchingly.

A Crushing Paradox?

Russell noted that the logical system of Frege was open to a contradiction in connection with the paradox involving the class of all classes. This was recognized, by Frege, Russell, and others, as a crushing objection, requiring major repair work.

Do we have here a similar paradox? Competitive equilibrium has been proved—by Bergson, Arrow, Debreu, and earlier writers—to be Pareto-optimal, involving zero deadweight loss. I.e., not everybody can be made better off by a feasible departure from the competitive equilibrium position. Here, we seem to confront a similar contradiction: the free-trade equilibrium cum competitive profit differentials is alleged to be non-Pareto-optimal and to involve deadweight loss.

My own conclusion is otherwise. *No, there is not deadweight loss in the strict sense of the term. The contradiction is only apparent.* The argument founders on a subtle pitfall involved in stead-state comparisons.

There are many ways to explain this subtle point. Perhaps the simplest is to begin at the competitive equilibrium shown at E' in Figure 9-2. Show, if you can, that there is a feasible path of going from E' to E, the better steady-state configuration, so as to make *every* American and *every* Asian better off in the transition. I say, *You cannot find such a path; it does not exist.* Comparing A and E is really comparing cheese and chalk, comparing life as it is with life as it might be if popsicles grew on trees; or, more accurately, comparing E' and E is comparing life now with what it *could* be after someone has abstained from current consumption goods in order that somewhere in the world there would be a greater accumulation of goods-in-process or equipment in the clothing industry.

To be sure, if we let America lend to Asia, building up there the capital goods in clothing needed to make the E steady state possible, there would be enough extra output brought into existence by that lending process to enable the debt to be repaid with interest and still leave enough left over to make every Asian (and every noncapitalist and capitalist in America) better off than in the pre-lending equilibrium at E'.

In brief, as Joan Robinson has been warning economists for the last twenty years, you must not look at a steady-state locus like FEC in Figure 9-1, and think that the world is free to choose indifferently among the points on it. Such a locus implies synchronization of time-phased inputs and presupposes in the background requisite stocks of heterogeneous capital goods that are different in quantities at each point. To go from points inside such a frontier to the frontier will involve sacrifices of some goods at one time in return for more goods at another later date.[5]

Conclusion

Competitive profit differentials as such cannot create wht is literally deadweight loss, whatever they may do to the inequity of the distribution of laissez-faire incomes.

Notes

1. Monthly Review Press, New York, 1972, a translation of L'ÉCHANGE INÉGAL, (Paris: Libraire Francois Maspero, 1969), including two Appendixes by the distinguished Marxist, Professor Charles Bettelheim of the École Pratique des Hautes Études of the Sorbonne. The full English title is UNEQUAL EXCHANGE¾ A STUDY OF THE IMPERIALISM OF TRADE.

2. I deal with this in a forthcoming paper entitled "Illogic of Neo-Marxian Doctrine of Unequal Exchange."

3. If instead of the numbers 2-to-1 I had used 4-to-1, or 1 1/2-to-1, the gains in per capita productions would have been 66 2/3, or 20, percent. The extreme symmetry assumptions make such definite statements possible.

4. Cf. the cited work on UNEQUAL EXCHANGE, which does not quite reach the present findings.

5. Reswitching phenomena do not affect this argument. But we should be aware of the possibility that a point like E', although it may be dominated in the steady state by some point northeast of it, say A, might have a superior potentiality for getting to some other third point! The present argument is not critically affected by the question of whether intermediate goods themselves can be traded internationally. Thus, semi-fabricated cloth, if it can be traded, may get exported to Asia to be finished there.

Part III:
International Development

 # Economic Dependence and Policy in Developing Countries

Robert LeRoy West

Introduction

The study of comparative economic systems, which George Halm pioneered at the Fletcher School, attempts to explain differences in national economic structures and to account for differences among countries in economic goals and instruments employed to influence performance of the economy. It is necessarily a cross-disciplinary subject, entailing investigation of the different political processes by which goals are determined and administrative means by which they are implemented. In the forty years during which George Halm has contributed to the subject its range of contemporary observations has been greatly enlarged by interest in the economic policies and performance of less developed countries; concurrent interest in explaining differences in political structures and accounting for differences in political goals and instruments among less developed countries has enriched and systematized the study of comparativypolitical systems. The marriage of such a perfectly matched couple, with so many interests in common, seems virtually preordained.

Whether jointly employed in or out of wedlock, the methods of comparative economic and political analysis are uniquely fitted to study the conduct of foreign affairs by less developed countries. In the Third World foreign and domestic policies are closely intertwined. Actions affecting foreign relations generally have an immediate impact on domestic affairs, while the taproot of foreign policy reaches into the strata where the most critical domestic issues are encountered. There is no closed model which can adequately describe the behavior of economic or political systems of less developed countries; there are few, and only quite secondary, aspects of foreign affairs which are not managed primarily by reference to internal issues. Moreover, foreign political policies generally yield to an explanation in terms of economic interests and foreign economic policies are governed by political considerations. Characteristically, foreign and internal goals and instruments are adopted in "packages" which must satisfy dominant political preferences, rooted in economic interest.

If improved understanding of these relationships is of overriding interest to the managers of foreign and domestic affairs in less developed countries, it is also important to those in more developed countries responsible for the conduct of relations with developed societies. There is need for a more accurate appraisal of the available choices among goals and policy instruments in different less developed countries, and how these choices are affected by actions of the more developed countries with respect to trade, aid, and investment relations. This need may be especially acute with respect to the administration of foreign aid, where the donor seeks to employ economic resources as an instrument of its foreign policy, frequently to collaborate more or less purposefully with the aid-receiving government in altering domestic structures.

Unfortunately, the relationship of economic structure to the selection of national goals and the basis on which choices are made of instruments for implementing policies in less developed countries constitute a primitive area of knowledge. There is a substantial literature, but it is largely descriptive, often polemical, and low in analytical content. There are, however, notable exceptions, and this study is importantly indebted to two major comparative analyses of behavior in this area. First, Hollis Chenery and his associates have sought to identify the origins of differences in economic structure and their relationship to patterns or strategies of economic growth; in a series of papers over the past decade Chenery and his colleagues have summarized much of what is known about this relationship in less developed countries and have reported on econometric tests of the comparative importance of a number of factors in a large number of countries.[1] Second, the Committee for the Comparative Study of New Nations of the University of Chicago has published case studies and conclusions drawn from its exploration of development policy and planning, with special attention to the nature and influence of economic nationalism.[2]

This relatively uncharted area has been a major focus of investigation for the Fletcher School's International Development Studies program. Borrowing methodological tools from comparative economic and political analysis, the contributions of Chenery and his associates and the University of Chicago Committee, and other more or less verified hypotheses about the process of change in less developed countries, a framework has been established for study of the ways in which changes in economic and political structures are interrelated. This framework has been employed by research associates and graduate students participating in the program to prepare country studies, each based on research in the country or direct experience in working with the government of the country.[3]

In this paper we employ information supplied by twenty-eight of these country studies, for which an adequate and comparable range of data has been found. The twenty-eight countries are listed in the Annex. They include seven Middle East and Asian countries, three in North Africa, nine in Africa south of the Sahara, and nine in Latin America and the Caribbean. They have highly varied structures and have experienced a wide variety of changes in the past two decades; there are very substantial differences in observed goals and instruments of policy. They range in size from one to 100 million and together had a population of 536 million reported in 1965, about one-half the population of all

Third World countries other than India and China. There is no basis, however, for asserting that their experience is characteristic of or encompasses that of all less developed countries.

In this comparative study of the experience of twenty-eight countries we will concentrate on differences in the perception of economic dependence: how to account for the differences, how they relate to structural characteristics, and how they are associated with "packages" of foreign and domestic policies. We will explore the political factors which appear to define the perceived options with respect to economic goals and instruments to implement economic policies, and the economic factors which seem to guide the political process of choice. We will present some tentative hypotheses to account for the observed clusters of different countries' experience, why foreign and domestic policies appear to be adopted in a few discrete combinations, and why a country's path of policies through time is constrained.[4] We will conclude with some suggestions for applied uses of this kind of analysis.

Perceptions of Economic Dependence

We assume it is generally recognized that the attainment of economic independence is among the most persistently specified goals of developing countries. In all of the twenty-eight countries included in this study it appears among the most compelling objectives cited in the statements of politicians and the writings of political-economists.

Of course, definitional precision is not assured by frequency of use. But we think Reginald Green has captured, in his working definition of the term, what is generally meant by national economic independence: "a situation in which national institutions (including private business and interest groups) have the right, capacity, and power to take and to implement decisions affecting the national economy and its component units without a *de jure* or *de facto* veto power being held by foreign individuals, enterprises, interest groups, or governments."[5] So defined, the degree of national economic independence can be assessed by evaluating the areas in which and the degree to which national right, capacity, and power exist (to take and implement decisions) in contrast with the areas and degrees of foreign right, capacity, and power.

If we seek an operationally significant concept, national economic independence suffers from several sources of ambiguity.[6] Nonetheless, politicians and economists seem capable of distinguishing it from other goals. When it is cited as an objective a definite meaning is communicated—as well as an emotive reaction elicited.

The important differences appear when those who cite the objective identify the particular conditions in a developing country which are asserted to be most significantly divergent from the conditions of economic independence. We find that substantively different viewpoints are expressed when, with reference to a given country, different observers identify the central, defining characteristics of economic dependence of the nation. When generalizing about developing countries as a whole, the observers reiterate the different viewpoints as they specify the key differences between characteristics of present developing countries and characteristics associated with national economic independence.

The observers to whom we refer are politicians, economists, journalists, and civil servants in developing countries. We believe the viewpoints they articulate are those of the interest groups with which they are associated; when the spokesman is associated with a dominant interest group in his country, the viewpoint he expresses is generally the same as that of the political regime defined in official statements and actions of the state. We will discuss later the evidence that different observers' viewpoints are systematically related to interest and political circumstance, and that the statements and actions of a political regime are associated with particular aspects of the country's relations with foreigners. But our purpose here is to define the different viewpoints, show how each is believed related to the attainment of economic development, and how each is associated with a particular strategy to reduce the economic dependency of the nation.

The twenty-eight case-studies which we have inspected generally confirm the observation of Dharam Ghai about the concept of economic dependence in African countries:

When politicians and economists talk of the economic dependence of developing countries, they may be referring to some or all of the following features of their economies: (1) structural characteristics of production and trade; (2) foreign aid and private capital flows form a high proportion of both public and total investment in the country; (3) the share of foreigners in both the stock of capital in the modern sector and of skilled manpower is high; as a consequence of this, the foreign share in gross domestic income is high.[7]

In addition, but only in some cases, the reference may be to their countries' involvement in an international system of trade and production which is predominantly under foreign control or influence. It is the relative weighting of these features which results in different viewpoints with respect to the central characteristics of economic dependence.

We find there are three different perceptions of the meaning of economic dependence of developing countries. One viewpoint holds that the central explanation of economic dependence is the dominating presence of foreigners in the ownership of assets and in jobs of high skill and influence in the economy. This perception of dependence stresses reliance on external capital and man-power, both private and official. It is relatively unambiguous; in Ghai's words, "a country which draws heavily on foreign capital, enterprise and skills is dependent in the tautological sense."[8]

A second viewpoint is that the critical characteristics of dependence are those describing the structure of production and international transactions of the developing country—emphasizing the commodity composition, concentration, and technological level of the developing economy's output and foreign trade compared with those of industrial or rich countries. This perception of dependence, stressing the structure of production and trade, is less clear in application. With respect to the composition and concentration of national output, at least, not all developing countries are similar and not all rich countries are markedly different from many poor countries; there is similar ambiguity with respect to the proportion of foreign trade to total national production, and just how the composition of international trade is related to dependence is unclear. Recognizing these difficulties, nonetheless Ghai concludes that "in some weighted average sense, the poor countries can be shown to display greater dependence in the intensity and range of characteristics associated with (this perception) of economic dependence."[9] Whether this can be shown or not, many observers perceive national economic dependence in these terms.

A third viewpoint defines economic dependence as participation of the developing country in the international capitalist system of trade, organization of production, and division of labor; by this perception, dependence is a necessary, inescapable, and permanent characteristic of developing economies which adhere to the periphery of the international system organized and controlled at the center by the industrial, capitalist economies. This viewpoint is more often expressed by intellectuals than by other observers; in the twenty-eight case-studies it appears to be held by spokesmen for dominant interest groups in only two countries. But there is a rapidly growing literature defining this perception, which rests on an interpretation of the historical evolution of the international capitalist economy.[10] This evolution is believed to have produced two kinds of polarization, one domestic and the other international. The domestic polarization within a developing society is between groups which are related to high-growth sectors of the economy and marginal groups which are not, while the international polarization is between countries at the capitalist, industrial center of the system and developing countries on the periphery. The two kinds of polarization are related; high-income groups in the developing countries are linked to similar groups in the industrial countries through a worldwide technocratic bureaucracy. Because the priorities and needs of the industrial center of the system predominate, there is persistent evolution toward greater dependence of developing societies, growth of marginalism, and reinforced polarization. An interpretation of this complexity is, naturally, subject to various simplifications and versions.[11]

We do not propose to explore here the teleological aspect of these viewpoints, but to observe that, with a high degree of consistency in the twenty-eight case-studies, each of these three perceptions of national economic dependence is associated with a particular view of its relationship to the attainment of economic development and a specific preference among strategies to reduce the economic dependence of developing countries. While economic development of the nation is among the most frequently expressed objectives of observers in all the case-study countries, we find less agreement on the meaning of the term than on the definition of national economic independence. Generally, economic development seems to include, among ideas less universally expressed, the concept of growth in real assets and income of the nation at rates higher than those of the population or number of households. Almost as frequently, the term "development" is associated with particular kinds of changes in the composition of national output, exports, and the labor force.

Despite variations in the meaning assigned to the term, we attach importance to the evidence that each perception of national economic dependence is associated with a different conception of how efforts to reduce dependence are related to the attainment of economic development. When economic dependence is defined as the dominating presence of foreigners in the economy the observer generally conceives of independence and development as autonomous goals; at leas in the short run, the two objectives are believed to be in conflict and tradeoffs between the two are usually or frequently required. When observers perceive dependence in terms of the structure of production and trade they usually believe that achievement of rapid economic development is the necessary condition for reduction of national economic dependence; sufficient conditions are defined by the pattern of economic growth, which should result in diversification of production and international trade, localization of control over use of economic assets and performance of the economy, and more equitable distribution of economic opportunities and benefits. Finally, those who define dependence as participation in the international capitalist system generally hold the view that attainment of national economic independence is a prior, necessary condition for attaining economic development.

With a consistency that we find impressive, each perception of dependence is also associated with a preferred strategy for reducing the national economic dependence of developing countries. When the dominating presence of foreigners in the economy is believed to be the central characteristic of dependence, generally the preferred strategy seems to rest on the promise that developing countries can generally, and with high likelihood of success, attain accommodation of their most critical needs and goals through their international economic relations. Specific policies associated with the preferred strategy tend to focus on localization of jobs and asset ownership and on means of strengthening the international bargaining power of the developing countries, including often through functional integration of their economies.

Those who find the central characteristics of economic dependence in the structure of production and trade are much more likely to prefer strategies based on the assumption that developing countries can somtimes, but generally only at high risk, attain accommodation of their most crucial needs through their relations with the industrialized countries. High priority is assigned to policies which mobilize national resources to sustain international economic conflict, such as efforts to secure firm state control over modern-sector assets and influential jobs, methods of expanding domestic participation and equalizing benefits to undergird regimes of austerity, and exploration of prospects for the formation of militant international economic alliances of mobilized developing countries to support bargaining with the industrial center and to exploit any divisions which may appear among the more developed countries.

When participation in the international capitalist system is perceived as the definition of national economic dependence, it is usually associated with the search for ways to disrupt the system of international capitalism; if the adoption of revolutionary strategies is judged infeasible, preference may be for policies promoting national self-reliance and insulation from international economic influence.

In the next two sections of this paper we will inspect some aspects of a nation's economic structure which are closely associated with its international economic relations. From among these we will select a few not demonstrably related to the national level of per capita income. By reference to the twenty-eight case-study countries, we will find that there is internal consistency among a group of these structural characteristics and that they are associated with political-historical factors which influence the character of each country's international economic relations. We will employ the political-historical factors to array the twenty-eight countries in clusters along a continuum which will distinguish relevant differences in country experience and differences in the dominant perception of national economic dependence.

Classical Indicators of Economic Dependence

The international trade doctrine of classical political-economy had boundaries sufficiently broad to include consideration of many characteristics distinguishing the international economic relations of "grain" exporters from those of "cloth" exporters. Some of these characteristics, certainly all those predominantly reflecting political distinctions which bear on bargaining power, were purged from international trade doctrine when economic theory was purified to separate economic analysis from the study of political relations. At least after Heckscher-Ohlin they no longer appeared among the variables of orthodox trade theory, but survived in a sort of demi-monde of "socialist" economics, critiques of the distribution of gains from trade, and "structuralist" theories. More recently they have reemerged among the indicators of structural characteristics of less developed countries, as part of the descriptive content of development economics. In this role, both the political factors which influence the characteristics of developing countries' international economic relations, and the economic structural effects of those characteristics, have regained a measure of respectability.[12]

Observers in developing countries who perceive national economic dependence in terms of the structure of production and trade might be considered to be in this classical tradition, although the strategy for reducing dependence usually associated with this perception seems to owe more to Henry Carey and Gustav Schmoller than to the free-trade classical reformers. There is also another important distinction. The classical economist focused attention on the character of influences on the conduct of international economic relations, and how these influences exercised an effect on domestic economic structure. The contemporary observers who find the central characteristics of dependence in the nation's structure of production and trade generally concentrate on the defects they perceive in the domestic economic structure—concern is focused on how these defects impair securing national control over economic decisions and performance—and how these defects permit foreign influence to be exercised on the domestic economy. There is a significant area of concurrence on the structural indicators deemed relevant but, because the foci of concern differ, there are also differences in the indicators cited. Both the classical economists and contemporary observers, however, tend to mix together structural characteristics which are known to vary systematically with income per capita and structural features which have not been shown to depend on the level of income or other similar measures of economic development. Before we can adopt these structural indicators for our purposes, we must inspect their relation to income level.

Growth of gross national product and structural change, as Hollis Chenery and others have demonstrated, may be regarded as interconnected aspects of the process of development. That rising income is associated, among countries and over time, with systematic variations in many features of the economic structure "can be traced to similarities among societies in tastes, access to technology and to international trade, and common elements of development policy."[13]

If a structural characteristic identified with dependence, or the result of an aspect of the nation's international economic relations so identified, is typically found among countries or over time associated with a given income level, and if the characteristic systematically alters in the manner defined as leading to attainment of economic independence as the level of income rises, the distinction between the goals of development and independence may reduce to a question of rates of change or differential relationship to alterations in tastes, technology, foreign markets, and policies. Such may be the case with the identification of national economic dependence with some characteristics of the composition of output of developing countries: for example, that a large proportion of output consists of primary products, while manufactured consumer goods and capital equipment form a small proportion of domestic output. It can be shown that variance in the levels of total industrial output among countries is largely explained by differences in per capita income level, with significant but secondary effects attributable to population size, income distribution, factor proportions, and national policies. For individual sectors of industry, the relative importance of non-income variables in explaining differences in output among countries varies, but the level of income predominates for the average sector of industry.[14] A somewhat greater distinction between the goals of development and independence may obtain with respect to the composition of foreign trade: for example, the proportion of manufactures in total exports and imports. Variance in these ratios among countries is partly explained by differences in income level or "development," but more significant contributions are attributable to country size, population density, and other variables.[15]

Our purpose, to the degree possible, is to isolate the goal of reducing national economic dependence and to avoid confusing the indicators of dependence with those of low development. Therefore, we will concentrate on aspects of economic structure which reflect characteristics of the nation's international economic relations, but for which variance among countries is very little or not at all explained by differences in income level.

For the twenty-eight case-study countries, we have selected a sizable number of indicators of such aspects of economic structure and tested these indicators for the consistency with which they distinguish among the countries. If these indicators are to be useful as descriptors of national economic dependence, a country which ranks high by one indicator should generally rank high by all the other indicators in the group; a country ranking intermediate or low by one, should rank intermediate or low by all. If the twenty-eight countries are rank-ordered in terms of each indicator, the group of indicators should show rank-order correlation at a significant level and each indicator should show significant correlation with the rank-order sum of all indicators in the group.

We find that four structural characteristics of the kind indicated do meet the test of consistency: (1) the trade ratio (the sum of total exports and imports as a proportion of gross national product), a measure of the relative importance to the country of its participation in international trade; (2) the export commodity concentration ratio (value of the two most important export commodities as a proportion of total exports); (3) the trading-partner concentration ratio (value of exports to the two most important trading partners as a proportion of total exports); and (4) an indicator of the relative importance of foreign-owned assets in total productive assets of the nation.[16] Among a number of measures of foreign assistance received by the twenty-eight countries only one, the value of technical assistance services as a proportion of gross national product, was marginally significant in the test of consistency (i.e., significant at between the .05 and .10 level); we infer that it measures the relative importance of foreign technical and consultative personnel provided under official auspices. But we do not include this indicator, or any others which failed the test of consistency described in the paragraph above; we refer only to the four structural characteristics which did meet the test of consistency as the "classical indicators of dependence," and to the rank-order sum of the four indicators as the "classical dependency rank." The results of the consistency test are shown in Table 10-1.

For the twenty-eight case-study countries, the correlation of the four classical indicators of dependence is significant, and each indicator is significantly correlated with the group as a whole. Countries which rank high by reference to one of these structural characteristics tend to rank high by reference to each of the other characteristics. But size of the country, measured by population, makes a difference. Ten of the countries reported population in excess of 15 million in 1965, while eighteen of the countries had less than 15 million inhabitants. The four classical indicators of dependence are consistent for the small countries (with especially high significance for rank order association of the trade ratio, commodity concentration, and foreign-ownership of assets), but not for the large countries. For the large countries only the trade ratio and commodity concentration show significant rank order association, with both the foreign-ownership of assets and the technical assistance ratio marginally significant. Although we believe this result may in part be attributable to peculiarities of the large-country sample, because most of the large countries are closely clustered at one end of the distribution produced by the four indicators taken together, we will confine our inferences about the classical indicators of dependence to the eighteen small countries, only.

For none of the classical indicators of dependence is variance among

Table 10-1
Consistency Test of Classical Indicators of Dependence

N	Coefficient of Concordance	Spearmen's Rank Correlation Coefficients for Indicator and Rank Totals of All Indicators			
		Trade Ratio	Commodity Concentration	Trading-Partner Concentration	Foreign-owned Assets Indicator
28	(.40**	.76**	.50**	.39*	.77**
	(2.04)	(5.98)	(2.95)	(2.16)	(6.13)
10 Large	.31	.60	.66*	.35	.60
	(1.33)	(1.98)	(2.32)	(.99)	(1.96)
18 Small	.44**	.68**	.72**	.45*	.83**
	(2.36)	(3.82)	(4.28)	(1.90)	(6.14)
10 Large	.46	.73*	.68*		.58
	(1.70)	(2.85)	(2.42)		(1.90)
18 Small	.69**	.76**	.68**		.85**
	(4.49)	(4.81)	(3.84)		(6.56)

Note: Values in parentheses are: for Coefficient of Concordance, Snedecor's F; for Spearman's Rank Correlation Coefficients, *t*-ratios. *significant at .05 level. **significant at .01 level. All data are three-year annual averages, 1964-66. For definitions of indicators, see text.

countries significantly explained by differences in income level. This result is expected from the evidence of other investigators. None of the four indicators is significantly associated with per capita gross national product for the eighteen small case-study countries, and the "classical dependency rank" (rank-order of the four indicators taken together) is not significantly correlated with the rank-order of income level.[17]

Association of Dependence with
Political-Historical Factors

Expressed in terms of structural characteristics, the classical indicators of dependence measure the degree of involvement by foreigners in some areas of the domestic economy. If the degree of involvement measured by these indicators corresponds to the degree of foreign "right, capacity, and power to take and to implement decisions affecting the national economy," they would appear to be appropriate for assessing national economic independence, as this concept is generally defined.[18] Differences among countries in terms of the classical indicators may, consequently, distinguish different degrees of national economic independence or differences in the "presence" of foreigners exercising influence on the economy. This would seem to be very close to the classical economists' central concern with how foreign influences, working through the country's international economic relations, exercise an effect on domestic economic structure.

With respect to the "areas" in which foreign influence is exercised, we may attach importance to the features of their economies to which, as Ghai has found, politicians and economists of developing countries refer in assessing economic dependence: the structure of trade, the share of foreigners in ownership of capital in the modern sector and in the stock of skilled manpower, and the proportion of investment represented by foreign aid and private capital flows. The classical indicators of dependence correspond to aspects of the first two features and we have found that there is internal consistency among measures of the "presence" of foreigners exercising influence on these areas of economy such that, by reference to the case-study countries, differences among countries in the "presence" of foreigners in each area distinguishes in the same way different degrees of national economic independence. But with respect to the last area referred to, foreign aid and private capital flows as a proportion of current investment, we do not find that this measure of foreign involvement in the domestic economy is consistent with the classical indicators of dependence in distinguishing among the case-study countries. Foreign aid and private capital flows, which may be related to the level of income or to the rate of change in income, do not seem to indicate degrees of economic dependence in the same way as the classical indicators of foreign "presence" in other areas of the economy.

If, as we now argue, the classical indicators of dependence distinguish differences among countries in the presence of foreigners exercising influence on the economy, we should be able to account for variance in the dependence rank of countries by reference to the origins or causes of differences in the presence of foreigners. We can only regret that there is no standard guide or generally respected theory to help identify the sources and to measure the extent of foreign influence. Lacking such guidance, we are confined to a few propositions about the origin of differences in the exercise of foreign influence which seem to be securely grounded in the political history of the areas in which the case-study countries are located.

There is no doubt that the strength of foreign influence and the degree of foreign presence can be altered by dramatic, short-term events such as invasion, changes in the deployment of military forces, revolutions, formation of new international political alliances, significant technological changes, and shifts in the tastes, costs, and alternatives which underlie established international marketing arrangements. But we do not expect to find in such short-term factors a general explanation of intercountry differences in the areas and degree of foreign presence, the effects on economic structure of international economic relations, or the identifications and interests which shape the perceptions of social groups. These characteristics are generally described as relatively stable and persisting. We emphasize historical origins for the same reasons that students of comparative politics find it essential to stress historical sources of differences in political behavior.

A recurring thesis in accounts of the expansion of international commerce in the developing areas of the world is the search for raw materials and the organization of production and trade in price-elastic agricultural commodities. If the scramble for establishment of colonial dominion in the last century is inadequately explained in this way, the practice of strengthening both administrative and commercial facilities in dependencies with the most favorable fiscal prospects in this century supports this thesis. The first general proposition is that the distribution of foreign presence among developing countries is likely to be a function of the relative factor endowments of those countries. Second, we would expect a significantly different impact on economic structure and presence of foreigners in the areas of important colonization as compared with areas that did not experience large-scale immigration of colonists. Third, the history of petroleum exploitation strongly suggests that foreign presence is a distinctive phenomenon in those developing countries for which the production and exportation of petroleum products has become dominant in total output and foreign trade. Fourth, and independent of all the foregoing, is the difference in the domestic effects of international economic relations attributable to difference among nations in persisting qualities of political style and the characteristic form of political bargaining; these factors, which strongly influence the character of political organizations and institutions, also distinguish modes of dealing with foreigners. At one extreme are a few countries which, to much greater degree than other nations, have institutionalized and depersonalized management of the foreign presence; at the other extreme are countries in which the management of relations with foreigners is highly personalized and particular.[19] Finally, we would expect that the impact of the historical factors on economic structure and the effect of foreign presence on perceptions would be different in countries of large and heterogeneous population from the impact and effect in small countries.

Crude and tentative as the propositions must be, they suggest that variance in the dependency rank of countries should be associated with differences among the countries in size, resource endowment, experience with colonization, status as an "oil country," and mode of political style in dealing with the foreign presence.

The appearance of country size and resource endowment in this list of political-historical factors believed to be associated with differences among developing nations in structural indicators of dependence invites comparison with the investigation of development patterns. In testing the hypothesis that universal factors affecting all countries are reflected in intercountry growth paths, Chenery and his associates have found that population size and relative resource endowment establish categories of development patterns, each category characterized by a different pattern of change in the structure of production and trade. Size and natural resource endowment are seen to interact through comparative advantage to affect the timing of industrialization and, therefore, to establish different patterns of specialization in production—in primary commodities versus industrial products—and in the composition of international trade.[20] We argue here that the same two factors, taken together with other political-historical differences among countries, should be found to establish categories of perceived dependence, each category characterized by a different pattern of economic structural features identified by the classical indicators of dependence.

There is no standard criterion for classifying countries according to resource endowment; both statistical and theoretical problems are encountered.[21] We have computed two indices: arable land and land under permanent crops per capita, as a measure of relative endowment of agricultural resources, and mineral exports per capita, as a measure of other natural resources under exploitation.[22] We array the case-study countries by each of the two indices and take the sum of ranks to determine the combined land and other natural resource endowment. Discriminant values have been assigned each country for colonization experience, status as an oil country, and mode of political style in dealing with foreigners. Division of the countries into categories of large or small is at a population of 15 million reported in 1965.

For small countries our findings can be expressed in two regression equations:

(10.1) $I = .237 + 1.006\,R + .128\,C + .212\,O + .079\,M$ $(R^2 = .751)$
 (2.85)   (2.22)   (3.68)   (2.20)

(10.2) $I' = .037 + .458\,R + .048\,C + .069\,O + .043\,M$ $(R^2 = .586)$
 (2.05)   (1.74)   (2.56)   (2.36)

where: I = "dependency rank," i.e. classical indicators of dependence:
 sum of rank orders ÷ 100

 I' = I + technical assistance received:
 sum of rank orders ÷ 100

 R = Combined resource endowment:
 sum of rank orders ÷ 100

 C = Significant colonization experience $(-1$ or $0)$

 O = Status as oil country $(-1$ or $0)$

 M = Mode of political style: "institutional strength" $(-1, 0, 1)$

t-values are shown in parentheses, where 2.16 is significant at the 5 percent level; all regression coefficients are significant at this level except resource endowment and colonization experience in the second equation. The regression relationship is significant at the 1 percent level for Equation (10.1) and at the 2 percent level for Equation (10.2).

Recognizing grave uncertainties about this method of demonstration, inferences must be cautious and tentative. But we believe it provides some evidence that differences among the small case-study countries in structural characteristics measured by the classical indicators of dependence are associated with differences in the political-historical factors.

If we employ the coefficients of the first equation, with the values of each variable observed in the eighteen small case-study countries, the estimating equation provides an array of the countries which we may divide into three categories (countries are numbered in ascending rank order of their overall "scores" supplied by the estimating equation):[23]

"Foreigners"	"Structure"	"International Capitalist System"
1. Libya	12. Tunisia	17. Tanzania
2. Trinidad-Tobago	13. Peru	18. Ceylon
3. Saudi Arabia	14. Ghana	
4. Sierra Leone	15. Ivory Coast	
5. Jamaica	16. Chile	
6. Uganda		
7. Morocco		
8. Ecuador		
9. El Salvador		
10. Malawi		
11. Kenya		

With the single exception of Malawi, these categories exactly correspond to the distribution of dominant perceptions of dependence in each of the small case-study countries, based on evaluation of viewpoints expressed by observers in each of the countries in the middle and late 1960s. In all of the ten large case-study countries the dominant viewpoints expressed were those associated with perception of dependence in terms of the structure of production and trade.

We may summarize our findings with respect to the twenty-eight case-study countries as follows:

1. Small countries which rank high with respect to the classical indicators of dependence (trade ratio, commodity and trading-partner concentration, and proportion of foreign-owned assets) tend to have relatively favorable resource endowments; countries with significant colonization experience oil countries, and countries characterized by a mode of political style resulting in personalized and particularized means of dealing with foreigners also tend to have high dependency ranks. Countries with relatively unfavorable resource endowments, without significant colonization experience, not oil countries, and with a mode of political style providing unusual institutional strength in dealing with the foreign presence tend to have low dependency ranks.

2. If we abstract from differences of colonization experience, oil-country status, and mode of political style, we find that population size and relative resource endowments crudely distinguish four different patterns of characteristics. All of the large countries we have studied have relatively unfavorable resource endowments; they also predominantly define dependence in terms of the structure of production and trade, and tend to have relatively low classical indicators of dependence and technical assistance dependence. Small countries with relatively favorable resource endowments generally perceive dependence, as the dominating presence of foreigners and tend to have high classical indicators of dependence but low technical assistance dependence; these countries may correspond to Chenery-Taylor small "primary-oriented" countries. Small countries with relatively unfavorable resource endowments generally perceive dependence in terms of the structure of production and trade, and tend to have low classical indicators of dependence and high technical assistance dependence; these may be Chenery-Taylor small "industry-oriented" countries. A few small countries with very unfavorable resource endowments perceive dependence as participation in the international capitalist system, have low foreign-ownership of assets and trading-partner concentration ratios, but have intermediate ratios, commodity concentration ratios, and technical assistance dependence.

3. Countries in which the dominating presence of foreigners defines the most widely held perception of dependence tend to be countries with structural characteristics resulting in high values of the classical indicators of depend-

ence; they are likely to be small countries, to enjoy relatively favorable resource endowments, to have had a significant colonization experience, to include the oil countries, and may have a personalized political mode of dealing with foreigners.

4. Countries in which the dominant perception of dependence is in terms of the structure of production and trade include the large countries. The category also includes small countries typically tending to have low values of the classical indicators of dependence and relatively unfavorable resource endowments, but unlikely to have had a significant colonization experience or to be an oil country these countries may exhibit a mode of political style that results in institutionalized management of the foreign presence.

5. Countries in which participation in the international capitalist system is the dominant perception of dependence tend to have low and intermediate values of the classical indicators of dependence; they are likely to be small countries with relatively unfavorable resource endowments, are unlikely to have had a significant colonization experience or be an oil country, but may have a mode of political style that results in institutional strength in dealing with foreigners. In a sense, countries in this category seem to be "extreme" cases of the political-historical experience of small countries which perceive dependence in "structural" terms; they are likely to have more of the characteristic political-historical features, or in greater intensity.

Dependence, Policy Choices, and the Roles of Foreigners

Comparative economic analysis of the twenty-eight countries studied appears to say that the pattern of a developing country's international economic relations, and the structural characteristics of its economy resulting from that pattern, are in a fixed relation to natural-physical features and historical experiences, all very largely beyond the discretion of short-term control of its present citizens. Moreover, the dominant perception of the central, defining characteristics of national economic dependence, how dependence is related to the attainment of economic development, and the appropriate strategy to reduce dependence are also associated with the same natural and historical factors. Structure, ideology, and preferred policy options all seem to be historically determined since the most likely speculation is that perceptions and economic relations are the product of such factors as population size, natural resource endowment, discovery of oil deposits, and colonization—rather than the other way around.

But no one familiar with the variety and volatility of developing countries can feel comfortable with such a rigid, deterministic mechanism and we believe the evidence from comparative political analysis of the case-study countries suggests an interpretation which is much less rigidly mechanical. We do believe that such things as the appreciation of the historical experience of a people, the perception of foreigners, and the structure of the economy are relatively immobile; they are not in the class of transient or ephemeral phenomena. But groups and individuals are not inevitably and forever the captives of their society's past experiences and accidents. Interpretations, perceptions, and structure do change—sometimes dramatically and suddenly, but more often slowly, uncertainly, and with irregular lags. The study of how and why these changes occur composes an essential part of the comparative analysis of political process in developing countries.

We have already stated our finding that observers in the case-study countries generally express viewpoints about economic dependence—that is, perceptions of the political-historical factors affecting their nation and the presence of foreigners in their country—which reflect those of the interest groups with which they identify. It is our hypothesis that the determinant interest groups are likely to be those defined by economic status or occupation, but in some countries and for some observers the identification with ethnic or regional groups may be equally or more important. Three corollaries are associated with this hypothesis.

First, we generally expect to find different viewpoints—with respect to the perception of dependence, of the country's historical experience, and of the foreign presence—expressed in the same country by observers identified with different interest groups; at least some political organizations in opposition to the government or the regime can be expected to express perceptions of national economic dependence different from that of government supporters.

Second, we expect the viewpoint expressed by an observer to change when his interest-group identification changes, but often with a lag. We also expect the characteristic viewpoint of an interest group to alter if the relative benefits the group derives from the foreign presence changes; but these alterations in group viewpoints are generally slow, uncertain, and with irregular lags. For both individuals and groups, we believe the most important (but not the only) cause of the change is the economic development of the country, which enlarges the total flow of benefits available for distribution, changes the primary distribution of at least the income and relative wealth component of benefits desired, and alters the size and composition of occupational groups.

Third, the dominant viewpoint in a country is generally that of the (most important) interest groups supporting the regime, almost always including the leadership of the bureaucracy which enforces and implements political decisions. We find that interest groups form an alliance, to the exclusion of other groups, which is based on a more or less explicit understanding about the distribution of benefits and which is the foundation of the country's political regime. The alliance generally survives changes of government, with marginal adjustments; fundamental changes in its composition are usually associated with profound changes of regime.[24] The day-to-day substance of politics is primarily concerned with the distribution of benefits and the maintenance of order, i.e., means of dealing with potential or active challenges to acceptance of the authority of the state by groups outside the alliance. Policies affecting foreign presence impinge directly on the distribution of benefits among interest groups and are generally adjusted to conform to the perception of the governing alliance, that is, to the relative benefits they derive from the foreign presence. Groups in opposition to the alliance are, therefore, very likely to define their proposals—and justify resistance to the authority of the state—in terms of national economic dependence and policies affecting the foreign presence.

This description of political process thrust to center stage the roles played by foreigners in the society. The community of foreigners varies greatly in different developing countries with respect to composition, size, visibility and identity of interests. There is usually, but not always, a dominant nationality among foreigners and the residents of the developing country are likely to perceive the whole foreign community in terms of the dominant nationality. In some countries there are large communities which do not consider themselves foreigners, but are so considered by other residents of the country.[25] In former colonies the dominant foreign group is likely to be the product of a wave of immigration which occurred in the colonial period and the group may or may not now have the support and association of the former metropole. In many countries the dominant group in the foreign community is identified with the foreign government or business firms most prominent in the foreign presence; in some cases the number of resident foreigners may be small but nonetheless be highly visible and influential. There are so many variances in the character of foreign communities in different developing countries that we are impressed with the uniformities we find in the twenty-eight case-studies with respect to the association of national policies and perceptions with the "roles" of the foreign community in each country.

The "roles" assigned to the foreign community appear to be defined by reference to three characteristics: (1) whether or not the dominant group in the foreign community is found to be closely associated with important interest groups in the governing alliance; (2) whether the dominant foreign group is found to be active in both public and private sectors of the developing country, or in the private sector, only;[26] and (3) whether or not the dominant foreign group is found to be highly visible (a sufficiently large number of resident foreigners insures visibility in small countries).

Employing the analytical framework defined by the hypothesis concerning interest groups and the three corollaries described above, we have inspected the political processes of the twenty-eight case-study countries to identify uniformities and the sources of differences in the policy choices each country has made. As we have indicated earlier, we find that the choice of foreign and domestic policies respecting both economic and political goals appear to be made in clusters or packages; the packages of policy goals and instruments adopted in the twenty-eight case-study countries appear in the cells of Table 10-2.[27] Of course, different options may have been chosen by other countries or at other

Table 10-2
Foreign Involvement and Policy Dependency in Developing Countries

		1. No Large Foreign Group in Residence or Visible	2. Foreign Group in Residence Large and Visible
		A. Foreigners Active in Both Public and Private Sectors	
I. Foreigners Associated with Governing Interest-Group Alliance		*Dependency perceives as:* wrong structure of production and trade: low level of development and inadequacies of public administration *Policy goals and instruments:* —target planning for growth to raise revenues and earn/save foreign exchange —expand local control of administration by reform of political system or "strongman" regime —maintenance of order —seek foreign assistance and accommodation	*Dependency perceived as:* dominating presence of foreigners *Policy goals and instruments:* —stimulate growth and foreign trade —maintenance of order —encourage foreign investment and aid —negotiate improved bargaining power and access to international markets
II. Foreigners Not Associated with Governing Interest-Group Alliance		*Dependency:* dominating presence of foreigners: perceived as neocolonialism, political dependency, "occupation" *Policy goals and instruments:* —nationalize or confiscate foreign-owned assets —revise agreements of treaties to reduce foreign presence; seceed; expel foreigners —perhaps seek substitute foreign group	*Dependency:* dominating presence of foreigners *Policy goals and instruments:* —localization of jobs in public bureaucracy —loctlization of jobs in economy and ownership of assets —government regulation and controls for ⁻redistribution —seek regional functional integration to improve bargaining power (likely to coincide with racial-ethnic conflicts)
		B. Foreigners Active in Private Sector Only	
I. Foreigners Associated with Governing Interest-Group Alliance		*Dependency:* wrong structure of production and trade: low level of development and poor domestic growth prospects *Policy goals and instruments:* —maintenance of order —fullest possible integration into foreign economic system	*Dependency:* wrong structure of production and trade *Policy goals and instruments:* —stimulate growth and foreign trade —planning and government regulation to maintain political control over growth and structural change —maintenance of order —encourage foreign investment —armslength relation with aid donors
II. Foreigners Not Associated with Governing Interest-Group Alliance		*Dependency:* participation in international capitalist system *Policy goals and instruments:* —enlarge state and cooperative enterprises; restrict private property, ownership and enterprises —emasculate, eliminate "native capitalist" interest group —extend political participation; social reform; austerity programs —insulate economy from international economic system —seek new international alliances	*Dependency:* wrong structure of production and trade *Policy goals and instruments:* —nationalization and forced divestment —government controls to alter economic structure: diversification and import substitution —emasculate, eliminate foreign interest group —extend political participation; social reform —seek militant regional unity to improve bargaining power

times, but the package of policies pursued in the twenty-eight countries we have studied are all included in Table 10-2.

Each country may be characterized by the description of its package of policy choices and by its dominant perception of national economic dependence. For the twenty-eight case-study countries we find that the packages of policies and the perceptions of dependence are systematically associated; in each cell of Table 10-2 is shown the definition of dependence together with the policy goals and instruments we found to obtain in the countries represented by that cell. Systematic association of policies with perception of dependence is what we would expect; unless some dysfunction of the decision-making process intervenes, the policy targets and instruments selected by the government of the day should correspond to the perceptions held by the most important interest groups supporting the regime with respect to the central characteristics of the nation's economic dependence, and how efforts to reduce dependence are related to the attainment of economic development. The association we have found illustrates in detail for each country the generalization we infer for all the case-study countries: each perception of national economic dependence is associated with a preferred strategy to reduce dependence.

Comparative study of the twenty-eight countries reveals several sets of variants of the perception of dependence and policy packages, but also that each set is associated with a distinctive combination of characteristics defining the role of foreigners in the nation. Table 10-2 identifies each perception-policies set with the particular combination of foreign-role characteristics obtaining in the countries represented by the cell. The inference we draw from this finding is that the characteristics defining the foreign roles in a country—whether or not the foreigners are closely associated with the governing interest groups, are active in the public as well as the private sector, and are numerous or highly visible—establish in palpable, concrete, local form the character of the foreign presence; it is with respect to this character of foreign presence that the perception of national economic dependence is specifically defined and strategies for reducing dependence are translated into concrete policies and particular choices of instruments. It is here that we find the key to the observation that in developing countries foreign and domestic policies are closely intertwined. Economic and political policy choices are shaped to the specific characteristics of the foreign presence, which includes foreign governments, with the explicit intent (and result) of granting advantages to or imposing disadvantages on the foreign community (and the domestic interest groups associated with the foreigners) with respect to the distribution of benefits.

Virtually every important policy choice has both a domestic and a foreign dimension insofar as it affects in some way the distribution of benefits among interest groups, including those associated with the foreign presence or the foreign community itself. The exact manner in which foreigners are affected by a policy choice depends on the specific roles of foreigners in the country; the extent to which they are affected depends on how extensive is the involvement of foreigners in the economy and society—that is, how important their interests are. If the involvement and interests of the foreigners in the economy are negligible compared with those of nationals of the country, we imagine that the nexus between foreign and domestic policies we have described would change in character or diminish in intensity. The association between perception of dependence and packages of policies would also weaken or disappear. Possibly this is why, for example with respect to the economic interdependence of the United States and Latin American countries, the United States does not perceive itself dependent on Latin American countries and does not shape its policies into packages systematically adapted to the roles played by Latin Americans in its society, while Latin American countries do perceive national economic dependence on the United States and appear to adopt policy-packages which correspond to the roles of the United States in their countries.

We believe that these two relations—the association of policy-packages with the dominant perception of the foreign presence in the economy and the association of the latter with the characteristics defining the roles of foreigners—describe ways in which economic factors guide the policy choices of a developing country. Political determinants of the selection of economic policies may be illustrated by inspecting the viewpoints and programs of opposition groups.

In some of the case-study countries many observers considered themselves in opposition to the regime and expressed a variety of viewpoints; interest groups judged to be outside or only marginally associated with the governing alliance proposed different programs and seemed to perceive national economic dependence in various ways. But our appreciation of the evidence is that significant and persisting expression of opposition viewpoints with respect to the foreign presence in their nation and the preferred strategy for reducing dependence, including translation into more or less coherent packages of proposed policies, does tend to correspond with the reference group's realized or expected benefits from its relationship to the presence of foreigners. The opposition policy-packages generally are consistent with their perception of the specific foreign roles which would result in a relative improvement in the benefits accruing to the reference interest group. Opposition groups clearly outside the governing alliance almost invariably advocate changing one or more of the characteristics defining the foreign roles in their country. Our finding is that important opposition groups hold sets of perceptions of dependence and preferred packages of policies as shown in Table 10-2, and that these are associated with specific combinations of proposed roles of foreigners defined by the relative benefits perceived as accruing to the interest group, also in the same relationships shown in Table 10-2.

It should be evident that among the policies included in the packages both of the regime and of the opposition groups are those which are intended to realize or strengthen the preferred specific roles of foreigners. The roles of foreigners can be changed by determined and persistent implementation of such policies in at least some cases. Foreigners can be admitted or enticed into close association with (almost any) regime desiring to establish such an association, and foreigners can be excluded from association with the alliance interest groups. Foreigners can be confined to activity in the private sector or induced to be active in the public sector as well. Resident foreign groups can be compressed in numbers and their visibility reduced; the reverse movement, however, is not accomplished easily and is often not a realistic option for change. Indeed, a number of these possible changes in foreign roles require time, resources, and the concurrence or restraint of foreign governments. This is another reason why foreign and domestic policies tend to be adopted in discreet packages. But assessment of realism or feasibility is not decisive. The opposition groups do believe that changes should and can be made in the roles of foreigners and both the risks and costs should be borne by the nation. It is our observation that differences in the preferred roles of foreigners is very frequently at the heart of political conflict between significant opposition groups and the regime, and is also frequently the issue most forcefully articulated. It is the idiom of conflict over the appropriate strategy to reduce national economic dependence. A change in the role of foreigners is generally associated with a change of regime and composition of the governing alliance.

Because conflict over the preferred roles of foreigners, and the packages of policies to realize or strengthen those roles, is generally the central political issue in developing countries, the path which a country may follow in changing from one set of policy goals and instruments to another is constrained. The relevant alternative sets of policies are those proposed by significant opposition groups, and these packages are defined by reference to the change in the roles of foreigners desired by the opposition groups. A governing alliance which attempts to accommodate an opposition group must adapt its preferred package of policies in ways approximating the specific change in the roles of foreigners which the opposition believes in its advantage.[28] Thus the relevant options can be defined by reference to the specific roles of foreigners which the opposition groups wish to change, and the path of policy changes open to a country is established by these options.

We have arranged Table 10-2 to place the relevant options—the significant opposition group programs and preferred status of roles of foreigners which we have found in the case-study countries—in cells adjacent to that occupied by each country. The relevant options, often only available through a change of regime, are found in the column of the cell describing the present set of dependency-perception and policy package of the regime. The most important options, advocated by the significant opposition groups, are in the cell immediately below that occupied by the country and at the top of the column. For countries in the right-hand column of cells, with a large and visible foreign group is residence, there is also another option—an opening to the left, available if the foreign group can be reduced in size and visibility—described in the adjacent cell in the row. For countries in the left-hand column of cells, without a large or visible foreign community, an opening to the right, although sometimes desired by groups in opposition, is only very rarely available to a developing country.

Summary

We have sought in a hypothesized model of political decision-making an interpretation of the observed relationships among the patterns of international economic relations, structural characteristics of economies, political-historical factors, and perceptions of dependence. The interpretation in terms of the political process of choice by interest groups and the central importance of the roles of foreigners in choices among policy goals and instruments corresponds more with experience and accords with the evidence from our case-study countries. But conclusions of this generality cannot rest confidently on so few observations and on comparative political analysis at the macro-level. We have attempted to state the hypotheses and relationships in an explicit and testable form so that they may be refined in more extensive samples of experience and in more precise micro-level research.

The utility of this framework in our present state of knowledge is largely heuristic. But confirmation of the relationships we have found could serve the Fletcher School's companion objective of contributing to the evaluation of foreign affairs operations. The evidence suggests to us that in formulating many kinds of policies bearing on international economic relations the predictability of consequences will suffer from a failure to recognize distinctly different patterns and structures among developing countries—with respect to perceptions of dependence and development, sensitivity to the roles of foreigners, the domestic-foreign policy options realistically available, and the consequences that accompany acquiescence in the policies or programs foreigners may prefer.

Notes

1. See especially Hollis B. Chenery, "Patterns of Industrial Growth," AMERICAN ECONOMIC REVIEW, March 1960, pp. 624-54; Hollis B. Chenery and Lance Taylor, "Development Patterns: Among Countries and Over Time," THE REVIEW OF ECONOMICS AND STATISTICS, November 1968, pp. 291-416; Hollis B. Chenery, Hazel Alkington, Christopher Sims, "A Uniform Analysis of Development Patterns," Economic Development Report No. 148, Project for Quantitative Research in Economic Development, Center for Inter-

national Affairs, Harvard University, Cambridge, Mass., duplicated, July 1970; and Hollis B. Chenery, "Growth and Structural Change," FINANCE AND DEVELOPMENT, No. 3, 1971, pp. 16-27.

2. Harry G. Johnson, ECONOMIC NATIONALISM IN OLD AND NEW STATES (Chicago and London: University of Chicago Press, 1967). We will repay our intellectual debt to the Committee and its chairman in an ungracious manner; we will argue that the failure to take into account more variables, to distinguish among different cases (as the author of at least one of the case studies, Manning Nash, suggests), yields generalizations that divert attention from aspects of the political processes which are crucial in explaining the selection of policy instruments.

3. The graduate students have included a group of mid-career officers of governments in less developed countries and of the United States Agency for International Development.

4. All of the findings are tentative; greater confidence in the inferences will require testing observations of other and more countries, development of more reliable data and indicators, and inspection of additional variables.

5. Reginald H. Green, "Economic Independence and Economic Coopera-tion in the African Context: A Political Economic Model and Some Implica-tions," to appear in Dharam Ghai (ed.), ECONOMIC INDEPENDENCE IN AFRICAN COUNTRIES (London and Nairobi: Oxford University Press, forth-coming). This volume will contain a number of papers, hereafter cited as CODESRIA Papers, prepared for the Regional African Meeting of Directors of Development Training and Research Institutes, held in Nairobi, February 1971.

6. First, it is a multivariate concept and it is not at all clear how its various dimensions are related or, for purposes of measurement, should be weighted. Second, it only has utility in a relative sense; the effort to conceive of an absolute state of economic independence is positively misleading. Third, a behavioral basis to define the concept is elusive because, in any concrete case, it is pursued for a variety of motives, often contradictory and sometimes conflicting in implementation.

7. Dharam Ghai, "The Concept and Strategies of Economic Independence in African Countries," CODESRIA papers. In this connection Ghai cites Reginald H. Green and Ann Seidman, UNITY IN POVERTY (Baltimore: Penguin Books, 1968), pp. 91-98, and Kwame Nkrumah, NEO-COLONIALISM: THE LAST STAGE OF IMPERIALISM (London: Heineman, 1965).

8. Dharam Ghai, ibid., pp. 3-4.

9. Ibid., p. 5.

10. See, for example, Osvaldo Sunkel, "National Development Policy and External Dependence in Latin America," JOURNAL OF DEVELOPMENT STUDIES, Vol. 6, 1969; Theotonio Dos Santos, "The Structure of Depend-ence," AMERICAN ECONOMIC REVIEW, May, 1970, pp. 231-236; John S. Saul, "The Political Aspects of Economic Independence," and Osvaldo Sunkel,

"Trans-national Capitalist Integration and National Disintegration in Latin America," CODESRIA Papers. This perception draws heavily on the views of Latin American experience expressed by Andre Gunder Frank, CAPITALISM AND UNDERDEVELOPMENT IN LATIN AMERICA, New York: Monthly Review Press, 1969, and Celso Furtado, Development and Underdevelopment, Berkeley: University of California Press, 1967. Important sub-categories of the literature discuss critically the activities of multinational corporations and the role of "unequal" partners.

11. Among observers who generally adhere to this perception of economic dependence there is a fundamental distinction between those who employ a class basis of analysis and those who do not. Compare: Paul A. Baran, "On the Political Economy of Backwardness," THE MANCHESTER SCHOOL OF ECONOMICS AND SOCIAL STUDIES, January, 1952, and Markos J. Mamalakis, "The Theory of Sectoral Clashes," LATIN AMERICAN RESEARCH REVIEW, No. 3, 1969, pp. 9-46. Terminological confusion is almost unavoidable. Some terms we employ, e.g., "the developing countries," are offensive to the ideas of those who perceive dependence as participation in the international capitalist system.

12. This is shown by the standard measures of respectability; they are included in textbook descriptions of developing economies, have been recognized by the World Bank, and appear as variables distinct from the stochastic term in some econometric models. We do not insist on respectability for all variables we employ, but it does help to preserve our academic credentials.

13. Hollis B. Chenery, "Growth and Structural Change," op. cit., p. 16. The bearing of the "similar wants and production possibilities" on common features of development patterns is explored in the other works by Chenery and his associates cited above. Pioneering investigation of structural changes associated with growth was conducted by Simon Kuznets, summarized in his MODERN ECONOMIC GROWTH (New Haven: Yale University Press, 1966).

14. See, for example, the evidence in Hollis B. Chenery, "Patterns of Industrial Growth," op. cit., pp. 639-50.

15. See Bela Balassa, "Country Size and Trade Patterns: Comment," AMERICAN ECONOMIC REVIEW, March 1969, pp. 201-204, and Donald B. Keesing and Donald R. Sherk, "Population Density in Patterns of Trade and Development," AMERICAN ECONOMIC REVIEW, December 1971, pp. 956-61.

16. Reliable data on foreign-owned and total assets is not available for most of the twenty-eight countries. We use the ratio to GNP of investment income earned by foreigners (gross, on public and private account, from the balance of payments). On the heroic assumptions that, on the average, earnings are proportionate to the value of assets and total assets are proportionate to value of output, for purposes of international comparison, this may give some indication of relative foreign-ownership of assets. Or it may only be one measure of foreign debt and equity service. For all indicators, three-year averages of 1964-66 are

used. Variants of all the ratios were tested. For the trade ratio, exports only and total current account earnings and expenditures were substituted in the numerator. For the commodity and trading-partner ratios, one and three commodities and partners were substituted. For the foreign-owned asset ratio, for countries in which the United States is the dominant investor, value of U.S.-owned assets was substituted. The indicators employed provided the best test results, but in general it did not make much difference which variants were used.

17. The rank correlation coefficient is .42, not significant at the .1 level.

18. Some investigators, analyzing related questions, do seem to conclude that such a correspondence exists. Similar indicators have been employed to estimate the degree of United States "economic presence," shown to be associated with particular attitudinal and behavioral differences among Latin American countries. See Manus Midlarsky and Raymond Tanter, "Toward a Theory of Political Instability in Latin America," JOURNAL OF PEACE RESEARCH, No. 3, 1967, pp. 20-227.

19. The analysis of these factors, and the study of their bearing on both domestic and international political relations in the case-study countries, has been carried out by Professor Arpad von Lazar of the Fletcher School. See his "Taxonomic Factors Influencing the Character of Political Organizations and Political Institutions," (unpublished manuscript). He devised the discriminant variable used in this study to account for differences in these factors among the case-study countries.

20. See Chenery and Taylor, "Development Patterns: Among Countries and Over Time," op. cit. Among the principal results of the study are the following (pp. 415-16): "(1) Three distinct development patterns have been identified from intercountry analysis: large countries, small primary-oriented countries, and small industry-oriented countries. The variation of production levels with income and trade patterns is best described by separate regression equations for each group because scale and resource endowments interact differently in each." "(3) The preceding conclusions are supported by the regression results from individual industries. The effects of scale and resources show up strongly in the cross-section patterns for the sectors where they can be expected to be significant."

21. Various indirect indicators have been proposed. The Chenery-Taylor study divided the small countries into two equal groups on the basis of an index of trade orientation—toward primary or manufactured exports—modified in marginal cases by consideration of agricultural resources (arable land per capita) and the existing industrial structure. (Ibid., p. 396.) Keesing and Sherk use population density "as an admittedly imperfect proxy for the availability of natural resources per head." (Op. cit., p. 956.)

22. The argument is that natural resources which are not known or exploited should not be included in a measure of relatively favorable resource endowment since they do not affect economic structure or perceptions of dependence.

Known but unexploited natural resources may affect political policies and the selection of economic instruments, however. For countries reporting adequate statistical information, we found mineral exports was a reliable estimator of mineral output, but with different parameters for small and large countries.

23. Countries are distributed into the same categories when Equation (10.2) (fitted to I') is used as the estimating equation, but the rank-order of countries within categories differs. We do not assign importance to differences in order with categories.

24. Arpad von Lazar's study, op. cit., explores the differences among developing countries which account for variance in the parameters relating group interests to political decisions (policy choices) through the intermediation of political organizations and the country's political institutions.

25. We believe there is evidence in some case-study countries that some ethnic, religious, or regional groups are assigned the character of foreigners by other residents of the country although the groups have no homeland outside the nation. But this subject is beyond the boundaries of the present paper.

26. Foreigners may be "active" by owning assets or by occupying a significant number of influential posts. But foreigners include foreign governments; the foreign community may be active in the public sector through consultants and technical assistance personnel provided by a foreign government or through visible, persistent, and important influence exercised by the foreign government's representatives on those who hold important posts.

27. The "policy goals and instruments" listed in each cell represent our best characterization of the country's domestic economic, domestic political, and foreign economic policies (in that order) at the time of the case study, in the middle or latter 1960s. Several case-study countries occupy each cell except 1.A.II. and 1.B.I.; in these cases, we believe other countries do pursue the package of policy choices listed, and they correspond to the perceptions and programs of opposition groups in some of the case-study countries.

28. The governing interest groups may redistribute benefits, generally through state welfare programs. They may attempt to counter existing or potential dangers to legitimacy (acceptance of the authority of the state) in a variety of ways including enlargement of participation in decision-making on the part of members of groups not in the alliance. In some circumstances this is judged infeasible, undesirable, or dangerous in terms of the roles of foreigners; in these cases the packages of policies are likely to include measures to control, repress or weaken opposition groups likely to challenge the legitimacy of the system. These cases are identified by the phrase "maintenance of order" in Table 10-2.

Private Capital Markets
for Development

Ernest Stern

Much discussion has focused on the provision of concessional capital and technical resources to assist in the acceleration of economic and social growth of the developing countries. Resources for this purpose have been increasingly difficult to obtain, particularly in the United States. Yet little attention has been given to measures which might enable some developing countries to attract increasing capital resources from the private international markets. Since the advantages may initially be modest compared to the effort necessary to introduce the developing countries to the capital markets the problem is not at the top of priorities in development finance. Yet it is clear that:

1. The need of the developing countries for external capital will continue to grow while the volume of concessional capital transfers is inadequate now and will not rise much in the future;
2. The political cost of trying to raise concessional capital is great and overshadows other aspects of relations between rich and poor nations;
3. Independence from aid, for which many developing countries strive, is a function of their export potential and balance-of-payments management and of the other sources of capital available.

After twenty-five years of relying heavily on public capital flows to finance development, the more extensive use of international capital markets to provide capital to the developing countries is both possible and desirable.

The Volume of Concessional Capital

The flow of external resources to the developing countries consists of four basic categories:[1]

1. private capital, largely equity investment and suppliers' credits;
2. public commercial capital, i.e., usually trade-related loans from such institutions as export-import banks, and contributions to multilateral agencies at market terms;
3. grants, for technical assistance, humanitarian purposes, international organiza-

tions, budget support for former colonies or the economies of Indochina, and other purposes;
4. public concessional loan capital.

The respective importance of these categories, for 1969 and 1970, is shown in Table 11-1.

The first two categories of resource flows are provided at *market terms*. The principal motivation for their volume and geographic distribution is profit—either directly by the investor or indirectly through the promotion of exports—rather than financing of development, though, obviously, they contribute to the latter as well. In the third category, most types of grants have a strong, special constituency in almost every donor country—ranging from the desire to maintain politico-cultural ties with former colonies to the church group support of child feeding programs. They are excluded from this discussion not because they are less meaningful for development—though some are—but merely to recognize that the grant flows are treated differently in the allocation process by donor and recipient alike.

The last category, public concessional loan capital, is the most controversial aspect of development assistance. Of the $14.7 billion in resource transfers to the poor countries in 1970, less than a quarter—$2.9 billion—was public loan capital on concessional terms. The total volume of such concessional lending, on a net basis, has been stagnant, as shown in Table 11-2. The slight increase in

Table 11-1
Total Flow of Financial Resources to Less Developing Countries (Billion Dollars)

	1969	1970
Total Flows	13.7	14.7
Private capital, at market terms	6.5	6.8
Public commercial flows	0.6	1.2
Grants	3.7	3.8
Public concessional capital	2.9	2.9

Note: DAC data are for flows to less developed countries and multilateral development institutions. However, the latter group are only a conduit and its receipts become, after a time lag, receipts of developing countries. This time lag is not important for our purposes and total resource flows from donor countries for any one year are, therefore, treated as receipts by LDCs.

Table 11-2
Disbursements of Development Lending and Capital (Million Dollars)

1967	1968	1969	1970
2,634	2,574	2,860	2,926

current prices is more than accounted for by the shift in U.S. food aid from a grant to a loan basis, and by inflation during the period.

The Requirement for External Capital

Much has been written about the requirement for external capital in developing countries. While there is no consensus about the precise volume of external capital needed by the developing countries, there is general agreement that aid levels have been inadequate and that requirements are likely to grow more rapidly than availabilities. The conclusion which emerges from every study on the subject is that more capital is needed—and can be used effectively—than is now available. This conclusion is supported by the macroeconomic analysis of the type prepared by UNCTAD or by the UN Center for Development Planning;[2] by inspection of the restraints on investment and imports in many developing countries, as demonstrated in the country reports prepared regularly by international agencies such as the IBRD; by the conclusion of the Pearson Commission,[3] or by private analyses such as the one done by Paul Clark.[4] While most of these studies calculate the total volume of external capital needed by developing countries, they also provide an assessment of the amount of public concessional capital required. Invariably the amounts required are very much larger than present availabilities. In the objectives for the UN Second Development Decade it was assumed that Official Development Assistance would amount to 0.7 percent of the GNP of industrialized countries. In fact, by 1975 the figure is likely to be half that.

An Alternative Source of Capital

The provision of capital for development through public channels assumes that:

1. the capital market cannot supply an adequate volume of capital
2. the cost of capital in the market will be prohibitive for developing countries
3. the technical and policy advice which accompanies public capital flows is essential to assure effective use of resources.

None of these propositions is universally demonstrable, and there are at least grounds for considering a more active use of the international capital markets.

As we have seen, the volume of concessional lending to the developing countries is modest—$2.9 billion in 1970. According to the IBRD Annual Report for 1971 total official bond sales in private international markets totaled $6.2 billion in 1969 and $6.0 billion in 1970. Of this $1.3 billion and $1.6 billion respectively were floated by the developing countries, the IBRD and the Inter-American Development Bank. The bulk of the borrowing in these two years was done by the international financial institutions and developing countries which are well advanced in the industrialization process, but it also included bonds from such countries as Panama, Malaysia, Peru, and the Philippines. In 1968 the Ivory Coast and the Malagasy Republic were among the borrowers. Table 11-3 shows borrowing activity in the last three years.

Much of the borrowing by developing countries represents special situations such as U.S. bank purchases of Philippines bonds, Israeli bond sales to overseas Jewish communities, or bond sales in France from Francophone Africa. Nonetheless, the point remains that under the proper circumstances bond sales from developing countries are feasible.

Of course, access to the international bond market requires an assessment of creditworthiness which few developing countries possess today. But creditworthiness is a term of art—based on attitudes, hopes, preconceptions, and some facts—not a scientific conclusion. The developing country borrowers must establish their prospects and credibility and the investors must develop confidence in the acceptability of government or corporate bonds from developing countries. While this is no easy matter, industrialized countries could do much to ease the access to their bond markets, to educate investors, and to make the obligations of developing countries attractive.

The Cost of Commercial Capital

Access to the financial markets is important but leaves unanswered whether the price of capital would effectively exclude the developing countries from the international markets. The price of capital is generally thought to be a major deterrent to borrowing by developing countries, given the already heavy debt burden, but two points are particularly relevant in assessing this proposition. First, the cost of greater reliance on the international bond markets must be compared to the real costs—financial and indirect—of present resource flows to the developing countries and secondly the prospects for debt servicing capacity

Table 11-3
Foreign and International Bond Issues (Million Dollars)

	1968	1969	1970
Total	7,729	6,220	6,021
Industrialized countries and European Institutions	5,705	4,940	4,384
International Development Institutions	1,392	365	1,261
Developing Countries	632	414	377

Source: IBRD Annual Report, 1971

cannot be viewed in a static sense—they are very much a function of the trade policies of industrialized countries.

Comparing the cost of borrowing on the financial markets to the actual costs of the present resource flows reveals that a large number of developing countries pay near market terms for the bulk of their external capital. Only the poorest, with limited access to private supplier credits, little attraction for private investors, and unable to service commercial or near commercial terms, obtain a substantial portion of their external resources on a highly concessional basis. The total resource flows to developing countries in 1970, excluding technical assistance and other grants, was $10.9 billion, but the discount from commercial terms, i.e., the grant element, was only $1.6 billion. In other words, about 85 percent of the nongrant capital provided by the industrial countries was on commercial terms.

Of course, these aggregates do not imply that each individual developing country obtained the bulk of its capital at near commercial terms. The country situations obviously vary widely. For instance, Mexico obtained virtually all of its external capital on commercial or near commerical terms—from private investment, supplier credits, export-import loans, and loans from the World Bank and the Inter-American Development Bank. Only a portion of the resources from the latter are on concessional terms. By contrast, India relies heavily on concessional capital for its external financing. A shift to obtaining capital from the international bond market would have little impact on Mexico, or countries like it, but would mean a major departure from current practice for India at a significant increase in cost. In between there are a large number of intermediate countries which get both concessional and commercial capital.

It would, of course, be unrealistic to expect the poor developing countries, whose economic capacity will grow only gradually over the long term, to rely heavily on the international bond market. But increased use of the market can provide additional resources for development in three ways. For the relatively high income developing countries the use of the international bond market would provide additional capital for development at a price which is not significantly greater than what they now pay for most of their external capital. This in turn could release some of the highly concessional capital which they still receive for use in the poor countries. Secondly, for all countries who could get access to the international bond market this capital could, in part, substitute for the high-cost, relatively short-term supplier credits which are being used in ever increasing volume. Finally, intermediate income developing countries might gradually increase their use of the international bond market to supplement capital from other sources, thus either reducing the foreign exchange constraints on their development or releasing highly concessional capital flows for the poorest countries.[5]

Advantage of an International Bond Market

Since increased borrowing on the international capital markets would involve higher direct costs to the borrowing countries, the obvious question is why should the effort be made to broaden the international bond market. There are several reasons. From the viewpoint of both of the lender and the borrower the aid relationship is beset with political friction between the two governments and internally in each country. How much concessional capital is obtained, from whom, for what purposes it is to be used, and for whose benefit are not politically neutral questions. The converse of these questions often poses sensitive problems for the providers of the concessional capital. These domestic issues often affect the external relations of borrower and lender. Even debt incurred in the international bond markets will have to be serviced, but the political parameters of the indebtedness will have changed drastically. The discipline of the market may be a welcome substitute for the administrative efforts of donors to assure sound economic management through speeches, traveling missions and conditions.

Secondly, concessional capital assistance often is only available for selected purposes whereas resources raised on the capital market can be used more flexibly. For instance, the bulk of concessional capital is available only for new investments, for the foreign exchange costs of projects, for large-scale industries, and for projects implemented by foreign consultants. Capital raised on the bond market would be available for general imports, for the full cost of projects, for expansion and modernization as well as for new plants, and for the financing of recurrent costs. Thirdly, capital requirements of developing countries are growing rapidly but the supply of capital is not. While the lending capacity of the international organizations has expanded to offset, in part, the relative stagnation of bilateral development lending there are institutional limits beyond which the international organizations cannot go efficiently. Finally, it is not feasible to envisage an eternal reliance on public capital flows. These flows came into being as a postwar phenomenon motivated by reconstruction and, subsequently, development objectives. The public concessional capital flows evolved because there was alternative, in the absence of a private international bond market, yet an alternative to a permanent aid relationship—even if that aid relationship is limited to borrowing from the World Bank and the regional banks—is highly desirable. The re-creation of an international bond market provides such an alternative—limited in impact initially, but with considerable potential for growth.

Costs of Aid

While these general reasons may justify the increased financial costs involved in market borrowing there are important costs associated with public concessional finance which must be considered in any comparison with commercial capital. Some of these costs are direct, such as aid tying, and reduce the effective degree of concessionality. There also are indirect costs which reduce the effective benefits of concessional capital, e.g., the distortion of price structures.

The most obvious direct cost is involved in aid tying—the requirement that all procurement take place in the country which makes the loan. The cost of aid tying has been estimated to range from 15-20 percent. That is, a $100 million will buy only $80 million of commodities at world market prices.

While this estimate is not unreasonable as a global average, it understates the cost to some major aid recipients. The cost of aid tying is a function of normal trading patterns, distance from the principal aid donor, diversity of aid sources and the flexibility of the recipients' management, U.S. aid tying has not been very costly for Latin America (though it may be a great nuisance) because a large share of total Latin American imports are from the United States, aid flows as a percentage of total imports are generally small and trading relationships are well established. Latin American aid recipients have thus been able to identify competitive goods for aid financing. But in Pakistan or India, for instance, the import of U.S. aid tying has been quite different. Commercial imports from the United States were small prior to the aid program and commercial relationships limited. Substantial aid from the United States meant realigning trade relationships and little flexibility in choosing commodities since the bulk of imports from the United States was aid-financed. Moreover, the needed imports were relatively less sophisticated commodities, goods in which the United States was less competitive. For instance, for a number of years Pakistan imported its iron and steel requirements almost totally from the United States with a price differential, in some categories, of over 50 percent. The requirement that 50 percent of all commodities be shipped on U.S. vessels further added to the cost, as did the regulations covering insurance, audit, and documentation.

Loans financing the sale of U.S. agricultural commodities have similar hidden costs. A cash down payment of from 5 to 25 percent may be required and the borrowing country is prohibited from exporting "like" commodities. This means that it is impossible to export rice while importing wheat—which would be thought normal in commercial practice—or to export textiles while importing cotton. The loans appear attractive because of the high value attached to alleviating the current year's foreign exchange constraints; the loss in terms of efficiency and market development may be both long term and considerable.

Providing concessional capital also affects allocative efficiency although the impact varies with the stage of development and the economic management capacity of the borrower. Since the provision of aid is recognized as a political tool by both borrower and lender economic criteria do not always determine the specific investment to be financed. Even aside from this fact, the availability of aid resources can lead to investment in projects which are only viable because capital is obtained cheaply.[6] Beyond that, the availability of aid in certain forms—e.g., loans for projects—emphasizes new investment at the expense of effectively utilizing existing plants. This contributes to the frequent phenomenon of plants operating at 50 percent of capacity or less while new investment proceeds apace. Also, the availability of aid often permits countries to postpone major policy changes, and these delays can result in widespread long-term costs to the economy. For instance, the cost of maintaining an overvalued exchange rate, with the inevitable restrictions and controls, is less apparent if aid flows are ample. The real long-term cost in neglect of export development and distortions of the internal price structure does not become apparent till much later.

Similarly, subsidizing the cost of capital enhances the trend toward capital intensive technology—reducing the number of workers which can be employed per dollar of investment. The supply of concessional capital reduces the average cost of capital[7] and supports policies which keep internal interest rates low, provide tax holidays and extend other benefits which make capital investment more profitable, the employment of labor costly, and investment in adaptative technology less attractive. While it may be possible to correct by administrative measures the distortions created by cheap capital, this can only be partially successful. With capital more correctly priced, the structure of incentives will change. Technological innovation maximizing the use of the abundant resource—labor—will become attractive as will labor-intensive production techniques.

The availability of concessional capital also affects the choice of technology in the developing countries, exacerbating their growing unemployment problem. Many of the developing countries already have serious unemployment which will probably worsen since the growth of their manufacturing industries is not likely to be adequate to cope with the rapid growth of the labor force and increased urbanization. The provision of concessional capital is generally accompanied by technical assistance, ranging from engineering advice on a specific project to assistance in institution building and the training of personnel from developing countries. All these channels have tended to provide advice which reduces the employment-creating potential of investment. Engineers, educators, economists, and other advisors think in terms of their labor-scarce, capital-abundant economies when they are transplanted to the developing countries and their advice is generally accepted uncritically, in part because the personnel they deal with has been trained abroad and proceeds from the same assumptions.

Finally, there is a cost associated with the uncertainty component of aid. To some extent all calculations in a development plan are subject to a considerable margin of error, but in the case of aid the uncertainty is compounded. Most developing countries prepare their annual budgets with no, or limited knowledge of the likely receipts of foreign assistance. International coordination mechanisms—consortia and consultative groups—help some, but do not solve the problem. As a consequence, projects are delayed, foreign exchange allocations are erratic, speculation becomes profitable, and working stock requirements are exceptionally high. Thus uncertainty affects the cost of production and the climate for private investment, and it requires senior executives to spend an inordinate amount of time juggling resources.

But the hidden costs of concessional capital are not limited to developing countries. In donor countries a major indirect cost of concessional capital is that it distracts attention from all other aspects of development and leads donors to define relationships with developing countries in budgetary terms. In the United States, for instance, public discussion of developing countries is almost invariably in the context of "aid." Understanding of, or concern with, trade and political relations, the role of developing countries in the international community, cultural diversity, and the evolution of political and social structures are notably absent. Aid becomes the totality of foreign policy.

Measures to Broaden the Role of the Private Capital Markets

Even if the comparison of financial, political, and psychological costs suggests that greater use of the international bond markets is desirable for some developing countries, what are the steps necessary to build a broader market for foreign bonds in the industrial countries? The categories of action have been succinctly stated by Professor Kindleberger:

There are . . . positive advantages in reviving the private international capital markets for the less developed countries. These advantages are perhaps moderate . . . (but they are) more than trivial. To achieve them, action is required on three fronts: the less developed countries must be interested in establishing their creditworthiness, the lending countries must take action to stimulate the international capital market, and various governmental and institutional actions may be initiated, or extended, to stimulate the appetite of private investors for the obligations of developing countries.[8]

Establishing the creditworthiness of developing countries involves the education of investors, improved economic management by the developing countries and substantial changes in informational trade policies, since the capacity of developing countries to service their debts depends on their capacity to export.

The export potential of the developing countries must be seen largely in terms of manufactured goods. Demand for primary products rises only slowly and while the demand for fuels is expected to grow rapidly, this affects only few countries—particularly among those that require external capital. World trade in manufactured goods has doubled in the past decade, and continued growth at about this level is expected for the 1970s. There should, therefore, be ample scope for increasing exports from the developing countries. Yet, the manufacturing industries that are the most likely prospects for the developing countries are those which tend to be the declining industries in the industrialized countries. They are relatively labor intensive—agricultural products, textiles, shoes—which makes them relatively high cost in the industrialized countries. Yet, they are politically potent and can generate pressure, successfully, for import restrictions.[9] These restrictions, while they affect all exporters, fall most heavily on the developing countries because of their limited alternatives. The central point is that the degree to which the rich countries limit the structural transformation of their economies necessary to adjust to the international division of labor, to that extent the capacity of the developing countries to develop their "creditworthiness" in capital markets is limited. While the adjustment process is necessarily gradual and governments will continue to control the rate of change, progress is essential if the developing countries are to become economically and financially viable. Of course, more liberal commercial policies are not a prescription applicable only to industrialized countries. The potential growth of trade between developing countries is hampered by a level and degree of protection which often dwarfs comparable practices in industrialized countries.

An increased potential for exports by itself will not suffice to establish the creditworthiness of those countries which are potential borrowers in international capital markets. There have been too many cases of bad balance of payments and general economic management for investors to place faith in developing countries guarantees of payment. Yet the record of economic management has improved considerably in the past decade as countries have gained experience and as the supply of trained personnel has increased. Occasionally, the excessive use of suppliers credits, with the consequent short-term debt problems, resulted from the inability to obtain aid funds—for political or other reasons—and the absence of alternative sources of capital. Despite improvements in management capacity in developing countries, and whatever the explanations of past failures, investors are unlikely to be attracted to developing country bonds, within a reasonable risk premium spread, without special actions by governments of the capital exporting countries and by the international financial organizations.

There is a range of measures which can be taken to help make developing country bonds attractive to private investors and gradually build market familiarity. The incentives which will be necessary initially, are sound investments in a system which will reduce the political frictions inherent in the provision of finance for development and enable an increasing number of countries to make their investment choices on commercial and economic rather than on political grounds.

A first group of measures involves improved access to capital markets—still controlled in the industrialized countries and frequently severely limited. While these restrictions have outlived their usefulness,[10] even while they remain in force special provisions could be made for developing countries. While continued supervision of access to international capital by developing countries is essential to protect both the investors and the borrowers and to avoid the history of the defaults in the 1920s and 1930s, this screening should not be used as an administrative device to deny access to borrowers that meet reasonable criteria of security. Similar criteria are already in use in assessing the capacity of developing countries to borrow from international financial institutions and it should not prove difficult to extend that screening process. Although careful screening of borrowers would be essential, the bonds of those countries that meet the test should be permitted regular access to the financial markets.

Governments can also assist in creating demand for bonds of developing countries in a variety of ways. At a minimum they can be made legal investments for pension funds, insurance companies, and other large institutional investors. Many industrialized countries provide insurance for all but normal commercial risks of equity investment of their firms overseas. The same principle could be extended to portfolio investments. The insurance could cover risks of convertibility and/or default for either interest or capital or both. The extent of insurance coverage must be carefully assessed in light of what is necessary to attract investors balanced against the cost of coverage. The more extensive the coverage the greater the involvement of the governments of the borrowing and capital exporting country. While reduction of risks through insurance arrangements may be desirable, risk reduction should stop short of guaranteeing bonds from developing countries. Such guarantees would vitiate a central objective since they would substitute the credit of the guaranteeing government for that of the borrowing government. The effect might be to raise capital but it would neither educate the investors nor broaden the market for foreign government bonds. Because of the importance of building the market for foreign government bonds, governments of the capital exporting countries might, for an initial period, provide some degree of tax incentives (tax credits or partial exemption) for the interest earned. This would help to attract investors and reduce the cost to the borrower.

In addition to financial incentives governments and international institutions can provide technical assistance. The developing countries have virtually no experience in international capital markets. They will need advice and guidance on timing, the size and design of offerings, legal provisions, dealings with the underwriters and on the assurances which they must provide investors. The financial community can, of course, handle many of these aspects, but the developing countries need experience in dealing with market specialists on these matters. Financial institutions, either national or international, might also provide underwriting support, particularly in the initial years.

It is not the purpose here to spell out the scope and details of the incentive and assistance package, but to suggest the ingredients which should be explored. Together they can make select foreign government bonds attractive to investors. What will be necessary in practice depends on the borrowing countries involved and the condition of the markets.

Conclusions

Quite clearly only a small number of developing countries will be capable of borrowing from the international capital markets. The suggestion that this market be revived for developing country bonds is not a solution to the shortage of development capital nor a panacea for the problems inherent in the flow of resources from rich to poor countries. Rather it should be viewed as another component in a system which links the economies of the world. The direct advantages of reviving the international bond markets will be modest, certainly in the short term, but the attempt itself will be important because it will recognize that developing countries seek to end the "special relationship" inherent in the provision of concessional capital. Reviving the international bond market will supplement financial resources for development, focus attention on the problems of development instead of the difficulties of aid, and force political leaders to face the fact that the developing countries cannot be integrated into world commerce without gradually shifting from a reliance on noncommercial inputs to effective participation in world trade and finance.

Notes

1. All data relating to the resource flows to the developing countries are taken from publications of the Development Assistance Committee, OECD, which publishes detailed data annually. There are variations in coverage and definition between this material and that published by the UN, but such differences are not germane to the propositions in this article. The DAC and UN data are reconciled for 1961-66, in J.N. Bhagwati, AMOUNT AND SHARING OF AID, Overseas Development Council, Monograph No. 2, 1970.

2. The UNCTAD Study, based on projections for thirty-eight countries, was published in 1968 as TRADE PROSPECTS AND CAPITAL NEEDS OF DEVELOPING COUNTRIES; the UN Center Study was also published in 1968, entitled DEVELOPING COUNTRIES IN THE NINETEEN-SEVENTIES: PRELIMINARY ESTIMATES FOR SOME KEY ELEMENTS.

3. PARTNERS IN DEVELOPMENT, Report of the Commission on International Development, Praeger, 1969.

4. Paul G. Clark, AMERICAN AID FOR DEVELOPMENT, Praeger, 1972.

5. The premium that developing countries may have to pay depends on the borrower, the market, and timing. However, there is some evidence that the cost is from 1-1 1/2 percent over that of more accepted bonds. In 1968 the yield to maturity of an Argentina issue, maturing in 1973, was 6.65 percent compared to 6.10 percent on an IBRD issue maturing in the same year. A Mexico issue maturing in 1982 had a yield to maturity of 7.28 percent compared to 6.92 percent for an issue by Denmark. See R.N. Cooper and E.M. Truman,

INTERNATIONAL CAPITAL MARKETS AS A SOURCE OF FUNDS FOR DEVELOPING COUNTRIES, UN Document TD/B/C.3/64, 1968.

6. Of course, the availability of aid is not the only cause of poor investment decisions. A number of the developing countries have demonstrated considerable capacity for bad investments using their own resources and export credits from industrialized countries. Of course, contrary to popular belief, bad investment decisions are not a monopoly of developing countries.

7. This is true even when loans are made on a concessional basis to governments and then re-lent on commercial terms to the investors, since governmental decisions might be quite different if the full cost of capital had to be faced.

8. C.P. Kindleberger, "Less Developed Countries and the International Capital Market," in INDUSTRIAL ORGANIZATION AND ECONOMIC DEVELOPMENT, I.W. Markham and G.E. Papanek, Eds. (Boston: Houghton Mifflin, 1970).

9. In the United States, for instance, there now are import restrictions on textiles, shoes, glass, flatware, and tomatoes. For a discussion of limitations facing manufactured goods exports from developing countries, see H. Malmgren, TRADE FOR DEVELOPMENT, Overseas Development Council, Monograph Series #4, Washington, 1971.

10. The future of restrictions, many of which trace back to balance of payments problems in the capital exporting countries, depends to a large extent on the changes to be made in the international monetary system and the balance of payments adjustment process. Surplus countries should, in any event, permit liberal access. Even deficit countries could give priority to developing countries since for some time the volume of their borrowing is likely to be very small in relation to total capital transactions.

Government Finance and the Balance of Payments

Jonathan Levin

Introduction

This paper is concerned with the changing relationship over the years between two fields of economic thought and policy—government finance and balance-of-payments adjustment. As both fields evolved and come under the influence of powerful reorganizing movements in economic thought, the nature and closeness of their relationship has varied. Both fields have been faced—and sometimes divided—in recent years, by a single question: whether the body of theory built up in developed countries over the past two centuries is applicable to developing countries as well. While some portions of traditional theory have gained wide acceptance as applicable to developing countries, others continue to undergo adjustment and adaptation.

It is the thesis of this paper that in the recent balance of payments and government finance experience of many developing countries a heightened interaction of the two fields is discernible, with important policy implications. To examine this development, the following pages deal first, briefly, with the evolution of the relationship between the two fields in developed countries and turn them to the changes becoming evident in some developing countries today.

The Historical Relationship

Over the past two centuries, the concern of international trade and payments theory has been with (a) the most efficient allocation of resources between production for domestic and foreign markets; and (b) the adjustment mechanism by which external payment equilibrium—and internal—might operate. The conclusions on allocation of resources or the gains from trade in conventional (classical or neoclassical) theory were that the greatest advantage lay in each country concentrating on those products in which it had the greatest comparative advantage—that is, in which it was most efficient or least inefficient—and trading these products internationally for the products in which other countries' comparative advantages lay. To the rule of free trade few exceptions were

The views expressed in this paper do not necessarily reflect those of the International Monetary Fund, where the author is employed.

permitted—for infant industries, for optimum (or market advantage) tariffs, and for the correction of factor market distortions. For balance-of-payments adjustment, the flow of gold or foreign exchange was the mechanism contemplated as leading to monetary contraction in deficit countries and expansion in surplus countries, so as to bring corrective adjustment in price levels and/or economic activity.

How did government finance relate to these concerns? Basically in two ways: (1) through the effects of import and export duties on foreign trade; and (2) through the effects of government finance on interest rates and international money flows, in a role shared with monetary policy. These two particular aspects were not out of keeping with the main areas of interest to practitioners of government finance. While some modicum of concern with the general effect of government finance on the wealth of the nation was exhibited, the prime focus was on the effects of the particular, specific instruments of government action—mainly taxes. The principle of neutrality set for each tax—minimization of any disturbance to market allocation of resources—was in line with the guiding spirit of free trade. Theory was tempered in practice, however, as protectionism combined with revenue needs to keep customs duties the backbone of many national revenue systems.

The Keynesian revolution shifted the focus in both fields to aggregate demand management. To price and interest rate changes as a mechanism of balance-of-payment adjustment was added the more painful variation in levels of income and employment. Concern with particular taxes and expenditures meanwhile gave way to concern primarily with the aggregates. Total government revenues and expenditures and the deficit or surplus were the tools of the new fiscal policy, capable of stimulating national employment, income, and demand when a policy of monetary ease could find no willing private investors. With fiscal policy stimulating aggregate domestic demand, which could in turn spill over into imports and compete for the consumption of exports, the link between government finance policy and balance-of-payment adjustment was provided by aggregate income and demand.

In time, however, the same kinds of rigidities which earlier made price and wage reductions an ineffective means of balance-of-payment adjustment came to weaken the potential for contractionary fiscal policy as well. More of the responsibility for attaining domestic and external equilibrium came to rest once more upon monetary policy. While the fiscal containment of aggregate demand would operate through increased taxes or reduced government expenditures, however, monetary containment operated to reduce business investment, home building, and consumer installment buying through reduced availability of credit and an increase in interest rates. This had important implications when a growing international mobility of funds followed the return of convertibility in the late 1950s. The money flows attendant upon a monetary policy approach to attaining domestic and external equilibrium brought dissatisfaction with both the domestic effects of very high interest rates and the external effects of money flows upon other countries affected. This dissatisfaction was reflected in discussion of a proper fiscal-monetary policy "mix" for attaining domestic and balance of payment equilibrium.[1] This discussion could do little, however, about the political and social rigidities blocking fiscal restraint, and the focus of balance-of-payment adjustment shifted to exchange rate flexibility, capital controls, and incomes policy.

While it was fiscal policy in the aggregate which during the four decades following the Keynesian revolution provided the main link between government finance and concern with the effects upon balance-of-payment adjustment, several notable exceptions occurred which focused on the *components* of government finance. One of these grew out of the GATT regulation permitting the refunding at export of indirect taxes previously paid on a product, but not of direct taxes.[2] This distinction has been justified on the general grounds that indirect taxes—on sale or production—are passed forward and added to the price, while direct taxes—on income and property—are not.[3] Indirect taxes were to be levied on the destination principle, therefore, and direct taxes on the origin principle. To permit exported goods to compete with goods produced locally in the importing countries exports are freed of indirect taxes in their country of origin in the expectation that they will have to bear, like local goods, the indirect taxes of their countries of destination. The refunds of indirect taxes granted exports by some countries drew objections on grounds that as approximations of the total burden of turnover taxes they often overstated the tax actually paid and consequently constituted fiscal subsidies to exports. To meet this problem agreement was reached among European Common Market countries for adoption of value added taxation, making possible more accurate measurement and repayment of indirect taxes to exports under the "border tax adjustment." Less susceptible to easy agreement has been the objection challenging the assumption that indirect taxes are fully passed forward while direct taxes are not, and arguing that exports from countries more dependent upon direct taxation are left at a competitive disadvantage by the refunding of indirect taxes alone. Theoretical arguments that in the long run such effects upon competitiveness are resolved by changes in exchange rates may be correct, but seem to bring no lasting or satisfactory solution as these arguments have become only a part of the much wider controversy preceding such exchange rate changes.

Other notable examples of balance of payment concern with the particulars of fiscal action have involved the imposition of temporary import surcharges, seen as the equivalent of exchange rate devaluation for imports, the temporary reduction of refunds for indirect taxes on exports, equivalent to an upward revaluation of the exchange rate for exports, and the imposition of taxes on particular forms of capital investment abroad, in effect devaluing the exchange rate for such transactions or imposing quantitative controls when the tax rate is prohibitive.

One may note also as recent balance-of-payments concerns with the *components* of government finance in developed countries a number of attempts to analyze the effects upon the economy of the government's direct expenditures abroad as well as several other major categories of revenues and expenditures—direct and indirect taxes, consumption, transfers, and investments—believed to have different influences upon aggregate income and demand.[4] These categories are utilized to calculate a measure of the overall expansionary and contractionary effect of fiscal action upon the economy. They appear to represent, therefore, not so much a departure toward concern with particular effects of government finance directly on parts of the balance of payments as a refinement of the main line of thought, concerned with measuring more carefully the overall effects of government finance upon aggregate domestic demand and in consequence the balance of payments.

Relationship in Developing Countries

The interaction of government finance and the balance of payments has followed a somewhat different course in developing countries. While the evolution of economic thought described above has affected the framework of economic thinking in these countries as well, other elements have intervened to modify their government's approach and line of action taken.

This is evident first in the objections which have been raised to the application in developing countries of conventional international trade and balance-of-payments adjustment theory. Such objections have taken many forms, as economists with different geographic and historical points of view have sought to formulate more satisfactory explanations of the developments which they have examined. One author, for example, has based his analysis of the international trade of developing countries on a finding that they have been unable to produce domestically the raw materials, capital goods, and replacement parts needed for their new industries and unable to find adequate export markets permitting them to pay for the needed imports. The result, he finds, is an export maximum and import minimum which gives rise to a foreign exchange gap leaving domestic resources unemployed. This makes foreign exchange costs and benefits the single criterion by which production, trade and investment decisions should be measured, domestic resources—which would otherwise be unemployed—being in effect free.[5]

Another alternative to the conventional theory of international trade for primary producing countries was advanced some years ago by the present author.[6] On the allocation of resources between production for domestic and foreign markets, this study found that historically comparative advantage among existing and mobile factors of production within each country had not in fact determined the location of international production and trade, as factors of production had often proved immobile domestically and more mobile internationally. As a result

the location of [the overseas raw material] export industries followed the same general principles as did the location of domestic industry, being determined by the location of the least mobile factors of production—such as climate, soil conditions, or mineral deposits—and accessibility to market.[7]

The consequence for the balance of payment adjustment mechanism was quite significant, as the establishment of export industries by factors of production coming from abroad led to an adjustment mechanism quite different from that posited by conventional theory. In such developing countries, fluctuations in export earnings give rise to parallel and offsetting fluctuations in remittances abroad by foreign factors of production and in importation of high-income goods by groups of residents receiving export proceeds. The balance-of-payment adjustment mechanism, consequently, did. not operate through nationwide changes in price levels, monetary expansion and contraction, or the variation of aggregate domestic employment and demand.[8]

In recent years, however,[9] the impact of "domestic factor government revolts" has been reducing the ease and importance of such imports and remittances and with it the freedom from economy-wide price, income and employment adjustments which many developing countries previously enjoyed. In its place has come the conventional balance of payments mechanism, complicated by two elements: (1) the shifting structure of imports, including dependence on import requirements not always met by the proceeds of exports; and (2) restricted entry into necessarily limited raw material export industries and the resulting coexistence in the same economy of activities with highly disparate levels of productivity.

It has been largely as a consequence of this disparity of productivity levels within a single economy and exchange rate area that the role of government finance has taken on far greater importance in the international trade and balance-of-payment adjustment process of many developing countries. Indeed, government finance in such circumstances has often become an integral part of the exchange rate system. The genesis of this relationship may be found in the quandary of government exchange rate policy faced with such disparities of productivity. As noted by the present author some time ago:

The rationale for a single rate of exchange for all export transactions lies in the expectation that factors receiving lower returns will then shift to the more profitable areas of employment, that is, to those areas where they are most efficient. This shift toward optimum efficiency, however, depends upon a condition of domestic factor mobility under which factors respond to lower income by shifting to higher paying employment. In many of the export economies this condition of domestic mobility is not present. . . . As a result of either unwillingness to move or restricted entry, therefore, there may exist a domestic immobility of factors which prevents shifting from the less profitable to the more profitable areas of employment. Under these circumstances a lower return to the inefficient producer will mean not a shift to more profitable employment but continued production at a lower level of income.[10]

There were several ways in which governments sought to deal with the growing disparity which limited-entry export industry and a single rate entailed. Some governments apparently reflected the influence of the more profitable interests, in either a colonial or noncolonial setting, and permitted the discrepancy to grow.[11] Others, in what we have previously described as the "revolt of the domestic factor governments," took steps to derive heavy government revenues from the more productive export industries. This appreciated by the weight of the tax the effective exchange rate applicable to these export industries, while rendering the government quite often heavily dependent upon the export tax revenues. Other government measures sought through nonfiscal means to open entry into the export industry for national labor, capital, and entrepreneurship, private or governmental. Still other governments turned to heavy taxation of the high-income imports the profitable export industry made possible.[12]

In time, however, most governments took an interest not only in such means of tapping the limited-entry export industry, but in favoring the development of other sectors of the economy. Prominent among these sectors were domestic industries. Such industries, however, competed with goods importable at the relatively cheap prices made possible by the appreciated exchange rates appropriate to the efficient export industries while paying for domestic resources at prices set or affected by the profitable export sector. As for a variety of reasons development frequently focused first on production of such import substitutes, there was added to the traditional dependence upon a revenue tariff the desire for a protective tariff or quantitative import restriction. While such protection was first designed to provide an assured market for import-competing industries, it was later used to ensure the devotion of scarce foreign exchange resources to spare parts and raw materials for established industries and for the capital goods necessary for additional investment and growth.[13]

Where domestic markets were of limited size, the high cost structures set by heavy protection of domestic industry and by the factor-price levels influenced by major exports frequently left import-competing industries with unused capacity and difficulty in finding export markets for their potential production. Again the role of government finance became an important one, in the subsidization of new, nontraditional exports through multiple exchange rates, direct subsidies and indirect subsidies operating through tax remission provisions or import entitlement schemes of one kind or another.[14]

The result was often a complex foreign exchange rate system intricately interwoven in several ways with the government finances: (a) in direct budget revenues, (b) in hidden revenues used through exchange differential accounts to provide implicit subsidies for nontraditional exports, and (c) in hidden revenues used to support subsidized exchange rates for preferred imports, government foreign exchange transactions or capital payments. The gross flows, unreflected in the cash or budgetary accounts, are often obscured by the complexities of the system and difficult to estimate. Some flows, of course, do not move at all through government or special accounts, as when the higher prices paid by consumers for tariff-protected domestic goods flow directly to domestic producers. Alongside these private shifts in resources, however, the government itself has frequently become a heavily dependent third party in the equation of foreign exchange payments and receipts.

A diagram of a relatively simple exchange rate structure with some of these elements present is provided in Figure 12-1. The price of foreign exchange is plotted vertically (in units of local currency per dollar) and the volume of transactions horizontally (in millions of dollars). Each class of import and export transactions is plotted as a rectangle with the horizontal dimension showing its dollar volume and the vertical dimension measuring the distance between the official exchange rate and the *effective* exchange rate applicable to that class of transactions, as a result of explicit multiple rates, subsidies, export taxes, customs, etc. Government revenues are thus derived from customs (or relatively depreciated exchange rates) on free and licensed imports and from export taxes (or relatively appreciated exchange rates) on traditional exports. Government expenditures are required for subsidies (or relatively appreciated exchange rates) for favored imports and subsidies (or relatively depreciated exchange rates) for nontraditional exports. The overall gain or loss to the government on these transactions is measured by the area of the respective rectangles and in this case yields a considerable net gain to the government, primarily because the (horizontal) dollar volume of favored imports and nontraditional exports is relatively small. Another phenomenon may be noted toward the left of the diagram, however. For those imports under license, or quantitative restriction, an economic rent above the exchange rate plus customs applied by the government accrues to the holders of import licenses because of the scarcity—and high domestic prices—prevailing under conditions of restricted supply. At the extreme left of the chart lies a rectangle unlike others in the diagram. Representing domestic industrial production not exported it shows relatively high prices which, as a result of customs, quantitative import restrictions and hence a relatively more depreciated effective exchange rate, are distributed between higher costs and economic rent.[15]

While Figure 12-1 indicates government participation in the exchange rate system at a particular moment in time, it is necessary to consider also the elements which may influence decisions to change the level and structure of exchange rates. The normal array of those parties affected by the exchange rate system—in addition to the government's finances—may be seen to include on one side those who stand to gain by devaluation: exporters, both (1) traditional and

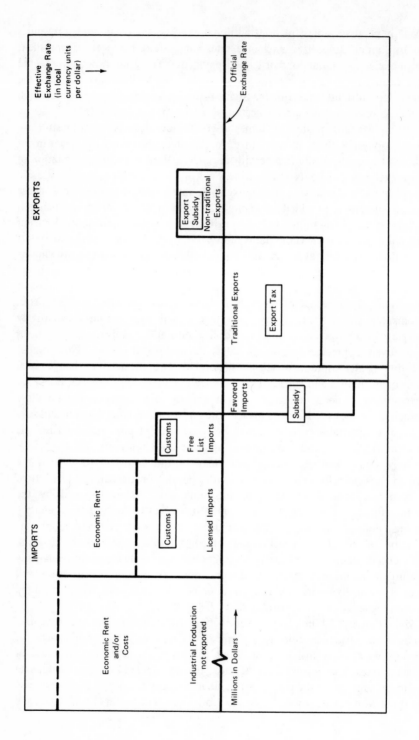

Figure 12-1. Hypothetical Structure of Exchange Rate, Foreign Trade Taxation and Subsidies

(2) nontraditional and (3) producers of import-competing goods; and on the other side, those who stand to lose by devaluation: (4) domestic consumers of potential exports, if any, and consumers of both (5) favored and (6) unfavored imports. The effects of any variation in exchange rates a government may choose to make will depend, of course, upon the elasticities of demand and supply of all six groups concerned. In any devaluation, therefore, a government may choose to intensify, modify, or annul the normal effects upon any of these groups through the application of special exchange rates, taxes, or subsidies. Indeed such countervailing measures accompanying a devaluation may offset all or much of the equilibrating balance of payment effects the devaluation may have initially been expected to produce. This erosion will of course reflect the complex of economic, social, and political influences brought to bear on any government concerned with growth, domestic equilibrium, the balance of payment, and the welfare of diverse groups.

An additional element of importance in exchange system decisions, however, will often be the finances of the government itself, in a sense as a separate party, though one with particular functions essential to many of the other affected groups as well. The importance of this element cannot be entirely revealed by examination only of the exchange system itself, as portrayed in Figure 12-1. The relative magnitude of government revenues generated in foreign trade must also be compared with other sources of revenue. Historical and cross-sectional studies have disclosed a pattern of tax structure development progressing from (1) traditional direct taxes, as upon land heads, or gross income, to (2) taxes upon foreign trade, to (3) taxes upon domestic trade, and finally to (4) the more modern direct taxes upon net incomes of persons and companies.[16] As these long-run, historical changes in structure take place, however, governments face serious political difficulties in the short run as they attempt to impose each new or increased tax, as upon domestic sales or income, for example. Under the influence of political, social, and economical factors, the mobility of resources available to government from different sectors of the economy is often highly uneven, and the government finds that resources from foreign trade can be more readily mobilized than those from other sources.

These elements have sometimes had interesting implications, serving to channel through government finance the broader economic pressures upon the balance of payments adjustment process. A brief examination of the dynamics of one kind of adjustment cycle may be instructive. It can be illustrated by the case of a government in substantial budgetary deficit, financed through expansionary central bank credit, contributing to aggregate demand pressures and serious balance-of-payment deficits. To redress the budgetary, domestic, and external balance, an increase in government revenues, or a decrease in government (or private) expenditures, would be warranted but may be judged politically inadvisable. A solution achieving essentially this same result may in fact be followed, however, by devaluing the exchange rate and diverting a part or all of the local currency gains of exporters to new export tax revenues for the government. As such a combination of devaluation gains and increased export taxes to absorb their "windfall profits" may leave exporters no worse off than before, assuming no immediate increase in domestic costs, it will be essentially from the consumers of imports, now paying higher local currency prices for their imports, that the government's new "export tax" revenues will actually be derived. In time, however, the added cost to import-consumers may through wage increases or other means lead to increased costs for exporters. The burden of the export taxes may then come to rest upon exporters, who may petition successfully for reduction of the export taxes. Should the government remain politically unable to raise the revenues elsewhere, it may find itself providing the necessary relief for exporters through resort once more to central bank credit. Thus a cycle of budget-induced domestic and external disequilibrium, devaluation, balance of payments adjustment, etc., may once more be generated. While the combination of circumstances contributing to such a cycle is by no means general, it has apparently been approximated on occasion.

Dependence upon foreign trade for marginal increases in government revenues may be quite substantial in the short run, so that the influence of government revenue needs upon foreign exchange decisions may sometimes assume considerable significance.[17] Indeed, the choice before governments with budgetary-induced demand and balance-of-payments disequilibrium has more than once come down to: "raise taxes or devalue (and generate foreign trade revenues)." The aggregate pressures of unbalanced government revenues and expenditures may thus come to bear at the margin upon a particularly susceptible revenue component linked to balance-of-payments adjustment. Indeed, one recent article has undertaken to calculate the permissible distortion of allocative efficiency by a revenue tariff, on the assumption that, politically, the tariff alone can serve to increase savings in an economy.[18] For the developing countries, it appears, the continued coexistence in the same economy of groups and activities with highly disparate levels of productivity has brought not only relatively greater susceptibility to taxation in foreign trade, but a more direct and intimate relationship between government finance and balance of payments adjustment than the more aggregative, and only occasionally direct, relationship which exists in developed countries.

Notes

1. See Alan Peacock and Graham Shaw, THE ECONOMIC THEORY OF FISCAL POLICY (London: George Allen and Unwin, 1971), Chapter 8.

2. A summary of the arguments is provided in Organization for Economic Cooperation and Development, BORDER TAX ADJUSTMENTS AND TAX STRUCTURES IN OECD COUNTRIES, Paris, 1968. See also Mel Krauss and

Peter O'Brien, "Some International Implications of Value Added Taxation," NATIONAL TAX JOURNAL 23, 4 (December 1970): 435-40, and Harry Johnson and Mel Krauss "Border Taxes, Border Tax Adjustments, Comparative Advantage, and the Balance of Payments," THE CANADIAN JOURNAL OF ECONOMICS 3, 4 (November 1970): 595-602.

3. An examination of the origins of the GATT rule suggests that this rationale for the distinction may in fact have come later. Unpublished paper by Robert Floyd, "The GATT Provisions on Border Tax Adjustments: A Background Note," 1972. This indicates that the GATT provisions were not originally intended to *permit* export rebates for general indirect taxes but to *limit* rebates with particular regard to selective excises.

4. Bent Hansen, FISCAL POLICY IN SEVEN COUNTRIES, 1955-65 (Paris: OECD, 1969); Joergen Lotz, "Techniques of Measuring the Effects of Fiscal Policy," OECD ECONOMIC OUTLOOK, July 1971, pp. 3-30.

5. Staffan Burenstam Linder, TRADE AND TRADE POLICY FOR DEVELOPMENT (New York: Frederick A. Praeger, 1967).

6. Jonathan Levin, THE EXPORT ECONOMIES, THEIR PATTERN OF DEVELOPMENT IN HISTORICAL PERSPECTIVE (Cambridge, Mass.: Harvard University Press, 1960).

7. Ibid., p. 167.

8. Ibid., pp. 186-202.

9. Ibid., pp. 308-309.

10. Ibid., p. 275.

11. For an interesting application of these principles to a case of regional differences, see Nathaniel Leff, "Economic Development and Regional Inequality: Origins of the Brazilian Case," THE QUARTERLY JOURNAL OF ECONOMICS, Vol. 86, May 1972, pp. 243-62.

12. EXPORT ECONOMIES, pp. 262-301.

13. See, for example, Daniel M. Schydlowsky, "Latin American Trade Policies in the 1970's: A Prospective Appraisal," THE QUARTERLY JOURNAL OF ECONOMICS 86, 2 (May 1972): 267-72.

14. United Nations Conference on Trade and Development, INCENTIVES FOR INDUSTRIAL EXPORTS (United Nations) New York, 1970, UN Sales No. E.70.II.D.8.

15. I am indebted to Mr. Tom Hutchinson of the Harvard University Development Advisory Service for perceptive comments on this subject.

16. Harley H. Hinrichs, A GENERAL THEORY OF TAX STRUCTURE CHANGE DURING ECONOMIC DEVELOPMENT (International Tax Program, Harvard Law School, 1966), pp. 97-109.

17. Distinguishable but not unrelated is the reciprocal influence which fluctuations in foreign trade may have upon government revenues therefrom and upon government decisions to raise or lower other, domestic, revenues. For a study of the effects of foreign trade revenue fluctuations upon fiscal perform-

ance and reform of one country's tax structure, see the author's "Import Cycle and Fiscal Policy in Colombia," NATIONAL TAX JOURNAL (Cambridge, Mass.) September 1968, pp. 314-25.

18. Jaroslav Vanek, "Tariffs, Economic Welfare, and Development Potential," THE ECONOMIC JOURNAL, Vol. 81, No. 324, December 1971, pp. 904-13. The role of the government has been wider than the generation of domestic savings, of course, and government's allocative and developmental responsibilities have provided strong political and economic arguments for the expansion of government and the search for additional revenues. Indeed, one may posit a potential government gap not unlike the savings and foreign exchange gaps in posing obstacles to economic development.

Index

About the Contributors

C. Fred Bergsten is currently a Senior Fellow at the Brookings Institution. From January 1969 until May 1971, he was Assistant for International Economic Affairs on the Senior Staff of the National Security Council. He remains a consultant to several government agencies. Dr. Bergsten was a Visiting Fellow at the Council on Foreign Relations in 1968 and again in 1971. From 1963 to 1967, he was in the Office of International Monetary Affairs at the Department of State. He has published several books and numerous articles on a wide range of international economic issues. He received the masters and Ph.D. degrees from the Fletcher School of Law and Diplomacy.

William G. Tyler is currently Assistant Professor of Economics at the University of Florida and Research Associate at the Kiel Institute of World Economics, Kiel University. He did his undergraduate work in economics at Dickinson College and his graduate study at the Fletcher School of Law and Diplomacy, where he was awarded the Ph.D. degree in 1969. From 1966 to 1969 he was Visiting Professor of Economics at the Brazilian School of Public Administration at the Getulio Vargas Foundation. He has also had experience as an economic consultant to the Brazilian Institute of Economics, the Agency for International Development (AID), and Acción International. In 1971 he was a Fulbright scholar in residence at the Getulio Vargas Foundation. He is the co-editor of *Contemporary Brazil: Issues in Economic and Political Development* and the author of numerous contributions to professional journals.

DISCHARGED

DISCHARGED

DISCHARGED 8-1987